comm CONTRACTS

a practical guide to
deals, contracts, agreements & promises

Revised Edition

C P THORPE MA LLB (CANTAB) BARRISTER

J C L BAILEY MA LLM (CANTAB) SOLICITOR

INSTITUTE OF DIRECTORS

KOGAN PAGE

First published 1996 by Woodhead Publishing Limited
This edition published 1999 by Kogan Page Limited

Kogan Page Limited
120 Pentonville Road
London N1 9JN

British Library Cataloguing in Publication Data

A CIP record for this book is available from the British Library.

ISBN 0 7494 2842 2

Contents

Preface

The prosperity of an industrial society depends on the health of the businesses operating in it, and the long term health of a business depends on the success of the deals and transactions which it enters into. The law of contract is the law of deals and transactions, and is the legal framework within which all business activity is conducted. For someone involved in business, in whatever capacity, an understanding of the principles of contract law is not a luxury but a necessity.

When we began our careers we knew a lot of law but very little about business, and we somewhat naively assumed that businessmen did understand at least the basic principles of contract law. Each of us was quickly disabused of that assumption.

Within a month of starting work as an in-house lawyer at a chemical company, Chris Thorpe met a commercial manager who thought that a contract was a formal agreement signed by both parties, and that in the absence of a signed document no contract could exist. For someone in his position that was a serious misapprehension, as he was in constant danger of committing his company to less formal contracts without realising that he was doing so.

Equally dangerous and mistaken was the proposition put to John Bailey by a director with whom he was working on the proposed sale of a subsidiary shortly after he began his career as a commercial solicitor: that by signing a sufficiently vague letter of intent with the purchaser, they could commit the purchaser to the transaction while the vendor itself remained free to change its mind if it wished.

To give one final example of a cardinal error, many businessmen routinely sign and return documents such as sales invoices or purchase orders which incorporate the other party's standard terms and conditions, usually without so much as a glance at the small print.

It is wrong to criticise someone's ignorance if he has no means available to enlighten it. The principles set out in this book are the stock-in-trade of the commercial lawyer, but the businessman has only two possible means of access to them. The first is to hire a commercial lawyer to advise him. While this makes sense where

the business is contemplating a major transaction such as an acquisition, the lawyer's fees (currently around £250 to £350 per hour
with a solicitor from a major London firm) make it uneconomic to
engage him on the more routine trading transactions which represent the bread and butter of the business. With transactions of this
type the businessman is generally left to his own devices. The only
remaining possibility open to him is to read one of the contract law
textbooks which the lawyers themselves use.

The lawyers' bible so far as contracts are concerned is *Chitty on
Contracts*, first published in 1826. The current 27th edition (1994)
published by Sweet & Maxwell consists of two volumes totalling
2,945 pages. Law students are generally introduced to the subject
by means of either the *Law of Contract* by Cheshire, Fifoot and
Furmston (13th edition 1996, 674 pages) or the *Law of Contract* by
Treitel (9th edition 1991, 973 pages).

The problem with these textbooks lies not so much with their
length as with their purpose and method. These are law books,
written by lawyers for legal practitioners and students, and as such
they conform to the convention for such books that every proposition must be supported by reference to authority. While this
approach makes them excellent reference books for the lawyer
wanting to check a particular point of law, it makes it very hard for
someone coming new to the subject to see the wood for the trees.
Perversely, you need to know the subject before these books can be
of use to you. We know a number of businessmen who have
acquired one of these textbooks, usually for the purposes of an
MBA, but we have never met one who claimed to have read it.

This book has two main purposes. The first is to set out in an
accessible way the principles of contract law applicable in England
and Wales, assuming no prior knowledge of the subject. The
second is to explain the practical significance of these principles
for the businessman.

This is not a law book in any conventional sense, still less an
academic treatise. What is of interest to us are those areas where
practical problems arise, and in those areas the aim is not only to
identify the precise nature of the problem, but also to examine the
possible solutions to it. Our experience is that the same contractual
issues recur time and again, and our hope is that having read this
book you will not only recognise those issues as they arise, but also
know what to do about them.

Both of the authors are practising lawyers. Chris Thorpe has his
own practice, specialising in oil and gas, although increasingly he
is involved in negotiating rather than traditional legal work. John

Bailey is in private practice and specialises in commercial and corporate law. They therefore see different aspects of business, although their separate careers have led them to a consistent view of business and of the legal topics which are important in business. That is the view set out in this book.

We have tried to write in a conversational style, where possible using real examples to illustrate the principles discussed, or failing that using imaginary examples expressed in terms of 'I' and 'you'. This we believe is the most direct and personal style of writing, and it is the natural way of explaining something to someone in person. The opinions expressed are however the opinions of us both, and the experiences recounted happened to one or other of us. The law stated is intended to be accurate as at 1 May 1999.

Under the Interpretation Acts 1889 and 1978, any reference in an Act of Parliament to the male gender includes the female, and vice versa, unless the context requires otherwise. Substantial written contracts usually have a section on interpretation which includes the same principle. In this work we too will use this principle of interpretation in order to avoid the clumsy and distracting use of 'he/she'.

Above all we have tried to keep the treatment of the subject simple and clear. This is due partly to our own conviction that if something is worth saying it is worth saying simply, but partly also to our perception that, for those who are most likely to benefit from this work, time is both valuable and short.

CHAPTER I

What is a contract?

1.1 CONTRACT DEFINITION AND THE PURPOSE OF CONTRACT LAW

1.1.1 Definition

The law provides no formal definition of what a contract is, a fact which you may find surprising. The closest equivalent in ordinary business language is the word 'deal', but the best definition we can offer, and the one we shall be using for the purposes of this book, is this:

> A contract is an agreement which the parties intend to be legally binding.

In this chapter we will consider this definition in detail. At first sight however it may seem to be an odd definition in that it does not provide any objective criteria to enable you to identify a contract, but only the subjective criteria of agreement and intention. The reason for this, and the reason why the law provides no formal definition of what a contract is, is to be found in the central principle of freedom of contract.

1.1.2 Freedom of contract

Freedom of contract is one of the few legal maxims which means exactly what you might expect it to mean, and has the additional advantage of being in English rather than Latin. It is entirely up to the parties involved to decide whether to contract, to decide the subject matter and the terms of that contract, and to decide whether and in what way those terms are to be recorded. The purpose of the law of contract is not to dictate to people what contracts they enter into, but to enable a party who has made a contract to enforce it in accordance with the original intention of the parties. To put it in more familiar terms, the purpose of the law of contract is to enable a person who has made a deal to hold the other party (or parties) to it.

1.1.3 Statutory intervention

In a number of areas Parliament has intervened to restrict the parties' freedom of contract, generally with the object of protecting the public against unscrupulous conduct. Examples of this kind of statutory intervention are to be found in the landlord and tenant legislation and in various statutes concerned with the protection of consumers.

Certain types of tenant have security of tenure under the Landlord and Tenant Acts, which means that the tenancy continues even after the stated expiry date of the lease. With agricultural tenancies this statutory protection can extend not only for the life of the original tenant but also for the next two generations.

In certain situations the Consumer Credit Act 1974 gives a consumer who has entered into a consumer credit agreement a cooling-off period, a period during which he is free to change his mind and back out of that agreement. A consumer who enters into various other types of contract as a result of an unsolicited visit at his home or place of work also has a cooling-off period and a right of cancellation under the Consumer Protection (Cancellation of Contracts Concluded Away from Business Premises) Regulations 1988.

Usually of course the parties are bound by the terms of a contract from the moment they enter into it, and neither party is free subsequently to change his mind. As a result this kind of statutory protection completely overrides the most fundamental contractual principles. But with trading transactions of the kind with which we shall be mainly concerned, and in particular where the transaction is between two businesses, there is very little statutory intervention and the parties' freedom of contract remains virtually complete. Here a party cannot generally look to the law for protection if he makes a bad deal or a deal which subsequent events lead him to regret. That is why it is so important for businesses and for businessmen to understand the principles we shall be discussing.

1.2 AGREEMENT

1.2.1 Meaning

A contract is an agreement. Lawyers themselves often use the word 'agreement' to refer to a formal document signed by the parties, and many people wrongly believe that that is what a contract is. In our definition however the word agreement is used in its ordinary sense. Two people are in agreement when they are in the same mind about something, and to say they are in agreement necessarily implies that they have communicated with each other. The law has a distinctive and useful way of analysing these communications in order to identify the precise point at which agreement was reached. These are the principles of offer and acceptance, which are discussed in section 3.1.

Not every agreement, in the ordinary sense of that word, is a contract. Two people may agree that the Conservative party will win the next general election, but this agreement is not a contract because it does not involve either party undertaking to do anything. The law of contract is concerned with agreements where the parties undertake to do something (or, sometimes, not to do something). With the vast majority of contracts each party undertakes to do something, and agreements where only one party undertakes to do something cause problems which are discussed in section 3.2.

Let us look at the simplest possible commercial transaction to identify the agreement and see what the parties undertook to do. Suppose that I go into a newsagents and see a row of Mars bars with price labels marked 30 pence. I say 'Mars bar, please'. The newsagent puts a Mars bar on the counter and says '30 pence, please'. I pay him the money and leave with the bar. The only piece of paper involved is the Mars bar wrapper, but the legal analysis of this transaction is that a contract has been both entered into and performed. The newsagent entered into an agreement with me, the terms of which were that he undertook to supply me with a Mars bar and I undertook to pay him 30 pence. To put it another way, he assumed the obligation to supply a Mars bar and I had a corresponding right to one, while I assumed the obligation to pay him 30 pence and he had a corresponding right to that sum. We each performed our obligations under the agreement a moment after we entered into it, and in all probability that will be the end of the matter.* With more substantial commercial contracts there is

* *The analysis of this transaction in terms of offer and acceptance is given in section 3.1.6.*

usually a much longer period between the actual agreement and the time when the parties are to perform their obligations under it.

1.2.2 Subject matter

Every contract can be seen in terms of the agreement reached and the respective rights and obligations of the parties under it. Because human activity is infinitely varied, the subject matter of contracts is also infinitely varied. If for example a company which markets portable telephones agrees to sponsor me to climb Mount Everest with one of their telephones and ring their chairman from the summit, the agreement between us is undoubtedly a contract, albeit an unusual one. (If I am sensible of course I will not undertake to climb Mount Everest but only to try to climb it. Obligations which are qualified rather than absolute are discussed in section 7.2.)

However, most contracts fall into well recognised categories, many of which have commonly used names reflecting the subject matter of the agreement. Here is a selection of some of the more common ones:

- Agreements for the supply of goods ('contract for the sale of goods').
- Agreements to perform services ('contract for services').
- Agreements for the hire of goods where the hirer has the option to purchase them ('contract of hire purchase').
- Agreements to transport people or goods ('contract of carriage').
- Agreements to work for someone ('contract of employment').
- Agreements for the loan of money ('loan agreement').
- Agreements for the construction of buildings or plant ('construction contract').
- Agreements for the hire of land or buildings ('lease').
- Agreements for the hire of equipment ('contract of hire').
- Agreements for the hire of a ship ('charterparty').
- Agreements transferring risks ('contract of insurance').

Which category a particular agreement falls into is not generally a question which has any significance. The significant question is what the parties respectively undertook to do, and not how their agreement should be labelled. As we shall see however, certain categories of agreement do have special rules applicable to them: for example the Sale of Goods Act 1979 applies only to contracts for the sale of goods. Here the question whether a particular agreement is or is not a contract for the sale of goods is significant because the answer to that question determines whether or not the Sale of Goods Act 1979 applies to it. That question can sometimes be difficult to answer, particularly where both goods and services are to be supplied.

If I agree to buy a second-hand Rolls-Royce, that agreement does not cease to be a contract for the sale of goods merely because the seller has also agreed to provide services in relation to the car such as cleaning and servicing it. At the other extreme, if I engage a firm of decorators to paint my house, that is plainly a contract for services notwithstanding the fact that they are to provide the paint as well as apply it. But if I engage a jeweller to design, make and supply a diamond brooch, it is difficult to decide whether this is a contract for goods or for services. Hybrid agreements of this kind are known as 'contracts for work and materials'.

It is worth noting that, despite the wide range of subject matter, the various types of agreement listed above have another thing in common. The main obligation of one party, and often his only obligation, is to pay money to the other. This is not true with every contract. A party may for example agree to supply goods not in exchange for money but in exchange for other goods, a transaction known as 'barter' or 'exchange' to which, incidentally, the Sale of Goods Act 1979 does not apply. But with most commercial transactions payment is the main obligation of one party.

1.2.3 Form

The parties are free to enter into an agreement in whatever form they choose. In our Mars bar example the agreement was an oral one, and with the very limited exceptions discussed below the parties are free to enter into any transaction orally, either face-to-face or by telephone. In practice of course more significant commercial transactions almost always involve some kind of paperwork because the parties want a written record of the transaction. Most transactions between businesses are entered into by exchanges of letters, telexes, facsimile transmissions or printed forms of some kind. Here, in order to find out whether an agreement has been reached and, if so, what the terms of it are, it is necessary to examine the various communications exchanged between the parties (some of which may be oral) in terms of offer and acceptance. This process is considered in detail in section 3.1.

If the parties wish to avoid any uncertainty about what the terms of their agreement are, they can either make a written record of those terms or else draw up a formal written agreement. In either case the end result is a document which formally records the terms of the agreement, which is usually (but not necessarily) signed by each party in order to authenticate the document. There is however a small but potentially important distinction between the two. In the first situation the document is merely evidence of the terms of an agreement which has already been entered into, and the agreement is said to be 'evidenced in writing'. In the second situation the document itself is the agreement, and no agreement exists until the document has been confirmed by each party usually by means of a signature. The practical difference can be seen if for some reason one party changes his mind and tries to back out before he has signed the document. In the second situation he is free to do so, but in the first he is not. Once the document has been agreed however it makes no practical difference whether this is an agreement evidenced in writing or a written agreement, and the phrase 'agreement in writing' is generally used to cover both, obscuring the distinction between them.

Although there is no difference in principle between an agreement in writing and an agreement in any other form, an agreement in writing has the great practical advantage of leaving no room for doubt about what the parties agreed and undertook to do. It is for this reason that really substantial commercial transactions almost always involve a written agreement which, having been fully negotiated and vetted by each party's lawyers, will usually be formally entered into at a signing ceremony. Often the signatory himself is a senior executive who has not been involved in the negotiation of the agreement and who has only the vaguest idea of what it contains.

The practical advantage of having an agreement in writing also appeals to businesses which are in a strong enough bargaining position to impose agreements willy-nilly on their customers. If you want to hire a car, get a new credit card or take out a loan, you will be required to sign a printed standard form agreement produced by the other party. You will probably not even have read that document, and you could hardly be said to have 'agreed' the terms of it in the ordinary sense of that word. The law nevertheless considers that you have entered into a contract on those terms, although as a consumer you are reasonably well protected if (as is almost inevitably the case) those terms are one-sided and unfair. That protection is discussed in sections 4.6 and 4.8, and the problems raised by standard form agreements are discussed in Chapter 5.

1.2.4 Deeds

The most formal kind of written agreement is a document under seal, known as 'a deed'. Deeds have been in use for centuries, and originally they were executed by the application of a wax seal. Today however, in order to qualify as a deed, a document has to meet two requirements. First, it must be expressed to be a deed, which is usually achieved by the use of introductory words such as 'Now this deed bears witness as follows ...'. Second, it has to be executed in a prescribed way. In the case of an individual, it must be signed by him in the presence of a witness who attests the signature, so the document bears the signature not only of a party but also of the witness. In the case of a company, the document must be executed in the way prescribed by the company's articles of association (discussed in section 2.2.5). In practice, this usually involves the application of a seal which indents the paper with the name of the company and is then attested by the signatures either of two directors or of a director and the company secretary. The Companies Act 1989 did away with the need for a seal, so that now a company can enter into a deed by means of the signatures alone. A deed is still however unmistakable because the document itself must say that it is a deed.

Most people assume that they are bound by a written agreement from the moment they sign it. Although as we shall see in section 3.1.7 this is not necessarily correct, in relation to deeds it is most definitely incorrect. For a deed to be binding it must (in the ancient phrase) be 'signed, sealed and delivered'. So it is not enough that the deed is signed and sealed: it only comes into effect when it is physically delivered to the other party.

As we shall see, certain types of agreement are required to be under seal, and so are various other documents which are not contracts at all such as wills and conveyances of land. Although an agreement under seal is not essentially different from any other written agreement, it has two peculiarities (discussed in sections 3.2.4 and 8.6) which may make it appropriate or desirable for a particular agreement to be executed in this way.

1.2.5 Agreements required by statute to be in a particular form

There are a number of examples of legislation requiring particular kinds of agreement to be in a particular form, and these are the exceptions to the general principle that the parties are free to enter into an agreement in any form they choose. Even the contract law textbooks do not attempt to list these statutory exceptions because most concern agreements of a specialised nature. To give just one example, regulations under Section 60 of the Consumer Credit Act 1974 not only require certain consumer credit agreements to be in writing, but actually specify the size of the lettering and the colours of the print and paper. Finance companies have to be aware of these requirements since an agreement which does not meet them may be invalid. There are however three examples of more general importance which we must consider, and these relate to long term leases, guarantees and contracts for the sale of land:

1. Section 52 of the Law of Property Act 1925 requires a lease for more than three years to be under seal.
2. Under Section 4 of the Statute of Frauds 1677, a guarantee cannot be enforced against the person who gave it unless he has signed the guarantee or some other document which records the terms of it. The word guarantee needs to be understood in its legal sense. The so-called guarantee given by a dealer when he sells a new car is not a guarantee in the legal sense but a 'warranty' (discussed in section 3.4.3).

   A guarantee is a contract under which one person undertakes to do something if another person fails to do it, for example if I undertake to meet my daughter's liability to the bank if she fails to repay a loan made to her. The primary obligation to repay the loan is on her, and I only become liable under the guarantee if she fails to do so. The obligations of a guarantor are therefore described as 'secondary obligations'.

   In practice guarantees are almost always in writing and also (for the reasons discussed in section 9.3.2) under seal. You will notice however that Section 4 does not actually require contracts of guarantee to be in writing, but only that the guarantor must have signed either the guarantee or else some other document which records the terms of the guarantee if it is to be enforceable against him. So an oral guarantee is enforceable if, for example, the guarantor confirms the arrangement in a signed letter. The name 'Statute of Frauds' gives a clue to its historical context, but today it is clearly anomalous that, while an oral contract for the sale of an oil tanker is enforceable, an oral guarantee is not.
3. Section 2 of the Law of Property (Miscellaneous Provisions) Act 1989 requires a contract for the sale of land to be in writing and

signed by each party. In legal terminology the word 'land' includes not just land but also buildings and parts of a building such as a flat. A contract for the sale of land must not however be confused with a conveyance: the contract is the agreement to sell, and the conveyance is the formal transfer of the land to the buyer. The complexities of land law and conveyancing are such that it is most inadvisable to enter into such a contract, or indeed any transaction involving land, without instructing a solicitor.

1.3 PARTIES

We shall be dealing with the subject of the parties to a contract in detail in Chapter 2. For the purposes of our discussion of the definition of a contract we need to note only a few points.

A contract must have at least two parties. It is not possible to have an agreement with yourself, nor to sue yourself. One consequence is that, if a tenant who has leased a flat from the freeholder subsequently buys the freehold from him, the lease is simply extinguished. It does not continue with his leasing the flat from himself.

The great majority of contracts do in fact have two parties, and for convenience they are called 'bipartite' or 'bilateral' contracts. Contracts with more than two parties are not however uncommon, and there is no maximum number. Some syndicated loan agreements (that is where the loan is provided by a syndicate rather than a single lender) have literally dozens of parties. Other types of contract may have hundreds or even thousands of parties. For example the memorandum and articles of association of a registered company (discussed in section 2.2.5) constitute a single contract to which each shareholder and the company itself is a party. Similarly the rules of a trade union constitute a single contract to which each member and the trade union itself is a party.

Most of the examples used in this book to illustrate the principles of contract law are examples of bipartite contracts, and only occasionally will it be necessary to refer to multipartite contracts. The principles discussed do however apply to all contracts, irrespective of the number of parties.

1.4 CONTRACTUAL INTENTION

1.4.1 Meaning

An agreement is only a contract if, at the time the parties entered into it, they intended that agreement to be legally binding. If they did, then either party can go to court to enforce the other party's obligations to him under the agreement, and the court will enforce those obligations unless there is some other factor which makes the contract invalid. These factors are discussed in Chapter 10. The word 'enforce' is however used in a specialised sense which is the subject of Chapter 8. If on the other hand the parties did not intend their agreement to be legally binding, then that agreement is not a contract and neither party can go to court to enforce it. The phrase 'contractual intention' is used to describe the parties' intention to be bound.

1.4.2 Inferring intention

The problem of course is that, while lawyers think in terms of contractual intention, other people do not. People enter into all kinds of agreements without stopping to think whether or not they intend them to be legally binding. Unless the parties have made their intention clear, it is necessary to infer what their intention was. If the parties had been asked the question at the time the agreement was entered into, would they have said that the agreement would be enforceable through the courts?

Generally speaking domestic arrangements are not intended to be legally enforceable, but commercial arrangements are. So my daughter cannot successfully sue me if I fail to pay the pocket money I agreed to give her, nor can I successfully sue someone who agrees to come to dinner but fails to turn up. On the other hand there is no doubt that the agreement with the newsagent for the sale of a Mars bar is legally enforceable: I can sue him if the bar turns out to have been injected with strychnine, and the newsagent can sue me for the purchase price if I fail to pay it.

Sometimes, however, the parties' intention can be extremely difficult to infer. In March 1994 the newspapers reported a case between two women neighbours who played bingo together. They had an oral agreement to share all their winnings, and over the years they had in fact shared numerous small wins. Then one of the women won £42,000 and refused to share it. The other sued her for half of that sum. The whole case turned on the issue of contractual intention: was the oral agreement between the two intended to be legally enforceable? On balance the court felt that it was, so the loser of the case was ordered to pay the winner £21,000 plus £6,000 in interest. The winnings had of course long since been spent, and it was reported that the loser would have to sell her house to meet the judgment. It was also reported that the winner of the case had been virtually bankrupted by her legal costs, and that the stress of the case had led to the failure of her marriage – a good demonstration of the unfortunate truth that litigation often has two losers.

1.4.3 Express intention

It is of course unnecessary to infer the parties' intention if they have expressly stated it. If a particular agreement is expressed to be legally binding (or is expressed not to be legally binding) that express intention is conclusive. There are of course other ways of putting it without using the phrase 'legally binding'. The words 'binding', 'enforceable' or 'contract' all serve to indicate contractual intention. On the other hand the phrase 'gentleman's agreement' indicates that the parties did not intend their agreement to be a contract, and you do occasionally find a substantial commercial transaction which has been entered into as a gentleman's agreement.

1.4.4 Commercial reality and the burden of proof

If a party to an agreement claims that it was not intended to be legally binding, the burden is on him to satisfy the court of that fact. With a substantial commercial agreement involving significant sums of money and valuable goods or services, it will be very difficult to convince the court that there was no contractual intention unless this was expressly stated. It is inherently unlikely for example that an airline would agree to buy a jet on the basis that it could not sue the seller if the jet proved defective, and it is equally unlikely that the seller would agree to sell it on the basis that he could not sue for the purchase price. In practice very few claims for breach of a commercial agreement are defended on the grounds that there was no contractual intention, and those that are nearly all relate to interim agreements.

1.4.5 The problem with interim agreements

With a large transaction such as the sale of a company, business or ship, it is common for the parties to reach agreement on the major commercial terms of the transaction, leaving the more detailed terms to be negotiated later and embodied in a full written agreement. The interim agreement itself is often recorded in a signed document known as a 'heads of agreement' or a 'memorandum of understanding' or some similar phrase, and at this stage lawyers may well not be involved. If the subsequent negotiations proceed smoothly and the full agreement is signed, the question whether the interim agreement was itself intended to be legally binding will never arise. But if the subsequent negotiations fail or one party decides for some reason not to proceed, the disappointed party may claim that the interim agreement itself was intended to be binding. If this is unclear, each party's lawyers can look forward to lengthy litigation and large fees.

When you are negotiating an interim agreement of any kind it is vital to ask yourself whether or not that agreement is intended to be legally binding and to say so clearly. Generally you will not want the interim agreement to be binding because important details remain to be agreed, but in some situations the need to tie up the deal will outweigh the need to be sure about details. Crude oil purchases and charterparties for example are regularly contracted by telex, leaving a formal and more detailed agreement to be concluded and signed later. The error is to leave the matter in doubt.

In our experience, the parties to an interim agreement are often reluctant to address the question whether it is to be legally binding. Each party really wants to be free to back out of the deal himself, but to hold the other party to it if it suits him. It is possible to have the best of both worlds, but this of course is an arrangement known as an option, and options tend to be expensive. Trying to have the best of both worlds by avoiding the question is a very dangerous game.

1.4.6 Options and conditional contracts

So far we have considered only the simple case where the parties either do or do not intend their agreement to be legally binding. More sophisticated arrangements where the agreement only comes into effect on the occurrence of a certain event are however common, the most common being options and conditional contracts.

Options in particular should be familiar as they are used in both the stock market and commodity markets. Suppose that A agrees to give B an option, exercisable at a future date, to buy (or to sell) a certain number of shares at an agreed price. This agreement is itself a contract, but it is not a contract for the sale of the shares. A contract for the sale of the shares only comes into existence if B exercises the option, and he will only exercise it if the market price of those shares on the option date makes it attractive to do so. This device can be used with any commercial transaction, and it gives the party with the option the best of both worlds: he can hold the other party to the transaction or he can abandon it. The corresponding disadvantage to the other party usually means that his price for granting the option will be high.

Suppose that the owner of a plot of land agrees to sell it to a land developer, but the sale is conditional upon the developer being granted planning permission by the local authority to develop the plot. This agreement is itself a contract, and neither party is free to back out of it. But it is not a contract for the sale of the land. A contract for the sale of the land only comes into existence if planning permission is granted, and the refusal of planning permission terminates the conditional contract leaving no obligation on either party. The conditional contract will probably require the developer to apply for planning permission and to use his best endeavours to obtain it. If this term has not been expressly agreed it will have to be implied: otherwise the developer can defeat the object of the agreement by not applying for planning permission. (Implied terms of this nature are discussed in section 4.7.2.)

Agreements which are subject to some condition are more common in the commercial world than might at first be supposed. Sometimes that condition is an external one such as the grant of planning permission or, in the case of certain types of export sale, the grant of a Government export licence. More often however the condition relates to the internal requirements of one of the parties. Large companies, for example, often require agreements negotiated by their salesmen or executives to be referred back for the approval of the credit control department or the board of directors. When an agreement is conditional upon internal requirements of this sort being met, it makes no practical difference whether the agreement is described as a conditional contract or a non-binding agreement: either way the company is effectively free to back out of the deal.

Problems can however arise if it has not been made clear to the other party that further approvals are required. He may consider that there is a binding contract, and the language that the parties will probably have used ('it's a deal then') may persuade the court that he is right, leaving the unfortunate individual concerned to explain to his board of directors why, in defiance of company rules, he committed the company to a binding contract without their approval.

When you reach an agreement which requires further approval or is subject to some other condition, it is important to make this clear to the other party, preferably in writing, no matter how eager you are to secure the deal or how confident you are that the condition will in fact be met.

1.4.7 'Subject to contract'

The practical problems discussed above all arise from the parties' failure to consider, or failure to make clear, whether or not their agreement is intended to be legally binding. When lawyers are negotiating an agreement which is not intended at that stage to be legally binding, they indicate this by including in all their communications to the other party the phrase 'subject to contract'. This phrase is of course entirely indiscriminate. It may mean that the agreement in question is not intended to be binding until it is signed (section 1.2.3), or is an interim agreement which is not intended to be binding at all (section 1.4.5), or merely that further approvals of some kind are required (section 1.4.6).

We personally prefer to be more specific and to make clear to the other party exactly what conditions must be met before a binding agreement exists: making your intentions clear at an early stage greatly reduces the possibility of a misunderstanding later on. But using the hallowed phrase 'subject to contract' is a very economical way of indicating that at that stage you have no contractual intention, and by using it consistently and correctly you can ensure that you are never involved in disputes of the kind we have been considering.

Sometimes however the words 'subject to contract' are mistakenly included on a document which is intended to be binding. This can happen because the author is so used to including the phrase that he does so even when he does not mean it, or else because the phrase appeared on the drafts of the agreement during the negotiation but is not removed when execution copies are prepared. If this goes unnoticed it will deprive the agreement of its intended legal effect.

In conclusion, an agreement is either binding or it is not binding. There is no grey middle ground. So the businessman must think, as the lawyer does, in terms of the black and white of contractual intention.

1.5 PRIVITY OF CONTRACT

1.5.1 Meaning

That concludes our discussion of the definition of a contract, but we cannot leave the subject of what a contract is without mentioning the most distinctive and important principle of the English law of contract, a principle known as the doctrine of 'privity of contract'. The principle can be expressed as follows:

> A contract cannot confer rights or impose obligations on anyone who is not a party to it, and nobody other than the parties can enforce that contract or have it enforced against him.

A person who is not a party to a particular contract is commonly referred to as a 'stranger to the contract' or else (irrespective of how many parties there actually are) a 'third party'. We shall be using these phrases in this sense from now on.

1.5.2 Consequences

While this statement of the doctrine of privity may seem unremarkable, its practical consequences can sometimes be bizarre.

Suppose that a friend and I go into a pub where he orders two pints of beer. The contract for the sale of the beer is between my friend and the proprietor of the pub, and as we shall see in section 4.8.1, that contract includes the implied terms that the beer will be fit for its purpose and of satisfactory quality. But since I am a stranger to that contract it cannot confer rights or impose obligations on me. If therefore my friend fails to pay for the beer, the landlord must sue him for the price. He cannot successfully sue me, even for the price of the pint which I drank. If on the other hand the beer is contaminated and we both end up in hospital, my friend can sue the proprietor for his breach of the implied terms. The principle of strict liability (discussed in section 7.1.1) means that the proprietor is liable for my friend's injuries even if the contamination was someone else's fault. But I have no rights under the contract and cannot successfully sue the proprietor for his breach of it.* Nor can my friend sue him on my behalf.

* In order to obtain compensation for my injuries from the proprietor I would have to sue him for negligence (an action which does not require there to be a contract between you), and I would have to show that the contamination was his fault rather than the brewer's or wholesaler's. If the contamination was a manufacturing defect I could sue the brewer under the Consumer Protection Act 1987.

1.5.3 Conclusions

While it is not surprising that a contract imposes no obligations on a third party, it is perhaps surprising that a contract confers no rights on a third party. In our example, my friend entered into the contract for my benefit as well as his own, and I had just as much interest in the proper performance of that contract as he did. It is anomalous that I have no rights under the contract, but that is unquestionably the position under English law. The law of Scotland does in fact allow a third party to sue under a contract which was entered into for his benefit, and there have been a number of proposals to alter the English rule of privity of contract to bring it into line with Scottish law.

There is a Bill currently before Parliament called the Contracts (Rights of Third Parties) Bill. This has cross-party support and is expected to become law during 2000. If enacted in its current form, the Act will abolish the English law of privity and give third parties rights under a contract which is intended to confer such rights on them.

We will encounter the doctrine of privity and its consequences at numerous points in our discussion. One of the most obvious of those consequences is that you have to be very clear about who the parties to a particular contract actually are, and it is the subject of the parties to which we must now turn our attention.

CHAPTER 2

Parties

To enter into a contract you must be a legal person with the capacity to enter into that contract. There are two important but distinct issues here which need to be understood. The first is legal personality (section 2.1) and the second is contractual capacity (section 2.2). We will then go on to consider the different types of obligations which can arise when two or more persons are acting as a group (section 2.3), and finally we will briefly discuss the principles of agency (section 2.4).

2.1 LEGAL PERSONALITY

2.1.1 Sole trader

Suppose that I decide to start a business selling and installing windows. The simplest option is for me simply to trade on my own behalf and in my own name. I would borrow money from a bank, lease premises and a van, buy the windows from a wholesaler and contract directly with my customers for their sale and installation. In this situation I might talk about 'my business', but in legal terms my business is not an entity distinct from me. My bank, my landlord, the vehicle leasing company, the wholesaler and my customers (and anyone else with whom I enter into a contract in the course of my business) would be contracting with me as an individual. If anything went wrong the other parties to those contracts would sue me personally. All the assets of the business would be owned by me personally and I would be personally liable for all the debts and liabilities incurred in the course of the business. Many small businesses are conducted by one individual in this way, and in the commercial world he is referred to as a 'sole trader'.

2.1.2 Registered company

The second possibility is for me to form a registered company to conduct the business. I would be the main shareholder of the company, its managing director, and also perhaps an employee of the company. The crucial point is that the company, no matter how small or how much of a one-man operation it is, is in legal terms an entity which is distinct from me. The assets of the business would be owned by the company and not by me. It would be the company and not me which entered into all the contracts and which was liable for all the debts and liabilities incurred in the course of the business. If anything went wrong the other parties to the various contracts would have to sue the company and not me personally.

The distinct legal personality of the company has a number of significant legal consequences. For example, I would not be free to help myself to the money or other assets of the business: that would be theft by me of the property of the company. Another consequence is that if the business fails I could let the company go into liquidation: the creditors of the company could claim against the assets owned by the company but not against any assets owned by me.* For tax purposes also the company is a distinct entity. The company will pay corporation tax on the profit derived from the business: I will have to pay income tax only on the money I receive from the company by way of salary or dividends. So for all legal purposes the company is a separate entity, even if the company itself is wholly owned by me.

2.1.3 Partnership

If more than one person is to be involved in running the business, there is a third possibility, which is the formation of a partnership. This will involve a contract between the partners ('a partnership agreement') which sets out the rights and obligations between the partners themselves. The important point for our purposes is that a partnership, unlike a company, is not a separate legal entity. Here it will be the partners who own all the assets of the business and who enter into all the contracts and who will be personally liable for all the debts and liabilities incurred in the course of the business. All solicitors' firms (other than sole practitioners) and many firms of accountants and architects operate as partnerships.

* The Insolvency Act 1986 *makes the directors personally liable for the debts of the company if they allow the company to trade when they know, or ought to know, that the company is insolvent.*

2.1.4 Limited liability of company

The main attraction of using a company rather than operating as a sole trader or a partnership should already be clear. The company is a separate legal entity and it is the company and not its owners (the shareholders) which is responsible for the debts and liabilities incurred in the course of the business. The liability of the shareholders is limited to the nominal value of the shares held by them. This is why most businesses, and virtually all the substantial ones, are run through a limited company.

A company which is trading with limited liability is obliged to make that fact clear by including at the end of its name the word 'Limited', 'Ltd', 'Public Limited Company' or 'plc', or in the case of a Welsh company the Welsh equivalents 'Cyfyngedig', 'Cyf', 'Cwmni Cyfyngedig Cyhoeddus' or 'ccc'. Although there is such a thing as an unlimited company, where the shareholders are personally liable for the company's debts and liabilities if the company itself is unable to meet them, they are extremely rare and so we will not consider them further.

There is a general belief that it is better to deal with a limited company rather than a sole trader or a partnership; the word 'limited' is seen as an indication of substance and reliability. In practice the reverse is often the case: if a limited company becomes insolvent while owing you money, you cannot recover that money from the owners of that company.

2.1.5 Groups of companies

Most really substantial businesses have a group structure. That is to say that there is a holding company with a number of subsidiary companies, which may themselves have their own subsidiaries. The BP group for example consists of several hundred companies. The holding company is The British Petroleum Company plc (whose shares are quoted on the Stock Exchange) which directly or indirectly owns all the other companies. Each of these subsidiaries is a separate legal entity.

If you enter into a contract with a subsidiary, the rights and obligations under the contract are between you and the subsidiary. You cannot enforce your rights against the holding company or any other company in the group, and if you try to do so your action will fail because you have sued a stranger to the contract. To put it another way, a group of companies is not a legal entity but a number of different legal entities linked by their common ownership.

2.1.6 Business names

A person who runs a business is free to trade using a business name different from his real name. So I may try to give my fledgling window business credibility by trading as 'Thorpe's Windows' or 'The Surrey Window Company'. The use of such a business name, also called a trading name or a trading style, does not in any way alter the contractual position as we have discussed it: everything depends on whether the legal entity running the business is a sole trader, a partnership or a registered company.

It would however be a mistake to think that only small businesses trade using a business name: some of the very largest do too. ICI, for example, does not operate through subsidiaries but through different divisions, each of which uses a trading name indicative of the nature of the business of that division, such as for example ICI Garden Products. These divisions are not separate legal entities. The suppliers and customers of ICI Garden Products are contracting not with the division but with the company Imperial Chemical Industries plc.

2.1.7 Establishing the identity of a party

The importance of knowing which legal entity you are contracting with should already be clear from the fundamental principle discussed in section 1.5 – namely that a contract can only confer rights and liabilities on, and can only be enforced by and against, the parties to it. While the use of a business name makes no difference from the contractual point of view, in practice it can cause problems because it can obscure the identity of the legal entity with which you are dealing.

The best time to establish the legal identity of the other party is of course before you enter into a binding agreement. At that stage you can usually expect an honest reply and you can record your understanding of the identity of the other party in the course of correspondence or, if there is to be one, in a written agreement. If the man representing The Surrey Window Company will not or cannot tell you the identity of the legal person or persons involved, then you would be well advised to have your windows replaced by someone else. You should never enter into a contract with someone whose identity is not clear to you. Unfortunately this happens all too often in the commercial world, under pressures to clinch deals, reach targets and earn commission. This represents the commercial equivalent of the (equally unreliable) show business maxim 'It'll be all right on the night'. Sometimes it is not.

Suppose then that you have already entered into a contract for replacement windows with an entity known to you only as The Surrey Window Company. As we have seen, this could be (i) a trading name used by an individual, in which case your contract is with him, or (ii) the name of a registered company, in which case your contract is with that company, or (iii) the trading name used by a company of a different name, in which case your contract is with that company, or (iv) the trading name of a partnership, in which case your contract is with the partners personally.

If something goes wrong, for example if The Surrey Window Company pockets your deposit or installs defective windows, you will need to identify the legal entity with which you contracted. If you sue the wrong legal entity, your action will fail. The fact that the word 'Company' is used does not help you at all. There is nothing to prohibit the use of that word in the trading name of an individual, a company or a partnership. What should however help you is a close examination of the correspondence received from The Surrey Window Company. In order to understand what the correspondence will reveal, we need to consider briefly two different pieces of legislation.

The Companies Act 1985 requires a company to include on all its business letters and order forms its name (including the word 'Limited' or 'plc' as appropriate), its place of registration, the address of its registered office, and its registered number (the importance of which is discussed in section 2.1.8 below). So the letters you received may say 'Surrey Window Company' in large embossed letters at the top, but 'CP Thorpe Limited registered in England no 123456 registered office 13 Acacia Avenue, Suburbia' in small letters at the bottom. If so, your contract is with CP Thorpe Limited, which uses 'Surrey Window Company' as a trading name.

The Business Names Act 1985 applies to any person who carries on business in Great Britain under a name other than his real name. For this purpose the real name of an entity means (i) in the case of an individual his surname, (ii) in the case of a partnership the surnames of all the partners, and (iii) in the case of a company its registered name (including the word 'Limited' or 'plc' as the case may be). Any person to whom the Act applies must give his real name or names on all business letters, orders, invoices and receipts, together with an address in Great Britain at which documents may be served on him. The only exception is a partnership of more than 20 persons, which does not have to give the names of all the partners on its business documents but can simply give the address of its principal place of business where a list of the partners' names is open to inspection.

You should therefore be able to work out, by examining any letter or other document received from The Surrey Window Company, what legal entity you are dealing with and the address at which you can serve legal proceedings if this becomes necessary.

2.1.8 Change of company name

In relation to companies there is one further issue to discuss. The shareholders of a registered company can change the name of that company at any time. That change of name has to be notified to the Registrar of Companies, whose head office is at Crown Way, Maindy, Cardiff CF4 3UZ, and the change will be recorded in the records held by him. These records are open for public inspection, and for a modest fee you can obtain a microfiche or a printout of those records, which record among other things the current name and all previous names of the company. However, the registered number of a company cannot be changed in any circumstances.

Most changes of name are made for perfectly respectable business reasons, in which case the company will notify all its suppliers and customers of the name change. Although in principle the contracts to which a company is party are not affected in any way by a change in that company's name, the device can be used to try and avoid debts and liabilities. Suppose for example that I am trading using two separate registered companies which have the same business address: CP Thorpe Limited and CP Thorpe Enterprises Limited. You contract with CP Thorpe Limited to install new windows in your house, but the windows are substandard and defective. You write to the company demanding compensation for breach of contract and threatening legal action. At this point I change the name of CP Thorpe Limited to CP Thorpe Enterprises Limited, and I change the name of CP Thorpe Enterprises Limited to CP Thorpe Limited. CP Thorpe Limited now replies to your letter denying that that company is under any liability to you. This is in fact true since your contract is with a different company which is now called CP Thorpe Enterprises Limited. If you sue the company which is now called CP Thorpe Limited you will have sued a stranger to the contract and therefore your action will fail.

Your clue to what has happened is that the registered number on the letter from the company denying liability will be different from the registered number on the letters received from the company with which you placed your order for the windows. This tells you that the letter denying liability is not from the company with which you originally contracted, despite the fact that it has the same name. When you have noticed the difference between the registered numbers you will inspect the records held by the Registrar of Companies, and these will reveal the double name change.

2.1.9   Asset sales and share sales

Let us suppose that, rather than being reduced to desperate measures to evade creditors, my window business thrives and in due course I decide to sell it and retire on the proceeds. The sale of the business may be effected in two quite different ways. The first possibility is for the owner of the business (whether that is me personally, a partnership, or a company owned by me) to sell the assets which comprise the business, including its stock-in-trade, the rights to its business name and the goodwill associated with it. If I run the business through a company there is a second possibility, which is for me to sell the company or, to be strictly accurate, the shares in the company. In either case the purchaser would be said to have acquired the business, but the effect of an asset sale is very different from that of a share sale.

With a share sale the business itself and the assets which comprise it remain in the ownership of the same legal entity throughout. Nothing has changed except the ownership of the shares in the company, so the existing contracts which the company has entered into for the purposes of the business are entirely unaffected. With an asset sale on the other hand, ownership of the business and the assets which comprise it has been transferred from one legal entity to another, and the seller will have no further use for the existing contracts which he has entered into for the purposes of the business. He will want to transfer all his rights and liabilities under those various contracts to the buyer, and this is a problem to which we shall return in section 11.2.

2.1.10   Other legal persons

In everyday language the word 'person' means a human being, while the words 'business' and 'firm' are used to describe any commercial enterprise regardless of whether it is being run by an individual, a partnership or a company. In legal terms however the word 'person' and the phrase 'legal person' are used to mean, in addition to human beings, any entity which has its own legal personality. In legal terms therefore a registered company is a person. When lawyers wish to refer to human beings as distinct from other legal persons they generally use the word 'individual' (or sometimes 'natural person'). In this book the words individual and person are used in their legal sense.

Registered companies are by far the most common legal persons in the commercial world, and we have spent some time considering the implications of a company's legal personality. There are however a variety of entities apart from individuals and registered companies which are legal persons and therefore have the power to enter into contracts. These include entities which are incorporated by royal charter (such as the BBC), entities which are incorporated by statute (such as building societies), local authorities, the European Union itself and European Economic Interest Groups (or EEIGs), which are companies formed under European law.

2.1.11 Sovereign states and trade unions

Two special cases need to be mentioned, and these are sovereign states and trade unions. A sovereign state is a legal person and can therefore enter into contracts, but the principle of sovereign immunity means that a foreign sovereign state cannot be sued in the courts of England and Wales. Legal advice should be sought before entering into any substantial contract with a foreign sovereign state or any agency of a foreign sovereign state. This problem does not however arise with contracts made on behalf of the British Crown: an action can be brought against the appropriate government department, although not against the Queen personally.

A trade union does not have its own legal personality as distinct from that of its members, but it is nevertheless empowered to enter into contracts under the Trade Union and Labour Relations Act 1974.

2.2 CONTRACTUAL CAPACITY

2.2.1 General principle

Any entity which has legal personality has the power to enter into contracts. A person's power to contract is referred to as his 'contractual capacity'.

The general principle is that a legal person has full contractual capacity. That is to say that he, she or it can enter into any kind of contract, without limitation. There are however certain exceptions to this general rule, and these exceptions relate to certain categories of individuals, to local authorities and to companies. The contractual capacity of an individual is restricted if he or she is a minor, mentally disordered or drunk.

2.2.2 Minors

A minor is an individual who is under the age of 18 at the time the contract is entered into. What matters is the individual's actual age and not his apparent age or the age he claims to be. The contractual capacity of a minor is as follows:

1. *Contracts for necessaries.* A minor can enter into a valid contract for necessaries, meaning goods or services that the minor actually requires. A minor can therefore validly contract for goods such as food and drink and services such as railway tickets and medical attention.
2. *Contracts of apprenticeship, employment, education or instruction.* A minor can enter into a valid contract for his apprenticeship, employment, education or instruction.
3. *Contracts for an interest in property of a permanent nature* with continuing obligations attached to it, such as for example a lease, a contract to buy land or a contract to buy shares. With a contract of this type, the minor has the right, at any time until his 18th birthday and for a reasonable period after that, to disclaim that contract. The contract is said to be voidable at his option, a phrase discussed further in section 10.1.2.
4. *Any other type of contract*, which would include a contract for goods or services (other than necessaries) or a loan, is not binding on a minor unless he or she expressly confirms it upon coming of age.

A party who enters into a contract with a minor (other than a contract within categories (1) and (2) above) is therefore in a most disadvantageous position. If the minor proves to have made a good deal he will affirm it, while if the deal turns sour he will disclaim it. There were a number of reports following the stock market crash of October 1987 of stockbrokers and financial institutions who had unknowingly been dealing with minors over the telephone. The minors disclaimed their contracts when the value of the shares fell.

Unfortunately there is no easy way to avoid finding yourself in this position. Businesses which deal with the public, such as mail order companies, generally require a signed declaration from each customer that he is over 18. That does not protect the business from the contractual consequences if the declaration is untrue, although it would enable criminal proceedings for deception to be brought against the individual concerned. If you are intending to enter into a substantial contract with an individual who may be a minor, the prudent course is to ask to see his birth certificate: but if in fact he is a fresh-faced 23, he may well take offence and take his custom elsewhere.

2.2.3 Mental disorder

An individual is mentally disordered if owing to his mental condition (whether temporary or permanent) he does not understand what he is doing. An individual suffering from a mental disorder can enter into a valid contract for necessaries, meaning goods or services which that individual actually requires. If however such an individual enters into any other type of contract that contract is voidable and the individual can disclaim it provided that the other party was aware of his mental disorder. The requirement of the other party's awareness makes this rule very much less dangerous than the rules applicable to minors. The moral of the story is that one should not take advantage of someone who does not appear to understand what he is doing.

An individual who is so drunk that he does not understand what he is doing can enter into a valid contract for necessaries but not any other type of contract. When a drunk enters into any other type of contract, it is not clear from the reported cases whether that contract is void, or whether it is merely voidable at the instance of the drunk when he sobers up. The courts will presumably apply the same principles in relation to other intoxicating substances such as drugs.

2.2.4 Local authorities

A local authority can only enter into contracts which relate to or are incidental to the functions of that local authority. If it enters into any other contract, that contract is void.

This restriction on the contractual capacity of a local authority was dramatically demonstrated in February 1990, when the Court of Appeal held that interest rate swap agreements* worth £6 billion

---

* *An interest rate swap is a complex device which allows a borrower to exchange a floating interest rate on its debt for a fixed interest rate, or vice versa. It is in effect a gamble on future interest rates.*

between the London Borough of Hammersmith and Fulham and a number of banks were void because the Borough was speculating with a view to a profit. It is not one of the functions of a local authority, nor is it incidental to those functions, to speculate on the financial markets with a view to a profit. Since the agreements were void, the banks were unable to recover money owed to them by the local authority under those agreements.

2.2.5 Registered companies

Each registered company has a written constitution. This generally consists of two documents, the memorandum of association and the articles of association. The memorandum of association lists the activities which that company is authorised to engage in (known as the company's 'objects'). A company only has the capacity to enter into contracts in furtherance of its objects. The rule used to be that if it entered into any other contract that contract was '*ultra vires*' (meaning beyond the powers of the company) and void. This meant that a third party had to be careful when contracting with a company to ensure that the company's objects were broad enough to give it the power to enter into that contract.

The Companies Act 1989 fundamentally altered the position. It provides that the validity of an act done by a company cannot be called into question by reason of anything in the company's memorandum of association. This does not mean that a company now has full contractual capacity: in principle its contractual capacity is still limited by reference to the objects set out in its memorandum. But it does mean that a third party dealing with a registered company in good faith no longer has to concern himself with the contents of that company's memorandum. Effectively therefore a third party can assume that a company has full contractual capacity as long as he is not actually aware of any limitation imposed by its memorandum.

2.3 MULTIPARTITE CONTRACTS

2.3.1 Different types of multipartite contract

We noted in section 1.3 that, although the vast majority of contracts are bipartite, there is no maximum number of parties. The principles discussed in this book apply to all contracts irrespective of the number of parties involved, so there is generally no need to deal separately with multipartite contracts. It is however necessary to make a distinction between: (a) multipartite contracts where each party has its own distinct rights and obligations as against each other party, and (b) multipartite contracts involving a number of persons who are acting as a group.

An example of a multipartite contract of the first type would be a joint venture agreement between a number of companies. That contract will set out the purpose of the joint venture, how it is to be run and the rights and obligations of each party. If one party fails to perform its obligations under the contract then any of the other parties can enforce the contract against him.

If the rights and obligations of the parties to such a contract between themselves are represented in a diagram, it looks like this:

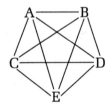

Although contracts of this type can be extremely complex, they raise no peculiar legal issues, and we need not consider them further.

2.3.2 Persons acting as a group

Contracts involving a number of persons acting as a group do however raise peculiar legal issues. We have already encountered two examples of contracts of this type. The first was a syndicated loan agreement (section 1.3), where the money to be lent is provided by a syndicate of banks. The second was a contract entered into by a partnership which, as discussed in section 2.1.3, is in legal terms a contract with the partners personally. If the rights and obligations of the parties to such a contract are represented in a diagram, it looks like this:

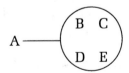

Here, B, C, D and E are all parties to the contract, but the contract is not concerned with the rights and liabilities between B, C, D and E themselves but with the rights and liabilities between A on the one hand and B, C, D and E on the other.

Suppose that the contract imposes an obligation on B, C, D and E to pay A the total sum of £100. If that sum is not paid, A faces an obvious problem: who does he sue, and for how much? The answer to that question depends on whether the obligations of B, C, D and E under the contract are joint, several or joint and several.

2.3.3 Joint obligations

A joint obligation is a single obligation owed jointly by all the members of the group. In our example this means that A can sue any or all of B, C, D and E for the £100, although of course he can only recover £100 in total. If therefore B has no money, A can still recover his £100 in full from C, D and E. This is the situation when a partnership enters into a contract: the obligations of the individual partners under the contract are joint obligations. Similarly the obligations of the other party are owed to the partners jointly.

2.3.4 Several obligations

A several obligation is an obligation which is split between the members of the group. The word 'several' originally meant 'separate'; there is a separate obligation on each group member to bear a specified share of the total obligation. Suppose in our example that B, C, D and E are each responsible for 25 per cent of the group's obligations under the contract. A must sue B for £25, C for £25, D for £25 and E for £25. If B has no money, A cannot recover B's share of the liability from C, D or E. This is the situation with syndicated loan agreements, which always specify what proportion of the loan is to be provided by each bank in the syndicate.

2.3.5 Joint and several obligations

A joint and several obligation combines the features of a joint obligation and a several obligation. If B, C, D and E owe A £100 jointly and severally, that means that there is one joint obligation for £100 and in addition a separate obligation for £100 on each of B, C, D and E. A can therefore sue any or all of them for his £100, although of course he cannot recover more than £100 in total. This is obviously the most advantageous situation from A's point of view.

2.3.6 Distinguishing between different types of obligation

Distinguishing between joint, several and joint and several obligations is a matter of interpreting the contract which gave rise to the obligations in question, but this is not generally difficult. If the contract specifies what share of the obligation is to be undertaken by each member of the group, then you are dealing with a several obligation. If no shares are specified you are dealing with a joint obligation. Joint and several obligations must be expressly created. If this does not actually involve use of the phrase 'joint and several', it will involve a very much more complex form of words which amounts to the same thing.

2.4 AGENCY

2.4.1 Meaning and significance

So far we have talked as if making a contract always involves direct interaction between the parties to it. In fact however it is very common for contracts to be entered into by an intermediary on behalf of one of the parties (who, as we shall see, may not actually be aware that the contract has been entered into). In legal terms the intermediary is known as an 'agent', and the party on whose behalf the agent is acting is known as the 'principal'. The word 'agency' is used to describe the relationship between the principal and the agent.

In everyday language the word agent is used in a number of senses other than its strict legal sense. For example estate agents and literary agents provide advice and services to their clients and often negotiate for them, but do not generally enter into contracts on their clients' behalves. They are not agents in the legal sense. Similarly a car dealer may describe himself as 'a main Ford agent', but in all probability he is buying cars from the manufacturer and reselling them on his own behalf rather than selling them on behalf of the manufacturer. In this book the word agent is used in its legal sense. The classic example of an agent in the legal sense is an auctioneer, who sells things on behalf of others.

The rules of agency are of great importance in the commercial world, and the main reason for this is that most businesses are run by companies. Although as we have seen a company has legal personality, it has no physical existence and it can act only through its agents, primarily its directors and employees. So any director or employee who enters into contracts or does anything else on behalf of a company is doing so as an agent of that company. Most individuals in the commercial world are therefore acting as agents rather than principals, and most commercial contracts (and virtually all the really large ones) are entered into by agents on behalf of both parties.

2.4.2 Essential principles

Let us take an everyday example from which the essential principles of agency should emerge. Suppose that I go into a branch of Dixons to buy a television set. The person I actually deal with is a member of the sales staff. He confirms that he has the model I want in stock, shows it to me and tells me about all its desirable features. He agrees to give me a 5 per cent discount for cash. I say that I will take the set and I give him the money. He gives me a receipt and I leave with the television.

Now this might look to a visiting Martian as if the contract for the sale of the television is between me and that member of the sales staff. It will be clear from the receipt that my contract is with Dixons Group plc and not with him, but this is of course already clear to both of us: we know that the television was not owned by him, and we know that the money I paid to him was not intended for him personally. If the set is defective I will demand a refund from Dixons and not from that member of the sales staff personally.

The legal analysis of this transaction is that Dixons has entered into a contract with me through the agency of that member of the sales staff. The important point is that, when an agent enters into a contract on behalf of a principal, it is the principal and not the agent who is party to that contract.

2.4.3 Authority of agent

Of course, one person can only enter into a contract on behalf of another person if that other person has authorised him to do so. The authority given by the principal to the agent may be general authority to carry out certain types of transactions, such as for example the authority given to an employee or salesman, or it may be special authority to carry out one specific transaction, such as for example the authority given to an auctioneer. The authority given by the principal to the agent is known as 'actual authority'.

An agent such as a door to door salesman or an auctioneer will usually have entered into a formal contract with his principal (an 'agency agreement') which sets out exactly what the agent is authorised to do and how he is to be paid for his services. Typically he will be paid a commission on sales.

By contrast, the shop assistant at Dixons who sold me a television is most unlikely to have entered into a formal agency agreement with Dixons. In all probability he is an employee of Dixons and the contract between them is an employment contract. That employment contract is most unlikely to set out in detail the authority given to the employee; it will probably say only that he is employed as a shop assistant (or perhaps these days a 'retail merchandising executive'), though it may provide for him to be paid commission in addition to his salary. Nevertheless, the fact that he is employed as a shop assistant necessarily implies that he is authorised to sell the goods in the shop to the public. His authority as an agent is no less real because it is implied rather than express. His actual authority may be expressly limited by the company's internal rules – for example, the branch manager's approval may be required before the shop assistant gives a customer credit in excess of £1,000.

At the other end of the scale the agent's actual authority may be entirely informal. Suppose for example that my wife asks me to telephone the local garage and arrange for them to service her car. When I make that arrangement I am doing so as my wife's agent: the contract for the servicing of the car is between the garage proprietor and her, rather than me.

The importance of an agent's actual authority is that the principal is bound by any contract entered into by the agent within the scope of the agent's actual authority. It does not matter how that authority came to be given or whether it is general or special or whether it is express or implied. The principal is bound from the moment the agent concludes the contract on his behalf, even if the principal is not aware that that particular contract has been entered into.

2.4.4 Apparent authority

Let us now turn to the position of the other party to the contract (usually referred to in books about agency as 'the third party' – an expression we will avoid since in this book we are using it to describe a stranger to a contract). In most cases the other party to the contract is simply not in a position to know what the actual authority of the agent is. If the agent enters into a contract which is outside the scope of his actual authority, it would be unfair to deprive the other party of the benefit of that contract if he was unaware that the agent had exceeded his authority. So the law has developed the doctrine of 'apparent authority', which means such authority as the other party might reasonably suppose that agent to have. The principle is that an agent, who as we have seen can commit his principal to any contract within the scope of his actual authority, can also commit his principal to any contract within the scope of his apparent authority.

Let us try to give some reality to these concepts. You will recall that in the example in section 2.4.2, the shop assistant agreed to give me a 5 per cent cash discount. Suppose that Dixons write to me saying that the shop assistant had no authority to give me a discount, and asking me to pay the extra 5 per cent. In legal terms they are saying that their agent exceeded his actual authority. In fact most shop assistants do have the authority to give a cash discount, and so it was quite reasonable for me to believe that this shop assistant had such authority. He was therefore acting within the scope of his apparent authority, and so Dixons is bound by the contract to sell me the television at a 5 per cent discount.

The outcome could have been quite different if, for example, Dixons had displayed a prominent notice in that shop saying 'our staff are not authorised to give discounts'. In that case I would (or should) have known that the agent's actual authority was limited. If the other party knows that the agent is acting outside the scope of his actual authority then he cannot rely on the doctrine of apparent authority.

We have in fact already encountered the distinction between an agent's actual and apparent authority. You will recall that in our discussion of conditional contracts (section 1.4.6) we considered the position when an executive concludes a contract on behalf of his company without making clear to the other party that some further approval (such as board approval) is required. The internal requirement of board approval is in fact a limitation on the actual authority of the company's agents. If in spite of that limitation the executive enters into a binding contract without board approval, the company is bound by that contract if the executive was acting within the scope of his apparent authority. The moral of that story could have been expressed in a different way, that is: when acting as an agent, be absolutely clear as to the extent of your actual authority and be careful not to exceed it.

In our earlier discussion of this example we did in fact assume that the executive had the apparent authority to commit his company to that contract. If he did not have that apparent authority the company is not bound by the contract. Whether or not a particular agent has the apparent authority to enter into a particular contract depends on whether, in all the circumstances, the other party might reasonably suppose that the agent has such authority. In general however it is safe to assume, and professionally we do assume, that:

1. A director or the company secretary of a company has the apparent authority to commit that company to any contract whatsoever.
2. A company's senior executives can commit the company to any contract of any size provided that the subject matter of the contract is related to that executive's title and function (which you can establish from his business card or, usually, from correspondence signed by him). In other words a sales manager can commit his company to any sales contract, a purchasing manager to any purchase contract, a commercial manager to any commercial contract, and so on.

The issue of apparent authority is directly raised whenever an individual enters into or offers to enter into a contract on behalf of a company. The other party needs to ask himself: is it reasonable for me to suppose that this individual has the authority to enter into this contract? If the answer is no, for example if an accounts assistant signs a major sale agreement, then the other party should either ask for evidence that the agent has the actual authority to sign (for instance by means of a board minute* evidencing that authority), or alternatively ask for a director or the company secretary to sign.

In our experience, however, it is very uncommon for a company to seek to avoid a contract on the grounds that their agents were not authorised to enter into it. This is partly because most directors and employees are in general very aware of the extent of their actual authority and are careful not to exceed it, but partly also because it is such an unattractive assertion to have to make. The courts do not look favourably on a principal who argues that the other party to a

---

* *A board minute is an extract from the minutes of the meeting of the company's board of directors at which it was resolved to give him that authority.*

contract should lose the benefit of it because the principal was unable properly to control his agent. The court is likely to hold that the agent was within his apparent authority and therefore that the principal is bound by the contract. This largely explains why the apparent authority of an agent tends to be extensive.

The distinction between the actual and apparent authority of an agent was dramatically illustrated in 1995 when unauthorised trading on the derivatives market in Singapore led to the collapse of Barings Bank. The individual who entered into these transactions was not authorised to do so: they were outside the scope of his actual authority. But it was taken for granted that the transactions were within the scope of his apparent authority, and it was never at any stage suggested that the Bank was not bound by them.

2.4.5 Consequences of unauthorised transactions

We need to consider further the legal consequences if an agent enters into a contract which is outside the scope of his actual authority. As we have seen, the principal is bound by that contract if the agent is within the scope of his apparent authority, but is not bound if the agent is outside the scope of his apparent authority. Let us consider these two situations separately:

1. *Agent within apparent authority – principal bound by contract.* In this situation the principal can recover from the agent any loss which the principal suffers as a result of the unauthorised contract. In our example of the Dixons shop assistant who gave me a 5 per cent discount, if he was acting outside the scope of his actual authority Dixons is legally entitled to recover the amount of the unauthorised discount from him personally. In our example of the executive who entered into a binding contract without board approval (section 1.4.6) the company is legally entitled to recover from him personally any loss the company may suffer as a result of the unauthorised contract. It is in fact very unusual for a company to bring a personal action against one of its employees except in cases where the individual concerned has acted fraudulently. But the possibility of such an action is a good reason for the employee to observe any limitation imposed on his actual authority.
2. *Agent outside his apparent authority.* In this situation the principal is entitled, if he so chooses, to ratify (i.e. adopt) the unauthorised contract by giving the other party notice to that effect. If he does so there is a valid contract between the principal and

the other party. If the principal does not ratify the contract, then the other party can recover from the agent any loss he suffers as a result, including the profit he would have made on the contract.

2.4.6 Undisclosed agency

So far we have assumed that the other party knows that the agent is acting on behalf of another person. However, the agent is under no obligation to tell him of this fact. He may choose to stay silent, in which case the other party may well assume that he is contracting with the agent himself. In this situation the principal is known as an 'undisclosed principal'. As and when the other party becomes aware of the principal's involvement, he has a choice: he can either accept that the contract is with the principal, or else he can hold the agent to the contract as if (as the other party thought when the contract was entered into) the contract was with the agent.

CHAPTER 3

Entering into a contract

Contract law textbooks usually begin with the principles of offer and acceptance and the requirement of consideration, and we must now consider these two subjects. The practical significance of these topics may not be immediately apparent, so let us begin with a brief explanation.

An understanding of the principles of offer and acceptance will enable you, in most but not all situations, to identify the precise moment at which a contract comes into existence. The importance of being able to identify that moment precisely should be apparent, because this is the moment at which both parties are committed to the transaction. Before this moment either party is free to pull out of the transaction, but from this moment neither is free to do so.

Consideration is a technical legal requirement for the formation of a valid contract. This requirement is supposedly the most distinctive feature of English contract law and is a favourite academic topic, but in practice there are only a few commercial situations in which the requirement of consideration causes problems. But in these situations it is important to recognise that there is a problem, because otherwise the parties may enter into an agreement which is unenforceable.

Once we have dealt with these two topics we can (as it were) get down to business. In the remainder of the chapter we will turn to the broader commercial realities of entering into a contract (section 3.3), to the problem of non-disclosure (section 3.4) and finally to tendering (section 3.5).

3.1 OFFER AND ACCEPTANCE

The law considers that every contract comes into existence as a result of the acceptance of an offer. An offer made by one party is accepted by the other party (or parties), and a contract is formed at the moment of acceptance. In section 3.1.8 we will question whether every contract can be analysed in this way, but we must begin by understanding what these terms mean and by taking a close look at the process by which every contract supposedly comes into existence.

3.1.1 Offer

An offer is a proposal which will result in a contract if the person to whom the proposal is made simply accepts it. This means that the proposal must be (1) complete and (2) made with contractual intention. We discussed contractual intention at length in section 1.4 and we need say no more here other than to note that a proposal made without contractual intention (the plainest example of which is a 'subject to contract' proposal) is not a contractual offer and does not result in a contract if it is accepted. We do however need to consider further the requirement that the proposal is complete.

In order for a contract to come into existence the parties must be in agreement not only on the basic terms of the transaction but also on all other matters which have been raised in the course of the negotiations between them. The basic terms of the transaction (discussed in section 4.2.1) are the minimum which the parties must have agreed if a contract is to exist: with for example a contract for the sale of goods the parties must as a minimum have agreed what goods are to be sold and what price is to be paid for them. But if in the course of their negotiation the parties have discussed other matters such as warranties, delivery date and the timing and method of payment, then no contract can come into existence until all these other terms have been agreed. It follows that a proposal only amounts to an offer if all the terms of the proposed transaction, and not just its basic terms, are clear. Notice however that the requirement is not that all the terms of the transaction are stated in the proposal, but only that they are clear.

Let us take three simple proposals to illustrate the requirement that, in order to amount to an offer, a proposal must be complete:

1. 'I offer to sell you this painting.'

2. 'I offer to sell you this painting for £10,000.'
3. 'I offer to sell you this painting for £10,000 payable in instalments.'

Proposal 1 is not an offer because one of the basic terms of the transaction, namely the price, is not clear. With proposal 2, the goods to be sold and the price to be paid for them are both clear, and this proposal is an offer: a contract for the sale of the painting will be formed if the other party simply accepts it. With proposal 3 however, although the basic terms of the transaction are clear, the proposal is that the purchase price is paid in instalments. But it is not clear how many instalments there will be, when they will be due or what interest (if any) will be payable. The proposal is incomplete and is not therefore a contractual offer.

Usually an offer is made to a particular person, but equally it may be made to a group of persons, any of whom may accept it, or to the world at large in which case anybody may accept it. The classic example of an offer to the world at large is an advertisement in a newspaper offering a reward for the return of some article of value. Anyone who returns that article in response to the advertisement will have accepted the offer and be contractually entitled to the reward. Obviously a person cannot accept an offer which is not made to him.

Lawyers refer to the person making an offer as the 'offeror' and to the person to whom the offer is made as the 'offeree'. We shall be using these useful but inelegant expressions from now on.

3.1.2 Termination of offer

There are a number of ways in which an outstanding offer may be terminated. To begin with, an offer which is stated to be open for a specified period lapses at the end of that period if it has not been accepted by then. If no such period is stated, the offer lapses if it has not been accepted within a reasonable period. Second, an offer terminates if the offeror notifies the offeree that he is withdrawing it, and the offeror can in fact withdraw an offer at any time even if it is stated to be open for a specified period, provided of course that it has not already been accepted. The only situation in which he cannot withdraw it is where he has entered into a contract with the offeree which obliges him to keep it open. Third, an offer terminates if it is rejected by the offeree, so an offeree who rejects an offer cannot change his mind and subsequently accept it.

3.1.3 Acceptance

Acceptance is the communication by the offeree to the offeror that he accepts the offer. Sometimes an offer will actually specify what the offeree must do to accept it, such as for example 'This proposal is open for acceptance by facsimile transmission to me at my office address before 5 pm today.' In this situation the offeree must follow the procedure specified if he wishes to accept the offer. Usually however no such procedure is specified, in which case the offeree can communicate his acceptance of the offer to the offeror in any way he chooses. The acceptance may be verbal (for instance 'yes' or 'OK' or 'it's a deal') or non-verbal (for instance by offering a handshake or countersigning a written proposal).

In principle however an acceptance always involves some positive act by the offeree. Silence can never amount to the acceptance of an offer. Suppose then that an offeror makes an offer which says 'I will assume that you have accepted this offer unless you tell me otherwise within seven days.' The offeree is free to ignore this offer, and if he does so his silence will not constitute the acceptance of the offer and no contract will be formed.

Whatever form the acceptance takes, a contract comes into existence the moment the offeror is aware that his offer has been accepted. Where the proposed transaction involves more than two parties, a contract only comes into existence when an offer made by one party has been accepted by all the others.

There is an anomalous exception to the principle that a contract only comes into existence when the offeror becomes aware of the acceptance, and this is where the acceptance is sent by post. Provided only that the letter is correctly addressed, a contract comes into existence at the moment it is posted even if the offeror never receives it. So if you return from the post-box having posted your acceptance of an offer, and the offeror telephones you to say that he is withdrawing that offer, he is too late since the contract has already been formed. This rule reflects a nineteenth century confidence in the postal service which is not widely shared today.

3.1.4 Rejection and counter offer

If the offeree does anything other than simply accept the offer, then he is taken to have rejected it. So the offeree may expressly reject the offer, but he is also taken to have rejected it if he responds with a counter proposal or a qualified or conditional acceptance. In section 3.1.1 we considered the following example of an offer: 'I offer to sell you this painting for £10,000.' Each of the following responses would in fact be a rejection of that offer:

1. 'I'll give you £9,000.'
2. 'It's a deal provided you have it professionally cleaned.'
3. 'It's a deal but you'll have to give me time to pay.'
4. 'I accept, subject to contract.'

Response 1 is a counter proposal at a different price. Responses 2 and 3 are qualified acceptances which introduce new issues into the negotiation. Response 4 indicates, as we saw in section 1.4.7, that the offeree does not at this stage intend to enter into a binding agreement. None of these responses results in a contract.

A response which counts as a rejection of the offer may itself amount to an offer (known as a counter offer) if it meets the requirements of completeness and contractual intention. If so a contract will be formed if the other party accepts the counter offer. Responses 1 and 2 above are both in fact counter offers, and they also illustrate the point made in section 3.1.1 that the terms of an offer do not have to be stated as long as they are clear: taken in context with the original offer the terms of the proposed transaction are perfectly clear. Responses 3 and 4 however are not counter offers. Response 3 is incomplete because the timing of payment is unclear, and Response 4 is made without contractual intention.

3.1.5 Illustration of principles

Analysing the communications between the parties in terms of offer and acceptance makes it possible (in theory at least) to identify (i) whether there is a contract and if so (ii) the precise moment at which that contract came into existence and also (iii) the terms of that contract, being the terms of the offer which was accepted. For the purposes of this analysis, any communication other than an offer or an acceptance is classified as an 'invitation to treat'. Treat is an archaic word meaning negotiate: the noun 'treaty' is of course still in use. Let us analyse in this way a simple oral negotiation between A and B for the sale of a car.

	Communication	*Classification*	*Comment*
A.	'Do you want to buy my Morris 1000 Traveller?'	Invitation to treat	Not an offer as price not proposed

B.	'How much?'	Invitation to treat	
A.	'£1,000.'	Offer	Basic terms now clear
B.	'I'll give you £700.'	Offer	Rejection of A's offer: counter offer
A.	'No. It's got eight months' road tax. I won't go below £900.'	Offer	Rejection of B's offer: counter offer
B.	'I haven't got that much cash.'	Invitation to treat	Rejection of A's offer
A.	'OK. Give me £700 when you collect and the balance later.'	Invitation to treat	Not an offer as not clear when balance of price is payable
B.	'OK. £700 when I collect it and the rest in 6 weeks.'	Offer	
A.	'Done.'	Acceptance	

A contract for the sale of the car came into existence when A said (or, strictly, when B heard him say) 'done'. If B had accepted A's first offer there would have been a contract for the sale of the car for £1,000. In fact however, in addition to negotiating on price, the parties brought three further matters into the negotiation. The terms of the contract finally reached include A's undertaking that the car has eight months' road tax and B's undertakings to collect the car and to pay the purchase price in two instalments. It is now too late for either party to raise any new concerns. B cannot for instance withdraw from the purchase on the grounds that the car has no MOT test certificate.

3.1.6 Application of principles

The principles of offer and acceptance have proved a powerful and adaptable way of looking at the formation of a contract. There is, for example, no difficulty in applying these principles to a contract formed between two parties over the Internet, a rapidly growing form of commerce.

Most ordinary situations lend themselves quite easily to this analysis. In our example of the sale of the Mars bar in section 1.2.1, when I said 'Mars bar, please' that was an offer which the newsagent accepted by putting one on the counter, a case of acceptance by conduct. But if no price had been displayed, my asking for a Mars bar would be only an invitation to treat: if the newsagent put one on the counter and said '£2.50, please', that would be an offer which I would certainly refuse.

Given a little thought, a purchase in a supermarket is equally straightforward. You might at first think that the display of a priced item is an offer which the customer accepts by putting that item in his basket. In fact however it is the customer's presentation of the item at the checkout which is the offer, and the cashier accepts it when he rings that item up: this conclusion is inevitable when you consider that until he reaches the checkout the customer is free to put the item back on the shelf.

Sometimes however the application of these principles can be very difficult, and a good example is the case of *Harvey* v *Facey* 1893 which concerned a negotiation over a plot of land called Bumper Hall Pen conducted by telegraph. Harvey asked Facey 'Will you sell us Bumper Hall Pen? Telegraph lowest cash price.' Facey replied 'Lowest price for Bumper Hall Pen £900.' Harvey replied 'We agree to buy Bumper Hall Pen for £900 asked by you. Please send us your title deed ...'. Harvey claimed that this exchange resulted in a contract for the sale of the property, and he sued to enforce it. The difficulty is to decide whether Facey's telegraph was an offer or only an invitation to treat. The court held that it was only an invitation to treat. Harvey's second telegraph was therefore an offer, but Facey had not accepted it, so no contract had been formed.

3.1.7　The significance of a signature

Since most major commercial transactions are entered into by means of signatures on a document, we must consider the significance of a signature.

Most of us sign a number of letters every day without giving it a second thought. A signature is a conventional means of authenticating a document, and it does not necessarily have any contractual significance at all. A contractual offer may be contained in a signed letter, but may equally be contained in a printed document, such as a circular or brochure, which is unsigned. The contractual status of any document must be judged from what the document says: the presence or absence of a signature does not in itself tell you anything.

A document may however make clear that the signature or

signatures on it are intended to have contractual significance. This can be seen with the standard form agreements produced by various types of businesses for their customers to sign, a subject to which we shall return in Chapter 5. Above the space where the customer is required to sign are some words like 'I agree to be bound by the terms and conditions contained herein', or perhaps just 'Accepted'. This makes clear that the customer's signature not only authenticates the document but also constitutes his acceptance of its terms. In principle of course the customer may accept those terms by some means other than signing the document, for example by letter or even orally. So while his signature on the document indicates that a contract has been formed, the opposite is not true: the absence of a signature does not necessarily indicate that no contract exists.

Negotiated written agreements invariably contemplate that the agreement will be signed by or on behalf of each party. The main body of the agreement is introduced by the words 'It is hereby agreed as follows' and ends with a statement along the following lines: 'In witness whereof the parties have caused this Agreement to be signed by their duly authorised representatives on the date first above written.' So the signatures serve not only to authenticate the document but also to signify the agreement of each party to its contents.* Again however it is possible in principle for one or more of the parties to commit itself to the contract by some means other than signing the document. As we shall see in section 6.4.3, this fact means that the parties have to tread very carefully from the time the text of the agreement is finalised until it is actually signed.

When the time comes for the agreement to be signed, execution copies (known as 'engrossments') will be prepared. Although in principle one engrossment is enough, in practice there will be the same number of engrossments as there are parties, so that each party can have a fully signed original for its records. For the sake of simplicity let us imagine a bipartite agreement, so two engrossments are prepared and signed by one party and sent to the other by courier for him to sign. This constitutes an offer, on the terms of

* *The signature section of the engrossments will often include the name and title of each signatory in print, and sometimes each signature will be attested by the additional signature of a witness. This can be very useful if it is ever necessary to find out who the signatories were, or if it is ever alleged that one of the signatures is a forgery. But none of this is actually necessary except where the document is in the form of a deed, the execution requirements for which are discussed in section 1.2.4. Unless the agreement is under seal, a simple signature on behalf of each party is sufficient to form the contract.*

the engrossments, from the first party to the second. He accepts that offer by signing the engrossments, so the contract is formed at this point. The second party therefore inserts the date of his signature in manuscript right at the beginning of the agreement: 'This Agreement is made the 15th day of February 1996.'

It follows from this analysis in terms of offer and acceptance that the signature by the first party does not commit him to the contract: he is not committed until the other party signs, so up until this moment he can notify the other party that he is withdrawing his offer. If in spite of that withdrawal the other party goes ahead and signs the engrossment, there is no contract despite the existence of engrossments signed by both parties. In reality of course in this situation only the offeree will know whether he signed before or after the offer was withdrawn.

If we try to apply the same principles to a multipartite agreement, such as for example a joint venture agreement with five parties, the waters start to become murky. The simplest analysis is that the first party to sign is making an offer to the other four, which they each accept in turn by signing the engrossments. The contract is formed when the last party signs: if one declines to sign, the signatures of the other four do not constitute a contract between them.* The problem with this analysis is that, although the law provides for the withdrawal of an offer, it does not provide for the withdrawal of an acceptance. So, if this analysis is correct, the first party can change his mind and withdraw his offer at any moment before the last party signs, but the next three parties to sign cannot subsequently change their minds.

This conclusion cannot be correct: if the first party can change his mind at any time before all the parties have signed, then surely so can those who sign second, third and fourth. We are therefore forced to conclude either that in this specific situation an acceptance can be withdrawn, or else that the signatures by the second, third and fourth parties somehow constitute offers rather than acceptances, so that the signature of the last party constitutes an acceptance of an offer made jointly by the first four.

As this is intended to be a practical book, we have throughout tried to deal only with problems which actually arise in practice. The absence of reported cases on disputes about signatures suggests that it is very rare for a party to change his mind after

---

* *The agreement may provide otherwise. In certain circumstances the parties may provide that there will be a contract between those parties who sign, even if one or more decline to sign.*

having signed the engrossments. In our experience however many senior executives are extremely nervous about signing agreements and are quite capable of having second thoughts at any point in the process.

A few years ago a friend of one of the authors told him one of those stories which is amusing provided that it happens to someone else and not to you: his commercial director changed his mind after having signed the engrossments of a multipartite agreement. As misfortune would have it they were in fact the last party to sign. When it was explained to the director that the contract had been formed and it was too late to back out, he proposed that they destroy the engrossments and tell the other parties that the documents had been lost without his having signed them. It had to be pointed out to him that the other parties might conceivably take the matter to court and ask him under oath whether he had signed the documents, and that to lie under oath constitutes the criminal offence of perjury. Of course the destruction of the engrossments after the contract has been formed would not affect the contractual position in any way. You cannot terminate a written agreement by tearing it up.

As we have seen it does not necessarily follow that because a party has signed a formal agreement he is committed to the transaction. In some situations engrossments are signed well before the parties intend to commit to the transaction, and are deposited with a third party (usually but not necessarily a solicitor) until the parties are ready to contract. This arrangement, known as an 'escrow', is particularly common with contracts for the sale of land. As we shall see in section 3.3.2, by convention a contract for the sale of land is formed only when the two engrossments, one signed by the seller and one by the buyer, are physically exchanged. This exchange (in which incidentally it is hard to find an offer and an acceptance) is usually handled by the parties' solicitors. Each party therefore signs his engrossment and deposits it with his solicitor, who holds it on escrow until the parties are ready to exchange. During this period the solicitor holds the signed engrossment to the order of his client, which means that the client can at any time require his solicitor to return it to him.

In practice of course a fully signed engrossment tells you virtually nothing about how the contract came into existence, and it is unlikely that a retrospective analysis of offer and acceptance will even be possible. This raises the practical question, when you are dealing with a formal written agreement, of how far you should go to satisfy yourself that this really is a contract binding on the parties. The first step is to check that the agreement has been signed on behalf of each party. If one or more signatures is missing, you will have to enquire further to establish whether the agreement was validly formed. Otherwise however, unless the validity of the agreement is itself in question, you have little practical choice but to assume that an agreement signed by each party binds each party.

Nevertheless we have seen that with signed agreements the strict application of the principles of offer and acceptance can have striking results. In some circumstances the parties can be bound by the terms of a formal written agreement even though one or more of them has not signed it. In some circumstances there is no contract despite all the parties having signed the engrossments. And, finally, the parties can be bound by the terms of a formal written agreement despite the fact that the signed engrossments no longer exist. As we said right at the beginning of the book, a contract is not a signed piece of paper: it is the meeting of minds.

3.1.8 The limits of offer and acceptance

In our discussion in the last section of the signing of multipartite agreements, we saw the principles of offer and acceptance coming under strain. In some situations they break down completely, and we will briefly consider three situations which cannot be satisfactorily explained in terms of offer and acceptance. The first two again relate to signed agreements.

1. As we have seen a bipartite agreement is very easy to explain in these terms if the engrossments are signed first by one party and then by the other. But at some signing ceremonies (including, according to television news pictures, the signing of some international treaties), events are ordered differently. Each signatory is given one engrossment which he signs. The documents are then swapped over, and each signatory signs the other engrossment. Not even the strictest legal purist could doubt that a contract has been formed, but which is the offer and which is the acceptance? This academic question would become important in practice if one signatory changed his mind after signing the first engrossment and declined to sign the other. Would everything depend on whether the second signatory had or had not signed the first engrossment?
2. Similar problems arise where a multipartite agreement is signed in counterparts. This is usually done when the parties are in a

great hurry, and do not have time to arrange a signing ceremony or to circulate the engrossments for signature by each party. Instead, one engrossment is sent to each signatory, so if there are five parties the end result is five engrossments each bearing a single signature. We do not propose even to attempt an analysis in terms of offer and acceptance. It is better to see this in terms of contractual intention: the parties intend that the five signatures will commit them to the transaction. They do.

3. The third situation concerns the contract which undoubtedly exists between the members of an entity such as a registered company or a trade union, which we mentioned in section 1.3. If I buy some shares in British Aerospace plc I become a party to a contract with that company and each of its existing shareholders, the terms of the contract being contained in the memorandum and articles of association of the company. But I have no idea who the other shareholders are, and it is very hard to see how there can be an offer and an acceptance between parties who are not even aware of each other's existence.

3.1.9   Practical significance

What then is the practical significance of the doctrine of offer and acceptance? The answer really depends on what form the agreement is in. At the two extremes of formality and informality, that is with agreements in writing on the one hand and with oral agreements on the other, the principles of offer and acceptance have little part to play. With an agreement in writing, any dispute between the parties is much more likely to turn on what the contract meant than on whether there was a contract or what the terms of it are. Although as we have seen difficult but potentially important questions can arise if something unexpected happens during the signature process, analysis in terms of offer and acceptance is not always helpful and it remains to be seen how far the courts will go in pursuing that analysis.

With a purely oral agreement such as our example in section 3.1.5, although in theory the negotiation can and should be seen in terms of offer and acceptance, in practice there is usually insufficient evidence to allow it. The parties' recollections of the negotiation are just not clear enough or consistent enough to allow analysis in these terms, so lawyers are reduced to asking questions like 'are you sure in your own mind that there was a deal?' and 'are you quite certain that the seller said the car had eight months' road tax?'

The principles of offer and acceptance come into their own in between these two extremes, where the transaction involves neither an agreement in writing nor an oral agreement, but is entered into in the course of a series of written communications of some kind. This of course covers the majority of commercial transactions, excluding only the very large and the very small.

When in this situation a dispute subsequently arises about whether there was a contract or what the terms of it were, the court will resolve those issues by a rigorous examination of those communications in terms of offer and acceptance. As we shall see in relation to standard terms and conditions, in some situations the analysis is pursued too far and can have unsatisfactory consequences. But if the court can identify an offer which was accepted it will conclude that there was a contract, and anything which the parties said or did after the acceptance is contractually irrelevant unless it amounts to a variation of that contract (discussed in section 7.4.1). The court will not be impressed by a party who claims that he did not intend at that stage to enter into a contract or that there were outstanding issues to be resolved.

3.2 CONSIDERATION

The words 'contract', 'deal' and 'transaction' all carry with them the notion of an exchange, typically the exchange of goods or services for money. An agreement which lacks this element of mutuality would not be called a deal or transaction and is not in legal terms a contract. So if A agrees to sell his car to B for £100, that is an enforceable agreement. But if A agrees to give his car to B, B cannot enforce that agreement against A. The legal expression of this requirement is that, for an agreement to amount to a contract, each party must 'provide consideration' for it.

3.2.1 The requirement of consideration

Exactly how 'consideration' should be defined is a favourite academic question, but the best way to think of it is this: a party provides consideration if the agreement involves him undertaking to do something. If each party undertakes to do something, then the requirement of consideration from each party is satisfied. But if one party has not undertaken to do anything, then the agreement is completely unenforceable because that party has provided no consideration.

In section 1.2.1 we analysed an agreement for the sale of a Mars bar in terms of what each party undertook to do: the newsagent undertook to supply me with a Mars bar and I undertook to pay him 30 pence. The newsagent's undertaking represents his consideration for the agreement, and my undertaking represents my consideration for the agreement, so the requirement of consideration from each party is satisfied and there is an enforceable contract between us.

An undertaking to do something is by far the most common type of consideration, but there is one other type. This is where a party to an agreement, rather than undertaking to do something, has already done something. We have already encountered an example of consideration of this second type in section 3.1.1: where someone returns a lost item in response to an advertisement offering a reward, the act of returning that item constitutes not only his acceptance of the offer but also his consideration for the agreement. He has no further obligations under the contract, but is entitled to the reward without having to do anything else.

3.2.2 What counts as consideration

The law is not concerned with the value of the consideration provided. As long as a party provides some consideration it does not matter if its value is minimal or else totally disproportionate to the value of the consideration provided by the other party. It is not uncommon for a lease to be granted at a peppercorn rent, and here the consideration provided by the tenant (that is his undertaking to pay the landlord a peppercorn) is sufficient. Nor does it matter if the undertaking which represents the consideration provided by a party is not actually performed. A single peppercorn has no practical value: it is unlikely that the tenant will actually give the landlord a peppercorn, and equally unlikely that the landlord will demand it. The undertaking to pay the peppercorn is sufficient consideration.

With most agreements consideration moves between the parties: A undertakes to do something for B and B in return undertakes to do something for A. The consideration provided by a party may however be in the form of an undertaking to do something for a third party: A undertakes to do something for B and B in return undertakes to do something for C. B's undertaking is sufficient consideration for the contract. The problem this situation raises is not lack of consideration but rather that C is a stranger to the contract and cannot therefore enforce it against A.

Sometimes one party, instead of undertaking to do something, undertakes not to do something, and a negative undertaking of this kind does satisfy the requirement of consideration from that party. One of the most common examples is where the parties to a legal dispute agree to settle it, a subject to which we will return in section 9.4.5. Suppose that A has made a claim for damages against B, and they eventually agree a damages figure in full and final settlement of the claim. B's consideration for the agreement is his undertaking to pay that sum to A, and A's consideration is his undertaking not to commence, or as the case may be not to proceed with, legal proceedings against B.

3.2.3 Existing contractual obligations

There is only one situation in which a party's undertaking to do something does not satisfy the requirement of consideration, and this is where he is already obliged under an existing contract with the other party to do that thing.

This principle was memorably illustrated in the case of *Stilk* v *Myrick* 1809 in which Stilk, a seaman, joined a ship for a voyage from London to the Baltic and back for £5 a month. During the voyage two of the eleven crew deserted and could not be replaced, so the captain agreed to share the deserters' wages among the remaining nine if they would work the ship back to London short-handed. On their return Stilk sued for his extra wages, but failed because he was already under a contractual obligation to sail the ship back to London. The agreement for the extra wages was not binding because Stilk had provided no consideration for it.

The principle that one party's existing contractual obligations to the other will not serve as his consideration for a subsequent agreement between them has significant implications which are considered in section 3.2.5.

3.2.4 Deeds

The requirement of consideration from each party does not apply to a deed (discussed in section 1.2.4). An agreement contained in a document under seal is binding even if one party has provided no consideration for it. In general, if A agrees to give B £1,000, B cannot enforce that agreement because he has provided no consideration for it. But if that agreement is in the form of a deed then B can successfully sue A for the £1,000 despite the absence of consideration from B. With a deed therefore the question of consideration simply does not arise.

It is common for people to make regular donations to charity by way of a covenant, which is another name for a deed. The attraction of this arrangement lies in its tax advantages: the donations are paid net of tax and the charity can recover that tax from the Inland Revenue. The arrangement does however have the side-effect of making the agreement legally enforceable by the charity.

3.2.5 Practical significance

Our discussion of the doctrine of consideration has been deliberately brief, and the reason for this should already be clear. It is very unusual indeed for a commercial entity to agree to do something for absolutely nothing in return, so with commercial agreements the requirement of consideration from each party very seldom presents a problem. But when it does it is important to recognise that problem before the agreement is entered into.

Suppose for example that for the purposes of negotiating a particular transaction it is necessary to reveal sensitive commercial or technical information relating to your business to the other party. You sensibly draw up a confidentiality agreement for the other party to sign in which he undertakes not to disclose any of that information to any third party or to use it for any purpose other than the evaluation of the proposed transaction. If that is all it says you will not be able to enforce this confidentiality agreement because you have provided no consideration for it. You can easily cure that fault when drafting the agreement either by putting the agreement in the form of a deed, or by including a token obligation such as the obligation to pay the other party £1,* or else by putting the agreement in a form which contains a real element of mutuality ('we will supply this information provided that you undertake not to disclose ...'). But if you overlook the problem it will probably only become apparent if the other party breaks his confidentiality undertakings and you try to enforce the agreement against him.

There is one situation in particular where the requirement of consideration tends to cause problems, and this is where the parties to an existing contract agree to vary it. An agreement to vary an existing contract is itself a contract, so a variation requires the agreement of and consideration from each party to the existing

---

* *The following formulation is very common: 'In consideration of the sum of £1 received from A, B hereby undertakes ...'. This is an example of consideration of the second type we discussed: A has done something rather than undertaking to do something.*

contract. But as we noted in section 3.2.3 a party's obligations under an existing contract will not serve as his consideration for a subsequent agreement between them, so a variation is only enforceable if each party undertakes some new obligation.

Suppose then that the parties to a construction contract meet to discuss a variation of that contract. If the builder agrees to perform work not required by the existing contract and the client agrees in return to increase the contract price, that is a valid variation of the existing contract. But if the builder agrees to perform extra work without charge, or the client agrees to increase the contract price for no extra work, then neither agreement is enforceable and the existing contract continues unaltered.

Exactly the same problem arises when a creditor agrees to accept a lesser sum in satisfaction of a debt owed to him. Suppose that A owes B £100,000, but being very close to the financial precipice is unable to pay that amount. He contacts B and explains that if B sues him for the full amount he will be forced into bankruptcy, with the likely consequence that B will receive nothing. Being a commercial realist B agrees that if A pays him £50,000 immediately he will write off the remainder of the debt. Unfortunately for A he has provided no consideration for B's agreement to accept a lesser sum in satisfaction of the original debt: he was already obliged to pay B £100,000, so his undertaking to pay a lesser sum will not stand as consideration for their subsequent agreement. The result is that there is nothing to prevent B, having received £50,000 from A, from suing him for the remaining £50,000.

In certain situations then the technical requirement of consideration from each party can have significant practical consequences, and it is for this reason that the businessman needs to be aware of it.

3.3 THE COMMERCIAL REALITIES OF CONTRACTING

A businessman entering into a contract is seldom much concerned with the legal technicalities of offer and acceptance or consideration. His concern is to get the right deal at the right price, and as long as he does not resort to criminal or otherwise unlawful means the law has very little to say about how he achieves that objective. The constraints on him are of a commercial rather than a legal nature, and the most significant of these constraints are the customary ways of contracting used in that particular trade or business (section 3.3.2) and the relative strength of his bargaining position (section 3.3.3). We must however begin by recognising the importance of commercial custom and practice in general, and by considering the relationship between commercial custom and commercial law.

3.3.1 Commercial custom and practice

Each different type of trade or business has its own way of doing things, its own customs, practices and traditions. Lawyers refer to this using the rather quaint phrase 'custom of the trade', and as we shall see commercial custom does have legal ramifications. But the scattered references in law books to custom of the trade hardly do justice to its enormous practical significance. The fact is that to operate effectively in any type of business you have to understand how that business works.

Suppose that an executive with 10 years' experience in advertising starts a new job with a shipping company. He will find himself in an alien world. To begin with he will find that people in shipping dress differently from people in advertising. He will also find that they talk differently and do business in a completely different way. He is likely to have a confusing and difficult time until he has learnt the vocabulary and practices of shipping, and is familiar with charterparties, bills of lading, certificates of quantity and of quality, documentary credits, demurrage and dead freight. It is precisely the enormous gulf between these two different worlds which makes it so unlikely that an individual will move between them, except curiously at the very highest level where complete inexperience is evidently no bar to a new job.

Commercial custom has played a very important part in the development of commercial law. Historically it was custom which came first, and the law followed it. Bills of lading provide an example of this from the world of shipping. Originally a bill of lading was simply a receipt, issued by the ship's master, to show that the goods described in it had been loaded on his vessel. In time however the practice developed of using the bill of lading as a document of title to the goods. This allowed the owner of the cargo to sell it, while the ship was still at sea, by transferring the bill of lading to the buyer. When the ship arrived at its destination the buyer could claim the goods on the basis that he held the bill of lading, without producing any other evidence to show that he now owned the goods. Commercial practice had therefore converted a simple receipt into a document of title, and furthermore into a document of title which was negotiable, meaning that title to the goods was transferred by means of the physical transfer of the document. In due course the courts gave effect to this practice and accepted and confirmed that a bill of lading was a negotiable document of title, so that he who held the bill owned the cargo.

Most of the common law of commerce was formed in this way. Today's law of insurance is essentially a codification of the practice originally developed by shipowners in seventeenth century London to protect themselves against marine risks, including as we shall see the most distinctive feature of that practice, which was the requirement of the full disclosure to the underwriters of all relevant matters by the person seeking the insurance. Effectively therefore much of the commercial law was originally developed not by lawyers but by businessmen, and the common law's ability to adapt to changing commercial circumstances and to absorb established commercial practice has always been one of its greatest strengths.

There are also a number of important statutes which simply codify commercial practice and the common law which developed from it. The Carriage of Goods by Sea Act 1992, which codifies the common law relating to bills of lading, is an example. Other examples include the Bills of Exchange Act 1882, the Marine Insurance Act 1906 and the original Sale of Goods Act 1896 (now repealed and largely re-enacted by the 1979 Act). The British Parliament usually legislates in a reactive and piecemeal way, so these statutes are unusual in that rather than changing the law they simply put the existing common law on a statutory basis. They are however models of clarity which put many more recent statutes to shame. During the hundred years or so in which they have been in force, they have required little or no amendment and have led to comparatively little litigation. That is the hallmark of good legislation.

In a well developed area such as shipping, commercial practice does continue to evolve but it does so slowly. In less developed areas commercial practice tends to develop very fast indeed. Information technology and reinsurance are two areas which are currently advancing very rapidly. Another is financial derivatives, such as futures and options, where the last 20 years have seen the introduction of ever more complex and exotic devices such as swaps, caps, collars, floors, straddles and strangles. The disastrous losses incurred at Lloyd's on reinsurance business since the mid-1980s, and the collapse of Barings Bank following huge losses in derivative transactions in Singapore in 1995, give the uncomfortable impression that the businesses involved did not themselves understand the risks their agents were taking.

Most of the customs which have developed in these fast moving areas have not yet come to the attention of the courts or the legislature. This does not however mean that they have no legal effect: the law will give effect to custom provided only that it is sufficiently well established, and it is sufficiently well established if it is universally recognised and adhered to by the individuals engaged in that type of trade or business. Where necessary the courts will hear evidence from experts as to what the customs are in the trade or business concerned.

Having discussed custom in general, we must now consider the practical significance of customary ways of contracting. We will however return to the subject of custom in relation to implied terms (section 4.7.3) and interpretation (section 6.2.5).

3.3.2 Customary ways of contracting

The customs of a particular trade or business often include a customary way of entering into contracts. It would be impossible to list all the various customary ways of contracting, but it is also unnecessary because the first thing an individual learns when entering a new trade or business is how deals are done. We will therefore consider only a few examples in order to demonstrate that here again custom has both commercial and legal implications.

Anyone who has household or motor insurance knows how contracts of insurance are traditionally entered into. The party wanting the insurance is required to complete and sign a printed proposal form, which in legal terms is an offer. If the insurer accepts this offer it will then issue a formal policy document recording the terms of the cover. Direct insurance, a relatively recent phenomenon where insurance is arranged over the telephone, may well signal the end of the traditional proposal form and thus the extinction of a custom. Our second example concerns construction contracts and engineering contracts. In these industries contracts are almost always awarded by means of a tendering procedure, which is considered in detail in section 3.5.

In principle the parties are free to contract in whatever way they see fit, and there is no legal requirement that contracts are entered into in the customary way. In practice however a well established custom is mandatory. Before direct insurance, the completion of a proposal form was mandatory in the sense that you could not get insurance without it. Similarly, a construction company which decides that it will no longer tender for contracts but deal only by direct negotiation with clients will soon find itself out of work and out of business, because its competitors will continue to tender in the usual way.

It is for this reason that, although we have spent much time dealing with different forms of contract, no general advice has been offered as to which form to choose in any particular situation. Very seldom will you have any choice. If you want a Mars bar you will have to enter into an oral contract, and if you want to buy a business you will have to sign a written one.

Two further examples will demonstrate the legal implications of customary ways of contracting. The first concerns auctions, a customary way of selling things which is of great antiquity. At an auction the auctioneer, acting as the seller's agent, solicits oral offers and accepts the highest with a tap of his hammer. The second concerns contracts for the sale of land, which as discussed in section 1.2.5 are required by the Law of Property (Miscellaneous Provisions) Act 1989 to be in writing and signed by each party. The universal practice with contracts for the sale of land is for two copies of the agreement to be drawn up, one to be signed by the seller and one by the buyer. The long established custom is that no contract is formed unless and until those two documents have been physically exchanged: it is exchange rather than signature which commits the parties to the transaction. This customary means of contracting for the sale of land is expressly recognised and preserved by the 1989 Act.

Everyone knows the procedure at an auction, and everyone involved in conveyancing knows the significance of exchanging contracts. In the absence of very clear evidence to the contrary the law necessarily assumes that the parties and their agents are conducting themselves in accordance with prevailing custom. So, while there is nothing to prevent you from bidding at an auction on a subject to contract basis, very clear evidence will be necessary to persuade a court that you really were bidding on that basis; and of course if you make this clear to the auctioneer he will ignore any bid you make. Similarly, if contracts for the sale of land have been signed but not exchanged, it is futile for either party to claim that a binding contract exists.

3.3.3 Bargaining power

The most important single factor in determining the outcome of any contractual negotiation is the balance of bargaining power.

Where one party's bargaining position is significantly stronger than the other's, this will be reflected in contract terms which are favourable to him. A business which has a monopoly, or an effective monopoly, in the supply of particular goods or services is of course in the strongest possible bargaining position: it can simply dictate the terms of supply to its customers. Most monopolies use standard terms which are slanted steeply in their favour, and simply refuse to contract on any other basis. Without an alternative supplier, the customer will have to accept those terms if it wants to do business with the monopoly. We shall return to the use of standard terms by monopolies in Chapter 5.

The position with a commercial negotiation for the supply of goods or services is seldom so one-sided. Generally there will be more than one contractor to choose from, and the various time-honoured methods of obtaining the most favourable contract price, such as sale by auction, sale by a process of sealed bids, and the tendering process used in construction contracts, all depend for their success on there being more than one person interested in the contract. Even where there is only one possible contractor, a party will still usually have the choice, if a satisfactory deal cannot be reached, not to contract at all.

The backdrop to any such negotiation is the state of the market for the goods or services in question, and a significant imbalance between supply and demand can have the most striking effects on the balance of bargaining power. In 1980 high oil prices led to a record level of drilling activity in the North Sea and a huge demand for drilling rigs. An oil company wishing to charter a rig could not use the usual tendering procedure. If it could find any idle rig it had to accept virtually whatever contract terms the rig owner demanded, and charter rates rose to nearly $100,000 per day. The oil price collapse of 1986 completely reversed the position. So many rigs were idle that charter rates fell to around $10,000 per day, and the oil companies could effectively impose whatever terms they chose.

Important as they are however, market conditions are not the only elements in the equation. Other more personal factors, like a party's reasons for wishing to enter into the contract, his circumstances, his expectations and his attitude, also enter into it. For example, commercial necessity and financial distress can both force a party into a deal on terms which would not normally be acceptable. Similarly a party taking a particularly bullish view of the future will be more keen to contract than market conditions alone might suggest. There are many examples of the acquisition of a business where the buyer inquired too little, paid too much, and obtained insufficient contractual protection from the seller. This is usually because the buyer, having set his heart on the acquisition, fatally weakened his own bargaining position by depriving himself of the option to say no. Any number of personal factors like this may be operating to tip the balance of bargaining power one way or the other.

The aim in any negotiation must be to maximise the advantage or minimise the disadvantage of your bargaining position. Bargaining power is however a relative matter rather than an absolute one. The question is not how much you want the contract, but whether you want it more or less than the other party, and while you will be aware of market conditions and of the strengths and weaknesses of your own position, you will not necessarily be aware of the personal factors affecting the other party. Although you can be sure that you will hear about the strengths of his position, he will of course try to obscure its weaknesses. So a negotiator should always try to look behind the other party's propaganda to the reality of his position, in order to establish where the balance of bargaining power really lies.

With a very substantial contract it is worth giving thought, before detailed negotiations commence, to the balance of bargaining power and in particular to the other party's position. Why does he want the contract, how much does he want it, and what other options are available to him? Is it possible to find the answers to these questions rather than just speculating about them? It is also worth giving thought, especially if your position is weak, as to how you might improve it. The classic means of doing so is to find some other option, in the form of another possible contractor or an alternative means of meeting your commercial objectives.

Following their privatisation in 1991, the UK's two main power generators were negotiating long term supply contracts with British Coal to replace the existing contracts after they expired in 1993; in terms of total value these contracts must be among the largest in the country. The coal price under the existing contracts was significantly higher than the price on the world market. In March 1992 it was announced that the power generators had pulled out of a project to construct a large deep-water coal import facility at Immingham on Humberside. The reasons for this decision were not made public. Obviously however the prospect of a new bulk import facility must greatly have strengthened the generators' bargaining position with British Coal, and it is possible that the project was abandoned when that purpose had been served.

3.4 NON-DISCLOSURE

3.4.1 No duty to disclose

A party entering into a contract is not legally obliged to disclose what he knows about the subject matter of that contract to the other party. Only if he says something which proves to be incorrect will the other party have any legal remedy against him. An example will illustrate the practical importance of this principle.

A purchaser P Ltd acquires all the shares in a small manufacturing company M Ltd from M's previous owner V Ltd. Following its acquisition of M Ltd the purchaser discovers a number of facts about the company which the vendor was aware of at the time the contract for the sale of the shares was entered into but did not disclose:

1. M Ltd had just lost its biggest customer and as a result is now unprofitable.
2. M Ltd's workforce is out on indefinite strike for better pay.
3. A large number of its past employees are suing M Ltd for damages on the grounds that they contracted asbestosis while working for it.
4. M Ltd's factory is badly affected by subsidence and is in need of expensive underpinning.
5. The local authority has made a compulsory purchase order in respect of part of the factory site in order to add a fifth lane to the nearby M25 motorway. The factory's administration and accounts block will have to be demolished and resited.

P Ltd would not have made the acquisition if it had been aware of these facts. Unfortunately however it has no legal remedies at all against V Ltd for failing to disclose them unless V Ltd gave assurances about these matters in the contract for the sale of the shares.

3.4.2 *Caveat emptor*

This is the significance of the phrase *caveat emptor* ('let the buyer beware'). The seller is in a much better position than his buyer to know the characteristics of the thing he is selling, but it is up to the buyer to ensure that the thing in question meets his requirements before he contracts to purchase it. There are two ways for him to do so. The first way is to make his own enquiries into the matters which concern him: in our example the buyer could have found out about the compulsory purchase order by inspecting the local land charges register kept by the local planning authority. The second way is to require contractual assurances from the seller. Such a contractual assurance is known as a 'warranty'.

3.4.3 Warranties

What warranties the seller should give is an important and contentious issue in the negotiation of any substantial contract of sale, whether for the sale of goods, land, a ship, a company, a business or assets of any other kind.

For his part the buyer cannot afford to leave any stone unturned: he will want warranties about any and every relevant matter and he will want them drawn in the widest possible terms. For his part the seller cannot afford to give any warranty which is or may prove to be untrue, since that would make him liable to the buyer for breach of that warranty.

Let us take just one example to show how this process works in practice. In the negotiation for the sale of a company the seller will have to provide the prospective buyer with the company's up-to-date accounts to show its current financial position. Often he will also provide his projections of the company's future profits to whet the buyer's appetite for the deal. The buyer will demand a number of warranties in relation to the accounts, including a warranty that the accounts provided are complete and accurate in every respect, and a warranty that the company's future profits will match the projections provided by the seller. The seller cannot reasonably refuse to warrant the accounts since that would indicate that he knows those accounts to be inaccurate, but he will try to water the warranty down, for example 'the seller is not aware of any inaccuracy in the accounts ...'. The seller will however be most unwilling to warrant the future profit projections because, if he does so and the company's future profits fall below the projections, he will be liable to the buyer for the difference. The two factors which will determine whether he has to give that warranty or not are the relative strength of his bargaining position and the degree of confidence which he has in those projections.

Warranties can therefore take a variety of forms. Some are assurances about past or existing facts while others are assurances as to some future state of affairs; some are assurances about facts while others are assurances about the state of mind of the party giving them. In demanding warranties the buyer is seeking information as much as contractual protection. His primary purpose is to get the seller to reveal what he knows and what he believes about the subject matter of the sale, and those revelations may lead the buyer to offer a reduced price or to pull out of the negotiations altogether.

3.4.4 Contracts other than sale

A buyer is not the only person who needs to protect himself against non-disclosure. For example, a lender is at risk if the borrower does not disclose relevant facts about his financial position. Lenders generally not only require extensive warranties from the borrower but also make their own enquiries into his financial position by examining his accounts and by checking his credit rating with an independent credit rating agency.

Similarly, an employer is at risk if the employee does not disclose relevant facts about his personal history, which is why prospective employers invariably require a full CV and independent references. My employer can dismiss me without notice if he finds out that I have spent the last two years in prison for fraud and not, as stated in my CV, working for a competitor;* but if he took me on without seeing my CV and without making any enquiries into my employment history, he would not have the right to dismiss me when he subsequently learns of my dubious past. Before entering into any contract it is vital to consider carefully what information you need about the subject matter of that contract and how you are going to obtain it.

There is one significant exception to the general principle that there is no duty of disclosure. With contracts of the utmost good faith, the most important example of which is a contract of insurance, there is an obligation to disclose relevant facts. This is discussed in section 10.2.3.

3.5 TENDERING

3.5.1 Outline of procedure

Finally we need to look in more detail at tendering. As we have already mentioned, this is the method by which virtually all substantial construction and engineering contracts are entered into, but it can be used by a party requiring goods or services of any description as long as there are at least two potential suppliers. It

---

* *This is in fact a misrepresentation, discussed in section 4.3.2.*

has become quite common for large companies to run tenders among commercial solicitors for the provision of legal services to the company, although in more buoyant times the major firms of solicitors might well shun any invitation to tender for work.

The first stage in any tendering procedure is to establish a list of the persons to be invited to bid. This can be done either by direct contact with potential bidders, or by advertising your intention to run a tender in a newspaper or trade journal, or both. All the parties who express an interest in bidding for the work are scrutinised to ensure that they are both technically and financially able to carry it out, a process usually referred to as 'pre-qualification'. The result is a tender list of persons each of whom is capable of doing the work required.

The next stage is for each person on the tender list to be provided with a set of tender documents, which will usually consist of (i) the specification, (ii) the contract terms and conditions and (iii) the instructions to tenderers. The specification is a precise description of the work required, and the contract terms and conditions are the detailed terms of the proposed contract. All reference in the tender documents to price will however be left blank.

The instructions to tenderers will set out exactly what each bidder must do if he wishes to bid. If a bidder fails to observe those instructions precisely this will usually result in his being disqualified, meaning that his bid will not be considered. Typically each bidder will be required to submit his bid in a specified form to a specified person by a specified deadline, and his bid will consist of a written statement of the price he would charge for the work together with a list of 'contract exceptions', that is any changes he requires to the contract terms and conditions set out in the tender documents. If all the bidders are happy with the contract terms and conditions and propose no changes to them, the party running the tender will simply award the contract to the lowest bidder. We shall return in section 3.5.3 to consider what happens when, as is usually the case, there are some contract exceptions.

That in outline is a description of a classic tendering procedure, and it should be sufficient to demonstrate both the attractions of tendering and its prevalence in certain important types of industry. A properly conducted tender is an elegant means of ensuring that you get a competent contractor to perform the work you require at the lowest possible price. On a practical level however the tendering procedure is open to abuse, for example if the bidders collude as to the price at which they bid, or if one bidder can induce someone involved in running the tender to give his bid preferential treatment or to reveal the level of the bids received from his competitors. The manipulation of the tendering procedure using an insider is probably one of the most common types of commercial fraud. Companies which often use the tendering procedure generally go to considerable lengths to avoid such manipulation by ensuring that the bids are sealed and are all opened and considered together by a committee often referred to as a 'tender board'.

We will not look further into the dark world of commercial fraud, but it is worth taking a closer look at some further contractual aspects of the tendering procedure.

3.5.2 Collateral obligations

The focus of the whole procedure is of course on the contract which will ultimately be awarded to the lowest bidder, which we shall refer to as the 'main contract'. It is however possible for other contractual obligations to come into existence in the course of the tendering procedure. Suppose for example that the tender documents state that the main contract will be awarded to the lowest bidder. This undertaking constitutes a distinct contractual obligation on the person running the tender, and the lowest bidder could enforce that obligation against him if for any reason the main contract is not awarded to him. In most situations however the person running the tender will not want to give this particular undertaking, because of course even the lowest bid may be unacceptably high, so most tender documents state explicitly that the person running the tender does not undertake to accept the lowest bid or any of the bids submitted.

Contractual obligations which are distinct from and independent of the main contract are known as 'collateral contracts', and the tendering procedure provides a further example of a collateral contract. Most instructions to tenderers require that each bid is in the form of a contractual offer, so that each bidder offers to do the work required at the price stated in his bid, and the bidder is required to confirm that his offer will remain open for a specified period, commonly 90 or 120 days. This gives the person running the tender time to evaluate the bids and to decide which to accept, and the main contract comes into existence when the successful bidder is notified that his offer has been accepted. In general however, as noted in section 3.1.2, a person who makes a contractual offer is free to withdraw it at any time even if the offer is stated to be open for a specified period, the only exception to that principle being where the offeror is under a contractual obligation to keep the offer open. In the tendering procedure there is a collateral contract under which each bidder undertakes to keep his offer open for the period specified, and this collateral contract prevents a bidder from withdrawing his offer during that period. In this way the person running the tender ensures that the bids remain open while he chooses between them.

We have used our discussion of the tendering procedure to provide two examples of collateral contracts. It is however important to appreciate that collateral contracts can arise in the course of any contractual negotiation. It is always open to one of the parties to a negotiation to give some undertaking which stands as a distinct contract. The case of *Andrews* v *Hopkinson*, discussed in section 4.3.1, provides a further example of a collateral contract.

3.5.3 Award of contract

Anyone who is familiar with the tendering procedure will have recognised that our brief description of it is in one important respect simplistic. The bidders are unlikely to find the contract terms and conditions included in the tender documents entirely acceptable, so the probability is that each bid will include a significant list of contract exceptions, which are the changes which the bidder requires to the contract terms and conditions to make them acceptable to him. It is equally unlikely that the bidders' contract exceptions will all be entirely acceptable to the person running the tender. So in reality, rather than simply awarding the contract to the lowest bidder, the person running the tender will have to negotiate with the lowest bidder in order to finalise the terms and conditions of the contract.

The other point to appreciate is that price and contract terms cannot be considered in isolation: some of the bidders' contract exceptions may be price sensitive. If for example the lowest bidder's contract exceptions would make the contract very much more favourable to him, it may be that one of the higher bids is in fact preferable. In reality therefore the person running the tender may have to negotiate finalised contract terms separately with a number of bidders before he can decide, taking account of both price and contract terms, which bid is the best. Only then will he be in a position formally to award the contract.

Once the contract has been formally awarded, the parties will usually draw up and sign a formal agreement to record the terms of the contract between them. As we have seen however the main contract generally comes into existence when the successful bidder is notified that his bid has been accepted, in which case it does not actually matter whether a formal agreement is subsequently signed or not. Such a formal agreement is therefore an example of an agreement evidenced in writing rather than a true written agreement, a distinction we encountered in section 1.2.3.

There are however good practical reasons for signing a formal agreement. As we have seen there will usually have been some form of negotiation on the successful bidder's contract exceptions, and those negotiations may have been conducted in writing or orally, whether by telephone or in a meeting, or a combination of the two. So it is prudent to formalise the agreement while those negotiations are still fresh in the minds of both parties.

3.5.4 Letters of intent

In section 1.4.5 we discussed the contractual problem which can arise with an interim agreement, namely the difficulty in telling whether or not that agreement was intended to be legally binding, and we saw the danger of sending any communication which refers to an agreement having been reached but does not deal explicitly with the question of contractual intention. Exactly the same problem can arise in relation to the tendering procedure.

It often happens that there is some delay in awarding the contract. This may be the result of delay in the finalisation of the contract terms or in the selection of the successful bid, or it may be that the schedule of the project to which the tender relates has slipped. Whatever the reason, the time approaches when the validity of the bids is due to expire. The person running the tender does not want to have to start the whole process again, so he sends the favoured bidder what is generally called a 'letter of intent', to the effect that he intends to award the contract to him. The idea is to keep that bidder on the hook, by giving him the impression that he will be awarded the contract notwithstanding the stated expiry date of his bid, but without actually awarding the contract at that stage. Any such letter of intent needs to be worded very carefully indeed: if for example it says 'we are pleased to inform you that yours is the favoured bid', this could well be interpreted as the acceptance of that bid with the result that the contract has been formed.

A much better solution to this problem is simply to ask the bidders to agree to extend the validity of their bids, a request which in our experience is seldom refused and which, if accepted, constitutes yet another collateral contract.

3.5.5 Subsequent price negotiations

We have touched on the possibility of the fraudulent manipulation of the tendering procedure by a bidder. The procedure is also open to a very different and less sinister type of abuse, involving further negotiation on price after the bids have been opened. This may be instigated by the person running the tender or by one of the bidders.

The first possibility is that the person running the tender, having seen the amount of the bids, decides to achieve an even lower price. He therefore contacts one of the bidders and tells him informally that his bid is too high to succeed, but that he will be awarded the contract if he lowers his price by £50,000. A bidder who receives such a proposal is in a difficult position. To begin with he cannot be certain that he is being told the truth: it may be that he is the lowest bidder and that if he declines to reduce his price he will be awarded the contract anyway. It is also of course possible, and perhaps even likely, that the other bidders have received a similar proposal, in which case the bidder concerned may agree to reduce his price but still not be awarded the contract. In an extreme case this can turn into a Dutch auction, with each bidder lowering his price in turn until only one player remains in the game.

The second possibility is that one of the bidders contacts the person running the tender and states informally that he is prepared to undercut the lowest bid. When this happens it usually means that the bidder concerned has obtained inside information on the bids and knows that his is not the lowest, although of course with a properly conducted tender he should not be able to find this out. Sometimes however a bidder who is desperate for work will make such a proposal without knowing what bids have been made, so if in fact he is the lowest bidder he is in the ludicrous and unprofitable position of undercutting his own price.

Negotiations on price after the bids have been opened are of course contrary to the spirit of the tendering procedure, and might well be considered unethical, but they are not necessarily unlawful. However, the person running the tender needs to be very careful if he is tempted to conduct such negotiations. The other bidders, and in particular the one who submitted the lowest bid in the tender, will be aggrieved if they discover what has happened and may consult their lawyers to see if they have any legal redress. The lawyers will scrutinise the tender documents, and if for example they find an undertaking that the person running the tender will accept the lowest bid, the lowest bidder could sue for breach of that collateral contract and recover in damages the profit which he would have made if the main contract had been awarded to him. Failing that the lawyers may be able to find an explicit or implicit undertaking that the tender will be conducted fairly or in good faith, and this could also provide a basis for legal action. There are even more alarming possibilities: if the strategy of the person running the tender involved actual dishonesty, such as telling the lowest bidder that his bid was not the lowest, he may well be guilty of the criminal offence of obtaining a pecuniary advantage by deception.

But the most compelling reason why the person running the tender should refuse to enter into subsequent negotiations on price is not ethical or legal but commercial. If it becomes known that he is prepared to deal behind the scenes, no future tender run by him will be taken seriously: no bidder will start with his best price if he expects to have a second bite at the cherry. As a means of obtaining the lowest possible price, the tendering procedure depends crucially on the bidders knowing that there will be no second chance.

3.5.6 European directives on public procurement

We cannot leave the subject of tendering without considering in outline the public procurement directives issued by the European Union. According to the European Commission, the public authorities in the different member states of the Union spend the equivalent of £574 billion per year obtaining works, goods and services of various kinds, but until recently only 2 per cent by value of these contracts were awarded to businesses from another member state. It appeared therefore that public authorities were routinely discriminating against businesses from other member states in favour of local suppliers, contrary to the fundamental precept of free trade within the Union.

To rectify this situation the Council of Ministers has issued a series of directives to the member states, which are required to enact them into local law. So far the relevant enactments within the United Kingdom are as follows:

1. The Public Works Contracts Regulations 1991, which deal with the award of works contracts (meaning contracts for building and civil engineering works) by public authorities and utilities.

2. The Public Supply Contracts Regulations 1991, which deal with the award of supply contracts (meaning contracts for the supply of materials) by public authorities and utilities.
3. The Utilities Supply and Works Regulations 1992, which deal with the award of both works and supply contracts by certain entities operating in the water, energy, transport and telecommunications sectors. (Unlike the other Regulations referred to, these Regulations are not restricted to the activities of state-owned entities. The justification for this is that the entities operating in these sectors do so under licences granted by the state, which is therefore in a position to influence their contract award procedures in favour of local suppliers.)
4. The Local Government (Direct Service Organisations) (Competition) Regulations 1993,* which deal with the conduct of competitive tendering for the carrying out of certain works by local authorities.
5. The Public Services Contracts Regulations 1993, which deal with the award of public services contracts by certain public bodies, including local authorities, government departments, Ministers of the Crown and fire and police authorities.
6. The Public Supply Contracts Regulations 1995, which deal with the award of public supply contracts (meaning contracts for the purchase or hire of goods) by certain public bodies (including those listed in (5) above).

Although we will not attempt more than the barest outline of this torrent of legislation, in substance most of these Regulations are very similar. The emphasis is on transparency. All contracts above a threshold value must be advertised in the Union's official journal. While the entity concerned is free to award the contract by means of an open tender, a restricted tender between bidders chosen by it, or by direct negotiation, it has to state in advance which procedure it will use and apply it without discriminating against suppliers from other member states. Where a tender is run a strict timetable must be observed and the entity is obliged to award the contract to the bidder making the lowest or most economically advantageous bid. The contract award has to be advertised in the official journal and a detailed report given to the authorities. Failure to observe these procedures can result in the contract award being set aside, and an aggrieved party can sue for damages for any loss he suffers as a result of that failure.

* As amended by the Local Government (Direct Service Organisations) (Competition) (Amendment) Regulations 1995.

While it remains to be seen whether these typically bureaucratic procedures will solve the problem of discrimination, it is clear that in the areas covered by these Regulations the character of the tendering procedure will be fundamentally altered. For the first time a potential supplier will have a means of forcing his way onto a tender list, and an unsuccessful bidder will have a means of reviewing and potentially overturning the award. So, in addition to the costs of meeting the bureaucratic requirements of the Regulations, public utilities will also have to meet the costs of defending legal actions from disappointed bidders. An eminent legal historian has said, not entirely in jest, that legislation never achieves its intended effect and often achieves the opposite effect from that which was intended. It may be that in the attempt to reduce the cost of public works in the European Union this legislation will make them more expensive.

CHAPTER 4

The terms of a contract

A contract consists of two types of terms. First, there are the express terms, meaning those terms which are expressly agreed between the parties. Second, there are the implied terms which, although not expressly agreed between the parties, the law will nevertheless imply to supplement the express terms. Before we begin however there are some important practical matters which require attention, and these are the problems of evidence.

4.1 PROBLEMS OF EVIDENCE

4.1.1 Disputes about terms

A significant proportion of contractual disputes are disputes about what the terms of the contract are. Let us take a very simple example. A buyer of goods sues the seller for late delivery, claiming that the contractual delivery date was the 14th but the seller did not in fact deliver the goods until the 28th. The seller admits that he delivered the goods on the 28th but claims that the contract did not require him to deliver before then.

The outcome of this dispute depends entirely on the evidence available as to what the terms of the contract were. What evidence is available depends on what form the agreement was in, and broadly speaking there are three possibilities. The first is that the agreement was an oral one. The second is that the agreement was entered into by an exchange of letters, telexes, facsimile transmissions or printed forms of some kind. The third possibility is that the agreement is in writing. We will discuss these three possibilities separately.

4.1.2   Oral agreement

We saw in Chapter 1 that, with only a few exceptions, any contract can be entered into orally. Samuel Goldwyn's observation, that an oral contract is not worth the paper it is written on, was witty but wrong. An oral contract binds the parties just as irrevocably as a formal written agreement, and can if necessary be enforced by legal action in exactly the same way.

Many transactions between private individuals are contracted orally, even when significant sums are involved. Even if someone is selling a second hand car or lending £1,000 to a friend, neither party is likely to insist on negotiating and signing a written contract. Oral contracts are also the norm with minor retail transactions. With more substantial commercial transactions oral contracts are unusual, but not unknown. Sometimes, especially where the individuals concerned know and trust each other or where the urgency is so great that there is no time for formalities, a very substantial deal is entered into orally.

The obvious problem with oral contracts, and the reason why the commercial world generally shies away from them, is the difficulty in establishing subsequently what the terms of the contract are. To return to our example of the dispute over the delivery date, suppose that the contract was entirely oral, having been entered into between an employee of the buyer and an employee of the seller in a meeting or over the telephone. It is important to appreciate that, despite the absence of documents, there is evidence available as to the terms of the contract: that evidence consists of the recollections of the two employees. If the dispute comes to court, each employee will be able to give evidence as to his version of events. If they each have a different recollection of what delivery date they agreed, the court will decide on balance whose evidence it prefers and this will determine the outcome of the case.

Even with an oral contract however there may be evidence other than the recollections of the parties or their agents. If for example others were present when the contract was made, they may be able to give evidence as to what was agreed. Alternatively there may be relevant documents, such as an internal memorandum prepared by one of the parties or correspondence between them which refers to the agreement. In a dispute over the terms of an oral contract, the evidence of the parties or their agents can be unreliable and tends to be self-serving, so the documentary evidence is particularly important. If for example the seller's employee sent a memorandum to his distribution department after the contract was made saying that delivery was required by the 14th, this will destroy his credibility if he subsequently claims that the agreed delivery date was the 28th.

Generally speaking a document sent by one party to the other is more convincing than a document drawn up by one party for its own purposes, and a document drawn up shortly after the contract was made is more convincing than a document drawn up after the dispute has arisen. So, if you do enter into a significant oral contract, it is worth sending a letter, telex or facsimile to the other party setting out the terms of the agreement as you understand them. If you receive such a document from the other party which does not accord with your understanding of the agreement, it is important that you reply to him without delay and in writing setting out your understanding, even if this results in a dispute about what was agreed. If there are differences about what was agreed, it is much better that they come to light before either party performs the agreement. In principle such a dispute does not affect the rights and obligations of the parties under their oral agreement, so either party can insist on performance and if necessary take the other to court. In practice however, provided that neither party has performed the agreement, the existing agreement may well be abandoned by mutual consent, in which case the parties may or may not negotiate another agreement to replace it.

4.1.3 Agreement by exchange of correspondence

The second possibility is that the contract was entered into in the course of an exchange of correspondence. In this situation, establishing what the terms of the contract are is a matter of analysing the correspondence in terms of offer and acceptance, a process which does not generally require oral evidence from the individuals involved. If the entire negotiation was conducted in writing there will be a complete paper trail, enabling the court to establish what the terms of the contract are without hearing any oral evidence at all. Often however part of the negotiation will have been conducted orally: if for example the parties were short of time, they may have resolved the outstanding issues and finalised the contract over the telephone (in which case it is strictly speaking an oral contract, although most of its terms will be evidenced by the prior correspondence). In so far as the paper trail is incomplete, the court will hear evidence from the individuals concerned to establish what happened in the oral part of the negotiation. Generally however the court will not be interested in hearing oral evidence about any part of the negotiation which was conducted in writing, on the basis that an individual's written words are the best evidence of what was in his mind at that time.

To return to our example of the dispute about the delivery date, this is much less likely to arise where the agreement was entered into in the course of correspondence than where the agreement was oral, except in one specific situation. This is where each party is claiming that the contract incorporates his standard terms of business. The seller is relying on his standard terms which provide for delivery within four weeks, while the buyer is relying on his standard terms which provide for delivery within two weeks. This intractable situation, known as the 'battle of forms', is discussed in detail in section 5.3.10.

4.1.4 Agreement in writing

If there is an agreement in writing (a phrase which as we saw in section 1.2.3 embraces both an agreement evidenced in writing and a true written agreement), the dispute in our example is most unlikely to have arisen in the first place. Suppose that there is an agreement in writing which provides for delivery on the 14th. In defending the case, the seller must be saying one of two things. First, he may be claiming that the document does not correctly represent the agreement he reached with the buyer, in other words that the document is inaccurate. Second, he may be claiming that the document is incomplete, for example that he had an oral understanding with the buyer that the delivery date would be put back by two weeks if manufacture of the goods were delayed by a strike. It makes no practical difference whether such an oral understanding is seen as part of the whole agreement, so that the contract was partly oral and partly in writing, or else as an entirely separate collateral agreement.

Whether the buyer is claiming that the document is inaccurate or is incomplete, the difficulty facing him is the so-called 'parol evidence rule', which is that where there is an agreement in writing neither party can produce oral or documentary evidence in court to contradict those written terms. This is really a matter of common sense rather than an absolute rule of evidence: if the parties go to the trouble to produce an agreement in writing, the presumption must be that the document is both accurate and complete. A party claiming that it is inaccurate or incomplete will need very convincing evidence to persuade the court of that fact and overturn that presumption. The chances are that he will fail.

If the seller is claiming that the reference in the agreement to the 14th is simply a mistake, it is open to him to bring an action asking the court to amend the agreement so that it reflects the true intentions of the parties. This is known as an action for 'rectification' of the document, but it is rare for such an action to be brought and even more rare for one to succeed.

4.2 CERTAINTY OF TERMS

4.2.1 The basic terms of a transaction

In our discussion of contractual offers (section 3.1.1) we saw that no contract exists unless the parties have agreed the basic terms of the transaction, and we saw that with a contract for the sale of goods the parties must as a minimum have agreed what goods are to be sold and what price is to be paid for them. If the parties have agreed to the sale of certain goods but they have not agreed a price, the court could only enforce that agreement if it were prepared to decide what the price should be. The court will not do so because that would be to impose a contract on the parties which they had not agreed themselves, contrary to the central principle of freedom of contract. For the same reason the court will not enforce an agreement for a loan if the parties have not agreed what rate of interest is payable, nor an agreement for the hire of land if the parties have not agreed what land is to be let, nor an agreement for insurance if the parties have not agreed what risks are insured against. None of these agreements is a contract.

The requirement that the parties themselves have agreed the basic terms of the transaction is known to lawyers as the requirement of 'certainty of terms', and they describe an agreement which is unenforceable because its basic terms have not been agreed as being 'void for uncertainty'. This is not however a technical legal requirement like that of consideration. It is simply a reflection of the parties' freedom of contract and the cardinal principle that it is for the parties and not for the court to decide what the terms of their transaction should be.

4.2.2 The context of a transaction

In order to identify the basic terms of a transaction it is often necessary to consider the context of the parties' words as well as their content. An item sold at an auction may be described only as 'a mahogany desk', which does not in itself identify what goods are being sold. But there is no doubt about what goods the successful bidder has contracted to buy: it is the desk labelled LOT 101 which was on display while the bidding took place. We considered a similar situation in section 3.1.5 with a contract for the sale by A of 'my Morris 1000 Traveller'. Provided that A owns only one such car it is clear what goods are being sold. But if he owns two, then unless it is clear from the context which he has agreed to sell the agreement is void for uncertainty.

In both of these examples the parties had specific goods in mind when they entered into the contract, but with most commercial contracts for the sale of goods this is not the case. When an oil refinery contracts to purchase 500,000 barrels of crude oil, the parties probably do not have any particular 500,000 barrels in mind, in which case the contract is said to be for unascertained goods rather than specific goods. As long as the buyer gets the quantity and quality he contracted for he is not concerned where or how the seller obtains it. The parties must however have reached agreement on quantity, quality and price if the agreement is to be enforceable. Their agreement on quality will usually involve a verbal description of the oil but, if the agreement does relate to a specific cargo of oil, the seller may provide the buyer with a sample rather than specifying its quality. The first situation is described as a sale by description, the second as a sale by sample.

4.2.3 Referential terms

Instead of agreeing the basic terms of their transaction, the parties may instead agree some means for determining one or more of those terms at a future date. It is common for shares and commodities to be sold at a price equal to their market value at some future date, and for land to be sold at a fair market price to be determined by an independent valuer. Architects and estate agents routinely charge a fee to be calculated on a percentage basis. Contracts for goods, services or both sometimes provide for payment on a 'cost plus' basis, although such contracts are notorious for cost overruns. In all these situations the price as such is not stated in the contract, but the contract is valid provided that the price can be ascertained by the time it comes to be paid.

Another common arrangement is to allow one party to specify one or more of the basic terms of the transaction. Most medium and long term loan agreements allow the lender to specify the interest rate from time to time, and this arrangement has never (so far as we know) been challenged on the grounds of uncertainty.*

Referential terms like this are especially common with long term supply contracts, which are used to secure long term requirements for raw materials such as steel, chemicals, oil or gas. Typically such a contract provides for the quantities of the goods to be supplied to be nominated monthly by the buyer within stated minimum and maximum limits, and for the price to be calculated by reference either to an indexation formula or to the price quoted for goods of that type during that month in a trade publication. An indexation formula usually involves an agreed initial price which is escalated monthly in accordance with some published figure such as the Producer Prices Index (or PPI). At the time such a contract is entered into neither the quantity nor the price of the goods to be supplied has been agreed, but the contract is valid provided that both quantity and price can be ascertained for each month's delivery.

Particular care needs to be taken with referential price clauses: where a clause refers to an outside source for an escalation index or for published commodity prices, it is important to identify the source and make sure that it does give the necessary information. The court will not select an appropriate publication if the parties have failed to do so, and will not guess which figure they intended to be used if the publication selected gives no such figure or else gives more than one. An apparently trivial oversight of this kind can invalidate the whole contract.

4.2.4 Agreements to agree

One consequence of the requirement of certainty of terms is that an agreement which leaves one or more of the basic terms of the trans-action to be agreed at a later date is not a contract. This means for example that an agreement to supply goods or services 'at a price to be agreed between us' is unenforceable. Similarly if a one year lease gives the tenant the option to continue the lease for a further year at a rent to be negotiated, that option is unenforceable and the landlord is free to ignore it, although this does not invalidate the lease for the first year.

It is however possible to make a contract which leaves some matters other than the basic terms of the transaction to be agreed at

---

* *The validity of provisions which give one party the unfettered right to vary the contract is discussed in section 7.4.2.*

a later date, which is the source of the problem with interim agreements considered in section 1.4.5. It is common for contracts for the sale of goods to provide for delivery on a date to be agreed. Even if the parties fail to agree a delivery date, the court can and will enforce the contract on the basis that the goods were to be delivered within a reasonable time.

4.3 STATEMENTS WHICH ARE NOT TERMS

4.3.1 Mere puff

A statement is not prevented from having contractual effect just because it is a statement of opinion or belief rather than a statement of fact. If a person sells 'an eighteenth century desk', he is in breach of the contract if the desk proves not to be eighteenth century. If however he says only that he believes it to be eighteenth century, he is in breach of the contract if he did not genuinely hold that belief, but he is not in breach just because his belief proves to be incorrect. It is of course easier for the buyer to show that the desk is not eighteenth century than to show that the seller did not honestly believe it to be, and this is why, as discussed in section 3.4.3, sellers always want their warranties to begin 'so far as the seller is aware ...'.

However, some kinds of statement have insufficient substance to have any contractual effect at all. For example the eulogistic statements often heard from salesmen, such as 'it's wonderful', 'you'll love it' and 'you won't regret it', have no real meaning. The buyer cannot sue just because, as things turn out, he does not 'love it' in the slightest. The law categorises such expressions as 'mere puff'. In practice though it can be difficult to decide whether a particular statement is mere puff or whether it has enough substance to amount to a term of the contract.

In the memorable case of *Andrews* v *Hopkinson* 1957, Mr Hopkinson, a car dealer, agreed to supply a used car to Mr Andrews on hire purchase. In the course of the negotiation Mr Hopkinson had said 'It's a good little bus. I would stake my life on it.' In fact the car had a steering fault, and a week later it swerved into a lorry wrecking the car and seriously injuring the unfortunate Mr Andrews. The court held that Mr Hopkinson's statement did have sufficient meaning to be a contractual term, so Mr Andrews won his action for breach of that term.* (See footnote on page 79.)

4.3.2 Misrepresentation

Sometimes a statement made by one party in the course of a negotiation is not included in the agreement which is ultimately entered into. Suppose for example that the owner of a veterinary practice persuades a purchaser to buy it by saying that the annual profit of the practice is £25,000 but, due to poor communication between the purchaser and his lawyer, the written purchase agreement contains no such term. The purchaser quickly discovers that the annual profit is substantially less than £25,000. If the seller's statement had been included in the contract, the purchaser would have had legal remedies against him for breach of that term, but in the event the purchaser has no remedies against the seller under the contract. He does however have legal remedies against the seller on the basis of his misrepresentation of the profits of the practice.

A misrepresentation is an untrue statement of fact which, although not included in the terms of the contract, nevertheless induced the other party to enter into that contract. There are three important points here. First, there must have been a positive statement which was untrue when it was made, or which became untrue before the contract was concluded. Mere silence does not amount to a misrepresentation. Second, the untrue statement must have been a statement of past or existing fact and not a statement of opinion or an assurance as to some future state of affairs. Third, that statement must have been at least partly responsible for inducing the other party to contract: if it played no part in his decision he has no grounds for complaint.

If these conditions are met there are two legal remedies which may be available to the victim of the misrepresentation. He may be able, if he so wishes, to 'rescind' the contract, meaning to set it aside. In our example this would involve the retransfer of the vet's practice to the seller and the return of the purchase price. Alternatively he may be able to sue the party responsible for the misrepresentation for the loss he has suffered as a result of it. In certain circumstances he can do both. The position depends,

---

* In our discussion of tendering in section 3.5.2, we looked at two examples of collateral contracts. Andrews v Hopkinson provides a further example. Since Mr Andrews was buying the car on hire purchase, the transaction was structured so that Mr Hopkinson sold the car to a finance company which then agreed to provide it to Mr Andrews on hire purchase. Mr Hopkinson's undertaking to Mr Andrews that the car was 'a good little bus' was a collateral contract between them quite independent of the sale agreement and the hire purchase agreement.

among other things, on whether the misrepresentation was fraudulent, negligent or innocent, but the rules governing remedies for misrepresentation are too complex for us to go into. If a misrepresentation is alleged against you, or else you are the victim of one, you will require legal advice.

The difficulties involved in a claim for misrepresentation mean that no business ever wants to become involved in one. There are two practical conclusions to bear in mind when negotiating a contract. First, make sure that any statement made by the other party which is material to your decision to contract is included in the terms of the contract. Second, be careful yourself not to make any statement in the course of the negotiation which is untrue.

4.3.3   Entire agreement provisions

We have seen that, even where the terms of an agreement are in writing, it is still possible for a party to claim that there are extrinsic matters to be taken into account. He may claim that the written terms are inaccurate or incomplete, a claim which the parol evidence rule (section 4.1.4) makes it difficult but not impossible for him to maintain. Alternatively he may claim that he was induced to enter into the contract by a misrepresentation which, by definition, was not recorded in those written terms. Substantial written contracts often contain what is known as an 'entire agreement' clause, which is an attempt to prevent any such claim being made. That clause will usually read along the following lines:

> This Agreement represents the entire understanding of the parties in relation to the matters set out herein, and each party hereby confirms that he has not entered into this agreement on the basis of any statement or representation other than those specifically mentioned herein.

Obviously this provision greatly weakens the position of a party who tries subsequently to contradict it, but it does not make it absolutely impossible for him to do so. What the terms of the agreement were, and whether a party entered into it as a result of a misrepresentation, are both questions of fact; no contractual provision can prevent the court from making its own decision on these facts on the basis of the evidence presented to it.

4.4 EXPRESS TERMS

4.4.1 Extent of express terms

As we saw in section 4.2.1, some matters are so fundamental that, if the parties have not agreed them, no contract can exist. It is entirely up to the parties to decide what further matters to cover in their agreement, and major commercial contracts generally go very much further.

To illustrate this we will consider an imaginary contract for the supply of a gas turbine which is to be installed in a new gas-fired power station. In practice a project like the construction of a power station would usually be carried out on a turnkey basis, which means that the generating company will appoint a main contractor to manage the whole project and to engage and supervise all the necessary subcontractors. In this case the contract for the turbine would be one of the subcontracts entered into by the main contractor, and in all probability the contract would be put out to tender. To keep the picture simple however we will suppose that the generating company is building the station itself and negotiates the contract directly with the supplier of the turbine.

The turbine itself will be an aero-engine which the supplier will buy off the shelf, but major modifications will be required to incorporate that engine into a power unit which can be installed into the new power station. The contract requires the supplier to design, manufacture and supply the complete unit. In the commercial world this would be called a procurement contract, although that phrase has no precise meaning, and in legal terms it is either a contract for the sale of goods or else a contract for work and materials. In all probability the agreement will be in writing and signed on behalf of each party, and the following is an outline of the matters which are likely to be expressly provided for in the agreement.

4.4.2 Contract between buyer and seller for the design, manufacture and sale of a gas turbine

Term	Outline of provisions
1. The contract	Statement of purpose of contract and brief summary of parties' respective responsibilities.
2. The parties	Warranties as to – parties' contractual capacity and internal approvals;

		– seller's skill, expertise and availability of personnel;
		– buyer's access to funds.
3.	Performance of the contract	Standard of performance required of seller. Compliance with applicable laws and regulations. Subcontracting of work by seller. Timetable for completion of various stages of the work. Appointment of each party's project manager, and the procedure for changing them.
4.	The goods	Specification – statement of buyer's requirements. Design – seller's obligations; approval by buyer; extent of buyer's involvement. Materials – sources, origins and standards of components and materials. Manufacture – place of manufacture; buyer's right to inspect. Testing – testing programme; performance criteria; buyer's right to be present. New technology – seller to incorporate any new technology which becomes available after the contract was made. Acceptance – written acceptance of goods by buyer. Warranties – seller's obligations if goods fail to meet performance criteria or are defective.
5.	Delivery	Time and place of delivery. Responsibility for delivery costs. Consequences of late delivery, including liquidated damages.
6.	Title and risk	Time of transfer of title to the goods. Retention of title provisions. Time of transfer of risk in the goods.
7.	Price	Determination of price: price escalation, cost overruns, acceleration payments. Payment for work outside original scope of contract. Buyer's right of audit.
8.	Payment	Method of payment. Stage payments. Retention of part of price by buyer. Interest on late payments.

9. Guarantees of performance	Buyer and/or seller to provide a guarantee of performance from parent company or bank, or else a performance bond.
10. Termination	Circumstances in which contract terminates, e.g. – cancellation by buyer; – in event of seller's default; – in event of buyer's failure to pay; – in event of insolvency of party. Consequences of termination: ownership of goods, payment for work completed. Identification of terms which survive termination.
11. Patents	Identification of relevant patents. Right to use patents owned by parties. Responsibility for obtaining patent licences from third parties. Responsibility for ensuring no patent infringements. Ownership of patents developed for the purpose of the contract.
12. Liabilities	Apportionment of liabilities under the contract. Exclusion of certain liabilities. Indemnities against certain types of claims or losses. *Force majeure* provisions.
13. Insurance	Requirement for parties to insure against certain risks. Levels of insurance. Responsibility for insuring the goods.
14. Confidentiality	Parties to maintain the confidentiality of the contract and all information acquired in the course of it. Exceptions for public information, disclosures to government departments or as required by law.
15. Assignment	Whether either party is permitted to assign the contract; the procedure for doing so.
16. Arbitration	Disputes to be settled by arbitration.
17. Law and jurisdiction	Choice of governing law; submission by parties to the jurisdiction of the courts (if no arbitration clause).
18. Notices	Names and addresses for service of formal notices under contract. Change of those names and addresses.

4.4.3 Contentious terms and boilerplate

Such a contract is likely to be the size of a book, with a text of over 100 pages and numerous technical appendices and drawings, and may well have taken months to negotiate.

The provisions relating to the goods, price and payment are of course the commercial heart of the contract. They will have been the focus of the parties' technical and commercial representatives, and if these crucial matters cannot be agreed no contract will be concluded.

Terms 14 to 18 are often disparagingly referred to as 'legal boilerplate' or just 'boilerplate'. These terms are not usually contentious and it is unlikely that the negotiation will fail because the parties cannot agree these provisions.

The most contentious issues will probably have been the seller's warranties in relation to the goods, the consequences of late delivery, and the provisions on guarantees of performance, termination, liabilities and insurance. It is interesting to note that all of these terms are concerned with what happens if something goes wrong: if nothing goes wrong it will not be necessary to refer to them. The main factor determining the outcome of the negotiation of these terms is the relative bargaining strengths of the parties. If for example the seller is the only company capable of manufacturing the goods, the buyer will not be able to insist that the seller gives extensive warranties of the goods and performance guarantees; conversely, if there are many other companies competing for the contract and the seller is short of orders, it will not be able to resist giving them.

Much of the rest of this book will be taken up with the discussion of these contentious contractual issues.

4.5 EXCLUSION CLAUSES AND INDEMNITIES

We now come to the important but unseductive topics of exclusion clauses and indemnities. For this purpose we need to make a distinction between two very different categories of liabilities. The first category is liabilities between the parties themselves, meaning liabilities which one party will incur to the other if he fails to perform his obligations under the contract. The second category is liabilities to third parties, meaning liabilities which either party may incur to third parties in the course of performing the contract.

The parties are free to agree contract terms which restrict their potential liabilities to each other: terms of this kind are called exclusion clauses and are discussed in section 4.5.1. The parties cannot however agree terms which effectively restrict their potential liabilities to third parties because, as we have seen, nothing in a contract can have any effect on a third party. The parties can however agree terms which set out how potential liabilities to third parties will be apportioned between them: terms of this kind are called indemnities and are discussed in section 4.5.3.

4.5.1 Exclusion clauses

The liability of a party who fails to perform his obligations under a contract is discussed in Chapter 8. For present purposes however we can assume that a party is responsible for all loss and damage suffered by the other party as a result of that failure. So if the seller of a gas turbine undertakes that the turbine will meet certain performance criteria but in fact it does not meet them, the seller is liable for all loss and damage suffered by the buyer as a result, including all the costs of redesigning, rebuilding or replacing the turbine and all the extra costs and lost profit resulting from the delay in the buyer's power generation project.

The terms of the contract may however restrict this potential liability. The seller's liability may be completely excluded ('the seller shall not be liable if the turbine fails to meet the performance criteria') or it may only be limited ('the seller's liability if the turbine fails to meet the performance criteria shall not exceed £1 million'). Alternatively the contract may exclude the seller's liability for certain types of loss or damage ('the seller shall in no circumstances be liable for the costs of any delay in the buyer's power generation project or for the buyer's loss of profit') or it may restrict his total liability under the contract ('the seller's total liability under this contract shall not exceed £5 million'). Any such term is known as an 'exclusion clause' or an 'exemption clause'.

It would be unusual in a contract like this to find a provision restricting the total liability of the seller under the contract. Such a liability cap is however commonly found in contracts for the sale of a company or a business, where the seller's total liability for breach of his warranties is often restricted to a sum equal to the purchase price. The rationale for this cap on the seller's liabilities is that, in the worst event, the seller may have to return the whole of the purchase price to the buyer in damages; effectively therefore he will have given the company or business away for nothing. But the seller will want to preclude the possibility of an even worse outcome where he finds himself liable for damages in excess of the purchase price.

In our turbine example the chances are that the supplier, rather than seeking a cap on his total liability, will try to exclude his liability for consequential loss. The phrase consequential loss is used to refer to indirect loss such as loss of profit, as opposed to direct loss such as physical damage or injury. If things go terribly wrong and problems with the turbine delay the buyer's power generation project, his claim for loss of profit will probably dwarf all the other claims he may have against the supplier, and the supplier is trying to preclude a really huge claim of this nature. Although lawyers themselves often use the phrase consequential loss, it is important to appreciate that it has no precise legal meaning. If the parties agree to exclude liability for loss of profit it is better to say precisely that.

The liability provisions are seldom the most stimulating or readable part of a contract, but they are important. They are not legal niceties with no real commercial significance, but an integral part of the transaction with major commercial implications. Failure to agree the liability provisions can destroy a deal just as finally as the failure to agree a price.

4.5.2 Liability to third parties

In performing (or failing to perform) a contract a party may of course incur some legal liability to a third party. Let us take two examples.

1. One of the buyer's employees is injured while he is at the seller's factory to witness a performance test. He claims damages for personal injury from the seller.
2. The design of the goods sold under the contract infringes a patent held by a third party. He sues the buyer for infringement of his patent.

A third party is a stranger to the contract and so the contract cannot impose obligations on him. So a term saying that 'the seller shall not be liable for any injury to the buyer's employees' cannot prevent such an employee from suing and recovering damages from the seller. Similarly a term saying that 'the buyer shall not be liable for any patent infringement' cannot prevent a third party from suing and recovering damages from the buyer for patent infringement. However the parties can achieve the desired effect by means of an indemnity.

4.5.3 Indemnities

An indemnity is an undertaking by one party to meet a liability which would otherwise fall on the other. The purest and most familiar example of this type of arrangement is a contract of insurance, which usually consists simply of the giving of an indemnity in return for the payment of a premium. Under a motor insurance policy for example, the insurance company undertakes to indemnify the motorist against claims by third parties for death, personal injury or property damage arising out of the motorist's use of his car. So if he is involved in an accident which damages a car belonging to a third party, and that third party makes a claim against him for the cost of the repairs, the contract of insurance requires the insurer to meet that claim. An indemnity is therefore a contractual device which the parties can use to apportion between them potential liabilities to third parties.

A major contract like the contract for the supply of a gas turbine which we have been discussing will generally contain a series of indemnities under which all potential liabilities to third parties are apportioned. To return to our earlier examples of third party claims, each party will typically agree to be responsible for the death or injury of its own employees, irrespective of the circumstances, and accordingly each party will indemnify the other against any such claim by its employees. As the supplier is responsible for the design of the turbine it is appropriate for him to indemnify the buyer against any claim by a third party for patent infringement. Generally the party giving an indemnity will be required not only to meet the claims in question but also to conduct the defence of them.

In our experience many people find the indemnity provisions in such a contract intimidating, and will defer any question relating to those provisions to their lawyers. Generally however such diffidence is unwarranted: with a clear head and an understanding of the principle of an indemnity, it is seldom difficult to work out how the parties have apportioned potential liabilities between them.

4.5.4 The proper use of exclusion clauses

There is nothing intrinsically objectionable in using exclusion clauses and indemnities to apportion the liabilities under a contract. There are indeed positive advantages in doing so. If a particular liability is placed squarely on one party, there is no room for argument subsequently about where that liability should fall. If for example liability for patent infringements is placed on the seller, that eliminates the risk of an infringement claim by a third party turning into a three-way court battle with both buyer and seller claiming that the other was responsible for the infringement and should therefore meet any liability to the third party.

The other advantage is that the party on whom a liability is placed can if he so wishes (or if the contract requires) insure against the risk of that liability arising. The apportionment of liabilities and the question of insurance cannot be dealt with in isolation; a company's insurance representatives should always be involved in the negotiation of the liability provisions of a major contract.

4.5.5 The abuse of exclusion clauses

The problem of course is that the parties' freedom to apportion the liabilities under a contract as they see fit makes it possible, at least in theory, for a party to contract on terms which impose no liabilities on him at all either to the other party or to third parties. This is the Holy Grail of commerce – doing business and making money without exposing yourself to any risks whatsoever. Two groups in particular have succumbed to the temptation and set off in search of this Holy Grail. The first group consists of those businesses which have a monopoly (or an effective monopoly) on the supply of particular goods or services. They are in a position to dictate the terms of supply. The second, much larger, group consists of those businesses which use standard terms and conditions. As we shall see in section 5.3, standard terms and conditions are intended to be incorporated into the terms of the contract without the other party even having read them. The terms used by both of these groups tend to include one-sided and wholly unreasonable exclusions of liability and indemnities. The worst offenders are of course monopoly suppliers which use standard terms and conditions.

4.5.6   The law's hostility to exclusion clauses

In principle exclusion clauses and indemnities are no different from any other contractual provisions: they are applied in accordance with the intentions expressed by the parties. The fact that such a term has been imposed by a monopoly supplier or has been incorporated into the contract as part of one party's standard terms and conditions does not in theory justify any departure from this general principle. In practice however the law has reacted to the abuse of exclusion clauses and indemnities with understandable hostility. This has shown itself firstly in the interpretation of such terms by the courts and subsequently in the passing of the Unfair Contract Terms Act 1977.

The courts tend to interpret such terms very narrowly indeed in order to avoid the manifestly unfair results of their application. If there is any ambiguity in an exclusion clause, that ambiguity is resolved against the party seeking to rely on the clause (a rule of interpretation discussed in more detail in section 6.3.1). Of course it is nearly always possible to find an ambiguity in any contractual provision if you are minded to do so.

Take for example the case of *Hollier* v *Rambler Motors (AMC) Ltd* 1972, which involved a contract between a garage and a private motorist for the repair of his car. The garage's standard terms of business included a clause stating that the garage 'is not responsible for damage caused by fire to customers' cars on the premises'. While on the premises the car was badly damaged by a fire caused by the negligence of the garage staff. The motorist sued the garage for compensation for the damage to his car, but the garage defended the claim on the basis that such liability was excluded. The Court of Appeal took the view that the clause was ambiguous: it was not clear whether the exclusion was intended to apply to a fire caused by the garage's negligence. It followed that the garage could not escape liability for the damage to the car on the basis of that clause. This case is a fine example of how justice can be done at the expense of a strained interpretation of an exclusion clause.

4.6   THE UNFAIR CONTRACT TERMS ACT 1977

A very much more direct attack on the abuse of exclusion clauses came in 1977 with the enactment of the Unfair Contract Terms Act.

Do not be misled by the title of the Act into thinking that it is about unfair contract terms in general. It is not. It is about certain kinds of exclusion clauses and indemnities, and certain other terms which undermine a party's contractual obligations. Unfortunately the Act is complex and technical, and while the following summary of it is intended to be accurate it is not a complete account of the Act.

4.6.1   Application of the Act

Not all contracts are covered by the Act. The Act is concerned with business liability (Section 1(3)), that is with contracts where one or more of the parties enters into that contract in the course of his business. So where none of the parties enters into the contract in the course of a business, as for example with a contract between two private individuals for the sale of a car or painting, the Act does not apply.

In addition, Schedule 1 to the Act lists certain types of contract to which the Act does not apply, the most significant ones being:

■ Contracts of insurance.
■ Leases.
■ Contracts for the sale of land.
■ Patent, trademark and copyright licences.
■ Contracts for the sale of shares of marine salvage and towage.*
■ Charterparties.*
■ Contracts for the carriage of goods by sea.*
■ International supply contracts (defined in Section 26, meaning essentially contracts for the sale of goods which are being imported or exported).

4.6.2   Operation of the Act

With contracts to which the Act does apply, the Act operates by making certain terms ineffective and by making other terms ineffective unless that term is reasonable. The Act does not prohibit the parties from agreeing these terms, but if they do so the terms do not achieve their intended effect.

The Act makes the following terms totally ineffective:

---

* Section 2(1) of the Act does apply to these contracts and the whole Act applies to them where one of the parties is a consumer.

1. Any term which excludes or restricts a party's liability for death or personal injury caused by negligence (Section 2(1)).*

The Act makes the following terms ineffective unless that term is reasonable:

2. Any term which excludes or restricts a party's liability for loss or damage (other than death or personal injury) caused by negligence (Section 2(2)).*
3. Where one party is dealing *either* with a consumer *or* on his own written standard terms of business:
   (a) any term which excludes or restricts that party's liability for breach of contract (Section 3(2)(a));
   (b) any term which entitles that party to render a contractual performance different from that which was reasonably expected of him (Section 3(2)(b)(i));
   (c) any term which entitles that party, in respect of the whole or any part of his contractual obligation, to render no performance at all (Section 3(2)(b)(ii)).
4. Where a party is dealing with a consumer, any term which makes the consumer indemnify anyone else against that party's liability for negligence[†] or breach of contract (Section 4(1)).

The Act also deals with terms which exclude or restrict various implied undertakings in contracts for the sale, hire purchase, hire or exchange of goods and contracts for work and materials. These provisions are discussed in the context of those implied undertakings in section 4.8.2 below.

4.6.3 Persons protected by the Act

The person best protected by these provisions is therefore the consumer. All four of the above items apply to him. A person is a 'consumer' if he does *not* make the contract in the course of a business but the other party *does* make the contract in the course of a business (Section 12 (1)).

---

* *'Negligence' is defined in Section 1 to include breach of a contractual obligation to exercise reasonable skill and care in the performance of the contract. If the parties have not expressly agreed to exercise reasonable skill and care in the performance of the contract, that obligation is likely to be implied – see section 4.7.2.*
† *See footnote on negligence above.*

Next best protected is a person who contracts on the other party's standard terms of business. Items 1, 2 and 3 above apply to him, and this is considered in section 5.4.

Otherwise only items 1 and 2 apply. This would be the case for instance with the contract for the supply of a gas turbine considered in section 4.4.2, which involved neither a consumer nor standard terms of business.

Terms covered by items 2, 3 and 4 above are ineffective unless that term is reasonable, and the Act amplifies what is meant by this test of reasonableness. The question is whether the term was a fair and reasonable one to include in the contract, having regard to the circumstances known to the parties when the contract was made (Section 11(1)), and it is for the person alleging that the term is reasonable to show that it is (Section 11(5)).

4.7 IMPLIED TERMS

4.7.1 The two kinds of implied term

Sometimes a term which has not been expressly agreed between the parties will nevertheless be implied into a contract. There are two situations in which this can happen. The first is where the parties must have intended that term to be included even though they did not say so (sections 4.7.2 and 4.7.3). The second is where an Act of Parliament requires that term to be implied into a contract of that type (section 4.8).

These two kinds of implied term serve very different purposes. With the first kind the purpose is simply to give effect to the parties' unexpressed intentions at the time the contract was entered into. By contrast the purpose of a statutory implied term is to give contractual protection to one of the parties, most importantly to the buyer of goods. In either case an implied term is just as much part of the contract as the express terms.

4.7.2 Terms the parties must have intended

Suppose that A enters into a contract with B, a carrier, in which B agrees to take a document from A's address in Manchester to an address in Southampton for a charge of £10. This is a very simple example of a contract of carriage. The parties have agreed the basic terms of the contract – namely what is to be carried, where from, where to, and the price – but they have not agreed any further terms. They have not agreed when B is to collect the document, what means of transport he will use, what route he will take, when he is to deliver it, or when and how the price is to be paid. Nor has the carrier expressly agreed to take care of the document while it is in his possession.

This does not of course mean that A must wait indefinitely for B to collect the document or to deliver it, or that B is free to carry the document by push bike or on an aeroplane flying from Manchester to Southampton via Rio de Janeiro. Nor does it mean that B must wait indefinitely for his £10. These matters are all covered by the terms which will be implied into the contract, and these are as follows:

1. B will collect the document within a reasonable time and deliver it within a reasonable time after that.
2. B will use a means of transport reasonably suited to the length of the journey (effectively limiting him to a motor vehicle, train or aeroplane).
3. B will carry the document by a reasonably direct route.
4. B will ensure that the document is not lost or damaged while it is in his possession.*
5. A will pay the £10 charge within a reasonable time.

The justification for implying these terms is that the parties must have intended the contract to be workable, and it is necessary to imply these terms if the contract is to be workable. The parties must therefore be taken to have intended these terms to be included, even though they were not expressly agreed. Another way of putting this is that, to be implied, a term must be so obvious that it goes without saying. So it is not enough that that term would have been a good idea or that prudent parties would have included it: a term will only be implied if the contract is unworkable without it.

There is of course no need for an implied term about a matter which the parties have expressly agreed. If in our example the parties had agreed that the document was to be carried on an aeroplane flying from Manchester to Southampton via Rio de Janeiro, there is no room for implied terms as to the means of transport or the route.

---

* *It was the desire of carriers to avoid this particular liability which led in the nineteenth century to the use of standard terms, as discussed in section 5.3.1.*

4.7.3 Customary terms

There is one other situation in which the parties may be taken to have intended a particular term or terms to be included even though they did not expressly say so. This is where it is the custom in the trade or business concerned, in a contract of that type, to deal on those terms. So custom, which as discussed in section 3.3.2 is important in relation to the formation of a contract, can also have a bearing on the terms of a contract.

A party who claims that a term is to be implied on the basis of custom is saying in effect that the term was so universal and therefore so obvious to both parties, at the time the contract was made, that it was not even worth mentioning. That custom will have to be very well established indeed if such an implication is to be justified. It is not enough that that term is commonly or usually found in contracts of that type.

4.7.4 The practical significance of implied terms

As we saw in our example, where the parties have agreed only the basic terms of the contract, the law will supplement those express terms with such implied terms as are necessary to make the contract workable. With common types of contract such as contracts of carriage and contracts for the sale of goods, the terms which are to be implied are so well established that it will be hard for either party to dispute them: a person who contracts to sell goods without a delivery date being agreed will not be able to deny the existence of an implied term that delivery was to be within a reasonable time after the contract. Any dispute between the parties is much more likely to turn on how long 'a reasonable time' was, and this depends on the circumstances of the transaction.

With a purchase from a shop, delivery generally takes place there and then. With a mail order purchase, perhaps 10 days would be a reasonable time, which is why the terms used by mail order companies generally specify a longer period ('please allow 28 days for delivery'). But where the goods are to be specially manufactured a reasonable time may be weeks or even months, depending on the complexity of the manufacturing process.

On the other hand an agreement in writing is generally intended to be comprehensive and is likely to make express provision for such significant matters as delivery and payment. This tends to leave little room for implied terms. If in this situation a party claims to rely on an implied term, this means of course that he is unable to point to an express term which serves his purpose. The existence of that implied term will probably be disputed, and more often than not such a term is not necessary to make the contract workable and will not therefore be implied. But even with a fully termed agreement in writing there may be room for an implied term, usually to correct an obvious omission. Let us consider one real example.

In *Gardner* v *Coutts & Co* 1967 the owner of a house entered into a written contract granting Mr Gardner an option to purchase the house if the owner ever wished to sell it. The owner subsequently gave the house to his sister without giving Mr Gardner the chance to exercise his option. Mr Gardner claimed that there was an implied term that he would be given the chance to buy if the owner wished to give the house away rather than sell it. The court held that this term was necessary to make the contract workable and Mr Gardner won his action for breach of that implied term.

4.8 TERMS IMPLIED BY STATUTE

The important examples of statutory implied terms relate to contracts involving goods or services, and are designed to protect the party contracting for goods or services against the supplier of them.

4.8.1 Contracts for the sale of goods

A number of such terms are implied into contracts for the sale of goods by Sections 12–15 of the Sale of Goods Act 1979 (as amended by the Sale and Supply of Goods Act 1994). In outline they are as follows:

1. The seller has the right to sell the goods.
2. No third party has any rights over the goods which the seller has not disclosed to the buyer.
3. The buyer will enjoy quiet possession of the goods.
4. The goods conform to their description, in a sale by sample. (Sale by description and sale by sample are discussed in section 4.2.2.)

Where the seller sells the goods in the course of a business, the following terms are also implied:

5. The goods are of satisfactory quality.
6. The goods will be fit for their purpose.

Terms 1 to 3 are designed to protect the buyer if the seller does not own the goods or if a third party has, or claims to have, some other right over them such as a pledge (discussed in section 9.2.1), a charge (section 9.2.2) or a lien (section 9.2.4).

It is however important to appreciate that despite this statutory protection the buyer is at risk if a third party does have rights over the goods. If it turns out for example that the goods had been stolen or else that the seller was in possession of them under a hire purchase agreement, the buyer will have to return the goods to their rightful owner: if the seller does not own the goods he cannot as a general rule pass good title to the buyer. The effect of these implied terms is to give a buyer in such a situation a legal remedy against the seller for his breach of the implied terms. But if the seller is a fraudster it is unlikely that he will be found and even less likely that he will be able to meet the buyer's claim for breach of contract.

The effect of term 4 is to give the buyer a legal remedy if the goods supplied do not conform to the contract. Terms 5 and 6 are concerned with the quality of the goods, but you will notice that these terms are only implied where the seller sells the goods in the course of a business. In a private sale therefore there are no terms as to the quality of the goods unless the parties expressly agree such terms. If they do not do so, the buyer has no legal remedy if the goods prove to be defective. This is why it is safer to buy a used car from a dealer rather than from a private individual, and it also explains why the dealer's price is usually higher.

4.8.2   Other contracts for goods or services

Terms virtually identical to those in the Sale of Goods Act are implied into contracts of hire purchase by Sections 8–11 of the Supply of Goods (Implied Terms) Act 1973,* into contracts for work and materials by Sections 2–5 of the Supply of Goods and Services Act 1982, and into contracts of hire by Sections 7–10 of the Supply of Goods and Services Act 1982. The only differences between these various sets of implied terms are those necessary to take account of the different nature of these various contracts.

---

* As further amended by the Consumer Credit Act 1974 and the Sale and Supply of Goods Act 1994.

Since 1982 therefore the terms implied into these various contracts involving goods, services or both have been for all practical purposes the same, and so the question of how a particular contract should be categorised (which we discussed in section 1.2.2) has ceased to have any practical significance.

A contract for services is of course different from the other categories we have discussed in that no goods are involved. With a contract for services, where the supplier is acting in the course of a business, terms are implied that the supplier will carry out those services with reasonable care and skill and within a reasonable time by Sections 13–15 of the Supply of Goods and Services Act 1982.

4.8.3   The exclusion of statutory implied terms

The statutory implied terms applicable to contracts for the sale of goods have changed little since they were first introduced by the original Sale of Goods Act 1893. At that time however it was possible for the parties expressly to exclude any of these implied terms from a particular contract. In a process similar to the abuse of exclusion clauses, the wholesale exclusion of these implied terms became common in the contract terms used by monopoly suppliers and in standard terms and conditions of sale. In this way the buyer could be deprived not only of any assurance as to the quality of the goods or their conformity with the contract, but even of the assurance that the seller had the right to sell the goods. The Unfair Contract Terms Act 1977 therefore limits the power to exclude these implied terms. As with the provisions discussed in section 4.6.2, the Act operates by making some such exclusions totally ineffective and others ineffective unless they are reasonable, and it also provides special protection for consumers.

With contracts for the sale of goods and contracts of hire purchase, the implied terms as to ownership (numbers 1, 2 and 3 in section 4.8.1) cannot be excluded or restricted (Section 6(1) of the Unfair Contract Terms Act 1977). When dealing with a consumer, the implied terms as to conformity, quality and fitness for purpose (numbers 4, 5 and 6 above) cannot be excluded or restricted (Section 6(2)). When dealing with someone other than a consumer, those implied terms can be excluded or restricted if it is reasonable to do so (Section 6(3)).

With other contracts involving the transfer of the ownership or possession of goods, the implied terms as to ownership (numbers 1,

2 and 3) can be excluded or restricted if it is reasonable to do so (Section 7(1)). When dealing with a consumer, the implied terms as to conformity, quality and fitness for purpose (numbers 4, 5 and 6) cannot be excluded or restricted (Section 7(2)). When dealing with someone other than a consumer, those implied terms can be excluded or restricted if it is reasonable to do so (Section 7(3)).

For the purposes of Sections 6 and 7 of the Unfair Contract Terms Act, the definition of 'consumer' is different from that given in section 4.6.3. A person is not a consumer merely because he does not make the contract in the course of a business but the other party does make the contract in the course of a business: there is the additional requirement that the goods supplied under the contract are of a type ordinarily supplied for private use or consumption. The provisions as to the scope of the Act (discussed in section 4.6.1) and the test of reasonableness (discussed in section 4.6.3) do however apply.

4.9   OTHER LEGAL PRESUMPTIONS

There are two other principles which, although not strictly involving implied terms, can conveniently be dealt with here. Both are legal presumptions which apply unless the parties have made some other arrangement. The first concerns the means of payment under a contract, and the second concerns the passing of title and risk under a contract for the sale of goods.

4.9.1   Means of payment

Generally of course a creditor does not care how he is paid as long as he does get paid. Strictly speaking however he is entitled to insist on payment in cash unless the contract provides for some other means of payment.

The original purpose of this ancient rule was to ensure that a creditor could not be forced to accept any sort of payment other than money of the realm. Today however the fact is that any large cash transaction is suspicious. A party who insists on being paid a large sum in cash may well be intending to defraud the Revenue, which as discussed in section 10.4.3 may mean that the contract is invalid. A party who insists on paying a large sum in cash may well be involved in some sort of illegal money laundering operation, which may also make the contract invalid.

To prevent either of these awkward situations from arising it is necessary, with any contract involving substantial sums, to provide expressly for payment by some means other than cash.

4.9.2 Passing of title and risk

To say that a party has 'title to' or 'property in' goods means simply that he owns them, while to say that he has the 'risk in' those goods means that it is he who must bear the loss if they are damaged or destroyed. If a person owns goods, it generally follows that he has to bear the loss if they are damaged or destroyed, but title and risk are distinct concepts and it is possible for title to be with one person while risk is with another. For example comprehensive motor insurance transfers the risk of damage to or destruction of the vehicle, but not title to it, to the insurer.

With a contract for the sale of goods, title and risk generally do pass to the buyer at the same time, and a series of rules is set out in Sections 16–20 of the Sale of Goods Act 1979 (as amended by the Sale of Goods (Amendment) Act 1995) for determining exactly when this happens. It is however open to the parties to make some other arrangement (including an arrangement by which title and risk pass at different times), and if they do so the rules in the Act do not apply to that contract. The rules in the Act, which are rather complex, make a distinction between specific goods and unascertained goods, a distinction encountered in section 4.2.2.

With specific goods, the general rule is that title and risk pass to the buyer when the contract is made. If however the contract is conditional, or the goods have to be weighed, measured or tested, or something else remains to be done to them before they are delivered, then title and risk only pass when that condition is met or when that thing has been done. So if you agree to buy an antique desk and the contract does not require anything else to be done to it before delivery, then unless you have made some other arrangement with the seller title and risk pass to you at the moment agreement is reached. This is unsatisfactory in that you are unlikely to have arranged to insure the desk before you agreed to buy it. The buyer's exposure if risk passes at this early stage is reduced by Section 7 of the Sale of Goods Act 1979, which provides that a contract for the sale of specific goods is avoided if the goods are accidentally destroyed prior to delivery. This does not however protect him if the goods are merely damaged prior to delivery rather than destroyed.

With unascertained goods, title and risk obviously cannot pass to the buyer until the goods are ascertained, that is until it has become clear exactly which goods are to be supplied. Subject to this, title and risk pass to the buyer when the goods are 'unconditionally appropriated' to the contract. Suppose then that a chemical company contracts to sell 5 tons of polyethylene to a plastics company, delivery to be by road tanker, and they have not agreed expressly when the title and risk are to pass. If the polyethylene is delivered in a single 5 ton tanker load, title and risk pass when the seller loads the tanker, which is the unconditional appropriation of the goods to the contract. But if the polyethylene is delivered from a tanker loaded with 20 tons, title and risk only pass when 5 tons are unloaded at the buyer's premises or, if earlier, when 15 tons have been delivered to other buyers so that only 5 remain in the tanker.*

It should be clear why substantial contracts for the sale of goods usually deal specifically with the passing of title and risk, rather than leaving those issues to be determined by the rather arbitrary provisions of the Sale of Goods Act 1979. Perhaps the most common arrangement is for title and risk to pass on delivery, that is the transfer of physical possession of the goods from seller to buyer. But if either party has sufficient bargaining power he may insist on a more favourable arrangement under which title and risk pass at different times. Ideally the seller wants risk to pass as early as possible while title stays with him for as long as possible. In the intervening period, although the buyer must bear the loss if the goods are damaged or destroyed, the goods are still owned by the seller, and this enables him to recover them if the buyer goes into bankruptcy or liquidation before title passes. The most common example of this kind of arrangement is the retention of title clause (discussed in section 9.2.5), under which a seller who supplies goods on credit retains title until he has been paid for them. The buyer of course would prefer the opposite arrangement: he wants title to pass to him as soon as possible while risk remains with the seller for as long as possible.

---

* *The buyer can obtain rights to part of the bulk before this if he has paid or part paid for the goods in advance, under amendments introduced by the Sale of Goods (Amendment) Act 1995.*

CHAPTER 5

Standard terms and conditions

A contract which incorporates a set of standard terms and conditions is not treated differently from any other contract, and there are no special legal rules applicable to such a contract apart from certain provisions of the Unfair Contract Terms Act 1977 (discussed generally in section 4.6 and in relation to standard terms in section 5.4). However, not only are such contracts extremely common, but they also raise a number of distinctive practical and legal problems. It is for this reason that we need to deal separately with them.

5.1 WHAT ARE STANDARD TERMS AND CONDITIONS?

'Standard terms and conditions' means a set of written contract terms which are intended to be incorporated into more than one contract. There are a number of different phrases used to describe such a set of terms: 'standard terms and conditions of business', 'written standard terms of business' (the phrase used in the Unfair Contract Terms Act 1977), 'terms and conditions' or just 'standard terms' or 'standard conditions' are all common variants. Although none of these phrases has a clearly defined legal meaning, a set of standard terms is, like an elephant, very easy to recognise when you see one. Standard terms are usually very lengthy, and they are often in very small print.

A set of standard terms and conditions does not refer to any particular transaction and, because it does not contain the basic terms of a transaction discussed in section 4.2.1, is not in itself a contract. The idea is that, when the parties enter into a particular transaction, they agree the basic terms of that contract and also agree that those standard terms will be incorporated into the terms of that contract. So the parties agree the bones of the transaction and the terms of the contract are fleshed out by the incorporation of standard terms and conditions.

5.2 THE USE OF STANDARD TERMS FOR CONVENIENCE

5.2.1 Negotiated standard terms

The incorporation of standard terms and conditions into a contract can be both useful and time-saving. Suppose for instance that a large company has a long term but intermittent requirement for a particular kind of goods such as desks and chairs. Instead of negotiating the terms of purchase with a supplier each time such goods are required, they may negotiate a set of terms and conditions of supply with a particular supplier. These terms will not deal with quantities and probably not with price but with secondary matters such as the specifications and quality of the goods, warranties, delivery, title and risk, payment and liabilities. Then, when the company requires a consignment of desks and chairs it only has to negotiate quantities and price, and agree to incorporate the agreed terms and conditions of supply into the sale contract. The civil service buys its furniture and stationery in this way.

There is a crucial difference between this arrangement and a long term supply contract such as we discussed in section 4.2.3. Here there is no contract until the quantity and price of a particular consignment have been agreed. Each time an order is placed and accepted a new contract is formed, but the buyer is not obliged to place any orders nor the supplier to accept them. So, unlike a long term supply contract, the buyer has no contractual expectation that he will get the goods he requires and this arrangement does not secure his future requirements. The point of a long term supply contract is that the seller is obliged to supply the goods required by the buyer in accordance with the contract, and so the contract does secure the buyer's long term requirements.

5.2.2 Published standard terms

Another common variation on the same theme is that, instead of negotiating a set of terms and conditions, the parties agree to incorporate a set of terms published by someone else. There are a number of professional and commercial entities which publish standard terms and conditions for particular types of contract. The Law Society publishes standard terms for contracts for the sale of land; Lloyd's of London publishes standard terms for contracts of marine insurance; the Institute of Mechanical Engineers and the Institute of Electrical Engineers publish standard terms for contracts for mechanical and electrical engineering work; the Joint Contracts Tribunal publishes standard terms for construction contracts; the Road Haulage Association publishes standard terms for the carriage of goods by road; and a number of ship owners publish their standard terms for charterparties. There are many other examples. Such published standard terms usually provide a fair balance between the interests of the parties. If they do not do so they are unlikely to be widely used.

So when two solicitors are acting in a house purchase, they generally draw up a contract which records the identity of the parties, the identity of the property and the price, together with whatever other terms have been specifically agreed between the parties. The contract specifies that the Law Society's standard conditions of sale are incorporated into it. These provide for such matters as the deposit and the formalities for completion (that is the conveyance of the house and payment of the purchase price). Very often solicitors will pick and choose from those standard conditions to meet the circumstances of that particular transaction: 'the Law Society's standard conditions of sale shall be incorporated herein except for conditions 5, 10a and 24'.

5.2.3 Practical issues

In the situations discussed so far standard terms and conditions are used as a matter of convenience, and the parties are (or should be) fully aware of what is contained in them. Their use in this way presents no special contractual problems. On a practical level, however, there are some points to watch out for.

First, although it does not matter whether a copy of the standard terms is attached to the contract or not, if no copy is attached it is important to make absolutely clear which set of standard terms is being incorporated. Most published standard terms are frequently updated and reissued, so it is prudent to refer to the date, edition or reference number of the standard terms to which your contract refers. Second, problems can arise where one of the standard terms is inconsistent with a term which has actually been negotiated. This problem can be avoided by providing that 'the ... terms and conditions shall be incorporated into this contract except in so far as those terms and conditions are inconsistent with the terms negotiated between us'. Third, if you are using standard terms in this way you do need to be sure what those terms actually say. You cannot escape the contractual consequences by saying that you never saw or never read the terms you agreed to incorporate.

5.3 THE USE OF STANDARD TERMS FOR CONTRACTUAL ADVANTAGE

Everyone has heard the expression 'the small print'. This derogatory phrase describes the most common and familiar use of standard terms, which is where a business produces its own standard terms and tries to incorporate them into all of its business transactions. The perception of the general public is, quite correctly, that the use of small print by one party is detrimental to the other, and that the effect of the small print is to undermine or even to contradict the terms expressly agreed between them. Generally such standard terms are not (whatever the businesses concerned might say) used for convenience but for contractual advantage, and the measure of this is that the terms are nearly always very one-sided. And generally the party using such standard terms does not want or intend the other to be aware of their contents, so long as they are incorporated into the contract. It is this use (or abuse) of standard terms with which we will be concerned for the rest of this chapter.

5.3.1 Origin of standard terms

The use of standard terms in this way was pioneered in the nineteenth century by the railway companies and shipping lines, but it did not begin as a grand scheme to exclude all contractual liabilities. It began because the carriers were concerned about one specific kind of liability, and this was their liability in respect of the goods they were carrying. We saw in section 4.7.2 that, unless the parties agree otherwise, a carrier is responsible if the goods are lost or damaged while in his possession. At common law a carrier can only escape such liability if that loss or damage resulted from an act of God or of the Queen's enemies; otherwise he is automatically responsible for all such loss or damage whether it was his fault or not. The only way to avoid this liability was to contract on terms which expressly excluded it, but with so many different contracts with so many different customers, how exactly was this to be achieved? The solution was to publish a set of standard terms to serve as the basis for every contract of carriage which they entered into.

Unfortunately what had begun as an exercise in excluding unacceptable liabilities turned almost inevitably into a much broader quest, which was to make the carrier's position as favourable as possible. So by the time the lawyers had finished drafting and the standard terms had expanded across several printed sheets, the carrier had excluded all potential liabilities and the customer was left without any contractual rights at all.

This is of much more than historical interest. The psychology of the process is still with us today, and is the root of all the problems to which standard terms have given rise. A party who decides, for whatever reason, to adopt his own standard terms is unlikely to be content with terms which fairly balance the interests of both parties. He will try to make his own contractual position as favourable as possible, and the most favourable position possible is to place all the risks and liabilities on the other party. Of course a wholly one-sided contract will not recommend itself to the other party or to a judge, and is unlikely to form a basis for satisfactory long term business relationships.

As we have seen however, since 1977 it has no longer been possible for a business which relies on standard terms to place all the risks and liabilities on the other party: under the Unfair Contract Terms Act some types of terms are automatically ineffective and some types are ineffective unless the term is reasonable. When dealing with a consumer further restrictions are imposed by the Unfair Terms in Consumer Contracts Regulations 1994.

5.3.2 British Rail's conditions of carriage

Although the use of standard terms has spread enormously, to this day it is the carriers who remain the finest exponents of the art, and it is worth looking back briefly at the terms and conditions used by British Rail immediately prior to its privatisation.

Every passenger ticket issued by British Rail had printed on it: 'This ticket is issued subject to the conditions shown in the (British Railways) Board's current Passenger Conditions of Carriage.' There was a different set of conditions for the carriage of freight. The Passenger Conditions ran to 23 printed pages. Most of this consisted of provisions relating to the validity and use of tickets, which placed numerous restrictions and obligations on the passenger. But as regards the obligations of British Rail, and the key question of what the passenger got for his money, the Conditions are silent except that in certain narrowly defined circumstances he may be given a refund of the cost of his ticket. The crucial provisions on liabilities are found in Condition 32 a):

> we will not accept liability for loss caused by delay and or cancellation of any train, by any missed connection or by the closure of the railway due to any strike, lock-out or other industrial action affecting our services. We will not, in any circumstances, accept liability for any consequential loss or costs that may arise from delay and/or cancellation of any train, the missing of any connection, or the closure of the railway (for whatever reason).

You will see that these provisions protected British Rail from liability even where the delay or cancellation was their fault, which would not of course be acceptable in a contract of carriage negotiated between two businesses of equal bargaining power. Under Section 2(2) of the Unfair Contract Terms Act 1977 these provisions are ineffective unless they are reasonable, so British Rail's lawyers evidently believed that a court might have been persuaded that these provisions were indeed reasonable.

The Passenger Conditions did not however seek to protect British Rail from liability if the passenger was killed or injured due to British Rail's negligence, since any such term is automatically ineffective under Section 2(1) of the Unfair Contract Terms Act.

5.3.3 Other users of standard terms

The businesses which are best placed to insist that all their contracts incorporate their standard terms are those which have a monopoly (or an effective monopoly) in the supply of particular goods or services. They can simply dictate to their customers that their standard terms and conditions are incorporated into the contract, and they do so on a 'take it or leave it' basis: if you attempt to reject or modify their terms they will simply refuse to contract with you.

Interestingly however some of the businesses which have a monopoly, and therefore unquestionably have the power to impose their terms on their customers, do not do so. Some at least of the regional electricity companies do not use standard terms in their dealings with their domestic customers. We do not know the reasons for this. It may be that, since the only significant obligation on the customer is the obligation to pay for electricity or gas consumed, and that obligation is easier to enforce by cutting off supplies than by suing for unpaid amounts, nothing is to be gained by forcing the customer to sign a written agreement.* Most businesses that have a monopoly position have no scruple about imposing very one-sided terms on their customers.

But it is not necessary to be a public utility or to be in a monopoly position to use standard terms to gain a contractual advantage, and the spread of this use of standard terms into all areas of commerce has been one of the most significant contractual developments of the twentieth century. Now, whenever you hire a car, book a holiday, put furniture into storage or check into a hotel, you are likely to be confronted with a set of standard terms and conditions. Since each business is free to adopt whatever standard terms it chooses, the terms used by a business can be quite revealing.

To begin with, those terms will be tailored to the main commercial activities of the business. Sometimes you are presented with a set of standard terms which bears no relation to the subject matter of the contract under negotiation, a sure sign that the business is acting outside its traditional sphere of activity. The contents of the standard terms will also tell you something about the commercial problems which that business faces.

Some years ago one of the authors had occasion to read the standard terms used by a conference and exhibition centre. Almost half of the document dealt with cancellation charges, setting out a tariff system under which a customer who cancelled his booking was charged a percentage of the conference fee which depended on how much notice of cancellation was given.† Obviously the conference centre had had problems obtaining compensation from customers who had cancelled their bookings.

Finally, the standard terms which a business uses reveal much about its commercial character. A business which is efficient and

---

* *In a case reported in* The Times *on 24 February 1995, the Divisional Court held that the arrangement between a regional electricity company and a domestic customer is not a contract at all. The reasoning was that, since the company is under a statutory obligation to supply, there is no scope for bargaining between the parties. We cannot believe that this is correct nor that the appeal courts will take the same view: if this arrangement is not a contract, then what exactly is it?*

† *This is in fact a liquidated damages provision, discussed in section 7.2.6.*

confident will often reflect this by using standard terms which are more positive, setting out what the customer's rights are rather than leaving him without any. However, the contractual position of a business is always more favourable under its standard terms than it would otherwise be, since there is no need for it to adopt standard terms at all unless it perceives some contractual advantage in doing so. And the advantage of the business is necessarily the disadvantage of the customer.

5.3.4   Terms of sale and terms of purchase

So far all our examples have involved standard terms used by businesses supplying goods or services to consumers. In order to see the full picture we need to consider the position of a business which is higher up the chain of supply, such as for example a company whose business is wholesaling. Wholesaling involves buying goods, usually though not necessarily from the manufacturer, and reselling them to retailers. So there are two distinct sides to this company's activities: the first is buying and the second is selling. Such a company will therefore usually be using two sets of standard terms. The first is its terms and conditions of purchase, which it will try to incorporate into all of its purchase contracts, and the second is its terms and conditions of sale, which it will try to incorporate into all of its sale contracts.

At the heart of both sets of standard terms is the issue of the liability of the supplier in respect of the goods supplied under the contract. Since the supplier is acting in the course of a business the contract would, if the parties did not agree otherwise, include the statutory implied terms that the goods will be fit for their purpose and of satisfactory quality. As discussed in section 4.8.3, as long as the supplier is not dealing with a consumer he can exclude those implied terms provided it is reasonable to do so. So typically the wholesaler's terms of sale will exclude those implied terms, and may or may not include a more limited warranty in respect of the goods – for example 'if the goods supplied are defective the seller will at its option either repair or replace them free of charge provided that the buyer notifies the seller of those defects promptly and in writing and returns the defective goods at his own expense to the seller within 21 days of delivery'. The wholesaler's terms of purchase on the other hand will seek to preserve the statutory implied terms, and may indeed go further by imposing extensive warranties from the seller in respect of the goods.

Although the liability of the supplier in respect of the goods is central, it is by no means the entire picture. Both sets of standard terms will also deal with other matters such as price, payment, delivery, and the passing of title and risk, and may include further provisions covering much the same ground as those outlined in section 4.4.2 in relation to a contract for the supply of a gas turbine. However, the terms of purchase will do so in a way favourable to the purchaser while the terms of sale will do so in a way favourable to the seller. So, to give only a few typical examples, the terms of purchase may provide that any agreed delivery date is firm and that the agreed price is fixed and payable within 60 days after invoice. The terms of sale on the other hand may provide that any agreed delivery date is only an estimate and that the agreed price, which will be increased in line with any increase in the seller's list price for those goods prior to delivery, is payable within 10 days after invoice.

Although each set of standard terms is tailor-made and therefore unique, businesses involved in the same trade tend to use similar terms. This is partly because businesses in the same trade will tend to encounter the same commercial and legal problems, but partly also because when a business drafts or updates its standard terms it can seldom resist the temptation to see what terms its competitors use. For example, although the main activity of a wholesaler is buying and selling goods it will inevitably require a variety of services as well, so the terms of purchase used by wholesalers are often drafted so as to cover contracts for services as well as contracts for goods. The most significant recent trend with standard terms of sale is the inclusion of a retention of title clause (discussed in section 9.2.5), as a result of a number of reported cases in the late 1970s which demonstrated that this device worked. So there is room for innovation with standard terms, but as always the innovators are few while the followers are many.

5.3.5 The incorporation of standard terms into a contract

We now come to the crucial issue in relation to standard terms, which is how they come to be incorporated into a contract. Where standard terms are used for convenience and both parties are aware of their contents, their incorporation requires no explanation: it is simply a function of the express intention of the parties. But where one party is using standard terms for contractual advantage, it is necessary to explain how the other party can be bound by those terms even if (as is usually the case) he is unaware of their contents. This comes about as a result of the application of the principles of offer and acceptance.

We saw in section 3.1 that the law considers that every contract comes into existence as a result of the acceptance of an offer, the terms of any contract being the terms of the offer which was accepted. So it is not enough for a party merely to insist that its standard terms are incorporated and that it always trades on that basis: it must ensure that those terms are incorporated into a contractual offer. Then, if that offer is accepted, the contract itself will incorporate those terms.

5.3.6 Offer

Let us deal first with the offer. Obviously the party seeking to incorporate its standard terms must bring those terms to the attention of the other party before the contract is made. If for example a contract is made over the telephone and then one party subsequently provides the other with a copy of its standard terms, it is too late for them to be incorporated into that contract.

The case of *Thornton* v *Shoe Lane Parking Ltd* 1971 illustrates the same point. In that case a motorist used a car park where the parking ticket was issued by an unattended machine. Having inserted his money into the machine, the motorist received a ticket which purported to incorporate a set of standard terms. The Court of Appeal decided that the machine being ready to accept the motorist's money constituted an offer, which the motorist accepted by inserting his money. It followed that the ticket referring to the standard terms arrived after the contract had been formed, with the result that the contract did not incorporate those terms.

It may well be that the tickets issued by British Rail, which as we have seen purport to incorporate the British Railways Board's current Passenger Conditions of Carriage, are only received by the passenger after the contract has been formed. However, British Rail would claim that their terms are incorporated by 'course of dealing', meaning that passengers receive a ticket every time they travel and must therefore be taken to have notice of those terms. However, this argument might well fail if the contract in question was the passenger's first journey on British Rail. No such argument was available to the owner of the car park in the Thornton case because it was the motorist's first visit to that car park.

Where a business deals with its customers face-to-face, another common technique for bringing its standard terms to their attention is simply to display those terms at its premises. This technique is less common than it used to be and it has an Achilles heel: it is always open to a judge, having considered the size, prominence and position of the notice, to conclude that the standard terms were not brought sufficiently to the customer's attention to have been incorporated into the contract. And the more one-sided those terms are, the greater will be the incentive for the judge to reach that conclusion.

The preferred technique therefore, whether the business deals with its customers in person or not, is to have the standard terms printed on some offer document which is handed or sent to them. The size of the print is reduced as far as is necessary to fit the standard terms onto a single sheet of paper. Modern business practice, with its reliance on computers and printed forms, lends itself very easily to this method, and it is hard for a customer who has actually had a copy of those terms in his hand to argue that he did not have notice of them. Then everything will depend on whether the other party's response to that offer amounted to the acceptance of it.

5.3.7 Acceptance

As we saw in section 3.1.4, when an offer is made it is either accepted in its entirety or else it is rejected. So a party who receives an offer which incorporates the other party's standard terms either accepts it (including those standard terms) or else rejects it, in which case no contract is formed. If he takes issue with all or any part of the standard terms, that counts as a rejection of the offer. The principles of offer and acceptance leave no room for the inter-mediate solution that the offeree accepted the main terms of the offer but not the small print.

The problem is that where the transaction has proceeded and money and goods or services have changed hands, there is a very strong inference that a contract has been formed; the conclusion that there is no contract at all is inconsistent with the subsequent actions of the parties and as we shall see has awkward legal conse-quences. So unless there is an express rejection by the offeree he is likely to be taken to have accepted the offer including the standard terms. He will certainly be taken to have accepted if he signs an agreement or says 'yes'. But he will probably also be taken to have accepted if he signs nothing and says nothing but allows the trans-action to proceed. Although in principle (as we saw in section 3.1.3) silence cannot amount to the acceptance of an offer, this principle tends to be displaced by the pressing legal need to conclude that a contract exists.

5.3.8 Dealing with a party which uses standard terms

So a party who receives an offer which incorporates the other party's standard terms is in a very difficult position. If he reads the terms he will probably find them unacceptable. If he takes issue with them, at worst the other party may refuse to contract with him and at best they may have to negotiate a full set of terms acceptable to both parties. But if he ignores the terms he will probably be taken to have accepted them.

For an individual dealing with a business which is using standard terms, there is no real solution to this dilemma. If you require the services of an entity with an effective monopoly, such as British Rail or the Post Office, you will have to sign anything they require you to sign. There is little point in even reading their standard terms if there is no alternative supplier. Where there are alternative suppliers, it is worth running fairly quickly through the standard terms presented to you. The purpose in doing so is not to look for objectionable provisions – you will usually find plenty – but to look for objectionable provisions which are not covered by the Unfair Contract Terms Act 1977. Only if you discover some of these is it worth considering an alternative supplier.

But where the recipient of an offer incorporating standard terms is itself a business which uses standard terms, then there is a solution to the dilemma. Assuming that the main terms of the offer are acceptable, the offeree ignores the other party's standard terms and 'accepts' the offer using a printed form which incorporates its own standard terms. Not only will those standard terms be completely incompatible with the other party's standard terms, but they will probably also expressly supersede them ('these terms and conditions shall apply to the contract to the exclusion of any terms and conditions relied on by the other party'). So although on the face of it this printed form looks and reads like an acceptance, it is in fact a rejection of the offer and a counter offer incorporating a different set of standard terms. In this way the tables are neatly turned on the party which made the original offer, who now faces the same dilemma in relation to the counter offer as the recipient of the original offer himself faced.* (See footnote on page 113.)

5.3.9 Practical example

Let us see how this technique works in practice. Suppose that the supplies manager of a large hotel telephones the sales department of a wine wholesaling company. The sales department confirms that their price per case for Château-Lafite 1966 is £1,500, that they have 10 cases in stock and that they can deliver to the hotel on the Wednesday of the next week. The supplies manager, careful not to enter into a contract over the telephone, concludes by saying 'OK, I'll send you an order'. He sends a printed purchase order which is addressed to the wholesaling company and reads as follows:

Please supply: 10 cases Château-Lafite 1966
Price: £1,500 per case
Delivery: Wednesday April 24th
This order is subject to the terms and conditions of purchase printed overleaf.

The purchase order may well also request the addressee to confirm the order by signing and returning one of the duplicate copies. The sales department of course does no such thing, since this would be an acceptance of the offer including the hotel's terms and conditions of purchase. Instead, they respond with a printed confirmation of order which is addressed to the hotel and reads as follows:

We are pleased to confirm your order for: 10 cases Château-Lafite 1966
Price: £1,500 per case
Delivery: Wednesday April 24th
This confirmation of order is subject to the terms and conditions of sale printed overleaf.

Now, unless the hotel responds with a further counter offer incorporating its terms of purchase, in taking delivery of the wine it will almost inevitably be taken to have accepted the wholesaling company's counter offer, in which case the contract incorporates the company's terms and conditions of sale.

* *There is of course no reason in principle why an individual cannot play the same game using his own standard terms and conditions, but we know of no individual (even a lawyer!) who does. In general consumers are adequately protected by statutory implied terms and by the Unfair Contract Terms Act 1977.*

You will notice that in both cases the document is stated to be 'subject to' that party's standard terms. This phrase means that, if that particular offer is accepted by the other party, the standard terms will take priority over the terms expressly agreed between them. So if the hotel does accept the offer contained in the wholesaler's confirmation of order, and the wholesaler's terms of sale allow him to increase the price in line with his list price at the time of delivery, the contract price may actually be higher than the £1,500 per case which was expressly agreed and recorded in the confirmation of order.

This example demonstrates why most trading companies now use standard terms. If a company is not using standard terms it will be taken to have accepted those of the other party, so its purchase contracts will incorporate its suppliers' terms of sale while its sale contracts will incorporate its customers' terms of purchase. If your customers and suppliers are using standard terms you cannot afford not to.

5.3.10 The battle of forms

Unfortunately however, the situation where both parties are using their own standard terms is, both legally and commercially, a nightmare. Failure to respond to an offer is to accept the other party's standard terms and lose the game. So every form received from the other party has to be answered by another form incorporating (or at least referring to) your own standard terms. So not only do standard terms now appear on every available document (including documents like delivery notes and invoices which really serve a completely different function) but new forms have had to be invented which have no real function other than to serve as a counter offer. So an order is met by an acknowledgement of order, which is met by a delivery request, which is met by a delivery note, which is met by an acceptance advice, which is met by an invoice, which is met by a payment advice, and so on even after the goods or services have been supplied and paid for. This increasingly common situation has come to be known, most aptly, as 'the battle of forms'.

A party can only be sure of winning the battle of forms if it has sufficient commercial power to insist that the other party signs and returns one of its forms (which represents an unconditional surrender in the battle). Few trading companies have such a degree of commercial power, so generally the best that a party can do is to try to ensure that it does not lose the battle by ensuring that no offer is either accepted or goes unanswered. But if both parties ensure that each offer they receive is rejected, the legal outcome is that there is no contract at all. This is a highly unsatisfactory outcome, since if there is no contract there is no legal framework to serve as a basis for the transaction: there are no express terms, no implied terms and no contractual obligations on either party. In this situation the only obligation which the law imposes on either party is the obligation on the customer to pay a reasonable price for any goods or services he actually receives (known as a *quantum meruit* payment, meaning 'for what it is worth', which is not necessarily the same as the price which the parties have agreed). So there is a strong incentive for the court to find an acceptance in order to avoid the conclusion that no contract exists.

The case of *British Road Services* v *Arthur V Crutchley & Co Ltd* 1968 demonstrates this tendency. In that case British Road Services, a carrier, delivered a lorry load of whisky for overnight storage in a warehouse owned by Arthur V Crutchley. The lorry driver had with him a delivery note which purported to incorporate BRS's standard terms (which were, incidentally, the standard terms published by the Road Haulage Association). At the warehouse the delivery note was stamped 'Received on AVC conditions' and returned to the driver. That night the lorry and its load were stolen from AVC's warehouse, and BRS sued AVC for failing to take proper care of it. AVC relied on a clause in their standard terms which limited their liability to £800 per ton. The Court of Appeal decided that the contract was formed when the delivery note was stamped and returned to the lorry driver, and so the contract incorporated the AVC terms including the liability limitation.

The decision in this case must be regarded as suspect. It is hard to believe that, on the principles of agency discussed in section 2.4, a lorry driver has either the actual or the apparent authority to commit his employer to a trading contract of this type. It does however show that the battle of forms can be won or lost by the activities of individuals like lorry drivers and warehousemen, who do not normally have any contractual function and are not likely to be trained in the art. The difficulty for such individuals is that a document like a delivery note may serve more than one function. It is primarily a receipt for the goods, but it may also serve as a vehicle for a contractual offer. The lorry driver may well be under instructions to refuse to unload them unless the document is signed, but in signing it the warehouseman may be taken to have accepted the contractual offer which it contains. One solution, as the British Road Services case shows, is for the warehouseman to be provided with a suitable rubber stamp. Another solution, which is common in the shipping world, is for him to sign the delivery note and add the words 'for receipt only', to make clear that his signature is intended only to confirm that the goods have been received.

5.3.11   Unpredictability of the battle of forms

If the court is unable to find any offer which is expressly accepted, it may nevertheless be able to infer acceptance by conduct. It may as we have seen regard the delivery or acceptance of the goods or services as the acceptance of the last offer made before then. Another possibility is to infer acceptance from the silence which follows the final shot in the battle.

When deciding such a dispute there is also an understandable human factor: a judge may wish to avoid the unjust results which would follow if he found that a very one-sided set of standard terms had been incorporated into the contract. It is relatively easy for him to avoid that result. One of the authors was involved in a case in which the judge refused to accept that a set of standard terms which had actually been signed by the other party had been incorporated. He did so on the basis that the print was too small for him to read, concluding that those terms had not been brought adequately to the other party's attention (see section 5.3.6).

In any particular battle of forms the outcome will therefore depend on the facts of the case, on a minute examination of each communication between the parties, and sometimes also on the personality of the judge. Unless one party has made the gross error of signing or expressly accepting one of the other party's forms, the outcome of any such battle is extremely unpredictable. It is highly unlikely that the parties will be able to resolve the situation without going to court. In our experience each party simply insists that its standard terms were incorporated since it trades exclusively on that basis. Tactically of course this is the correct position to take, but many businessmen seem to believe that this is true ('our terms of payment are 30 days'), which completely overlooks the problems of incorporation which we have been considering.

5.3.12   Conclusions on standard terms

In discussion with businessmen, we have heard a variety of attempts to justify the extensive use of standard terms, including that (1) it does away with the need to negotiate suitable terms, (2) it does away with the need for specialised staff who really understand contracts, (3) it is convenient and lends itself to computerisation, and (4) it provides a written record of the main terms of the contract and is therefore preferable to an oral contract. While there may be some truth in each of these arguments, our discussion points to a quite different conclusion.

We estimate that well over half of the contracts made between businesses in the UK involve the use of standard terms by at least one party, and that in around half of these cases both parties are using them. So in a very significant proportion of the commercial contracts made in the UK it is impossible, for the reasons we have discussed, to be certain what the terms of the contract actually are without a two or three year court battle. This uncertainty is not restricted to terms such as liability provisions, which only really matter if something goes wrong, but extends to such fundamental matters as the time of delivery, time of payment and the price. This must be regarded as a highly unsatisfactory situation, for which the law itself is indirectly responsible.

Where something does go wrong, the uncertain outcome of the battle of forms can be a matter of life and death for the parties. Several years ago one of the authors was involved in a legal action arising out of the sale of approximately £250,000 worth of cupronickel foil, which at that time was used for making electronic circuit boards. Defects in the foil resulted in the buyer suing the seller for losses amounting to over £3 million, a claim which if successful (and ignoring the substantial legal costs for which the loser would be liable) would put the seller into insolvent liquidation. The case turned almost completely on the issue of which party's standard terms had been incorporated into the contract. If the seller's terms of sale applied, the seller would win since those terms excluded all warranties and statutory implied terms in relation to the goods and limited the seller's liability in any event to the purchase price. But if the buyer's terms of purchase applied then the buyer would win since those terms included extensive warranties of the goods by the seller and provided no limitation of the seller's liability. The case was in fact settled out of court.

This case demonstrates the folly of a company relying on the incorporation of its standard terms in a contract of this size and importance. Although any business is well advised to have standard terms for the defensive reasons discussed in section 5.3.9, they must be used judiciously. The vagaries of the battle of forms may be acceptable when you are buying stationery, but not when you are entering into a contract with real significance for your business. With such a contract you must resolve with the other party what the terms of the contract are to be.*

Finally, let us record a personal view which many lawyers and businessmen evidently do not share. When advising a business on the adoption of standard terms we always try to persuade them that their terms should be balanced and reasonable rather than totally one-sided. There are three principal reasons for this. First, it gives a better impression of the business: an efficient business should not need to hide behind a forest of unreasonable small print. Second, it makes it more likely, for the reasons discussed in section 5.3.11, that those terms will be adjudged to have been incorporated if the matter should come to court. The third and most substantial reason is that some of those terms may well at some time be subjected to the test of reasonableness imposed by the Unfair Contract Terms Act 1977, to which we must now return.

5.4 STANDARD TERMS AND THE UNFAIR CONTRACT TERMS ACT

5.4.1 Outline of provisions

The provisions of the Unfair Contract Terms Act 1977, discussed in section 4.6, apply just as much to a contract which incorporates a set of standard terms as they do to any other contract. But some provisions of the Act apply specifically where one party is dealing 'on his own written standard terms of business'. So those provisions do not apply where the parties have negotiated a set of terms and conditions or have agreed to incorporate those published by someone else. They do however apply where one party has imposed his standard terms on the other or has won the battle of forms. The distinction is the same as the distinction we have been making between contracts where standard terms are used for

---

* There is one situation in which, even with a significant contract, this advice would not apply. This is where the other party has the commercial power to dictate the terms of the contract. Here the attempt to resolve what those terms are to be will result in your having to accept the other party's standard terms, so you may be better advised to engage in the battle of forms if the other party allows you to. The other side of the coin is of course that where you have the commercial power to dictate the terms, you must exercise it and on no account engage in the battle of forms. The relative bargaining strengths of the parties is, as we noted in section 3.3.3, the most important determining factor in any contractual negotiation.

convenience (section 5.2) and contracts where standard terms are used for contractual advantage (section 5.3). The provisions of the Act specifically related to standard terms apply only to contracts of the latter type.

These provisions are that, where one party is dealing on his own written standard terms of business, the following terms are ineffective unless they are reasonable:

(a) Any term which excludes or restricts that party's liability for breach of contract.
(b) Any term which entitles that party to render a contractual performance different from that which was reasonably expected of him.
(c) Any term which entitles that party, in respect of the whole or any part of his contractual obligation, to render no performance at all.

5.4.2 Analysis of provisions

Provision (a) set out in the previous section relates to exclusion clauses (discussed in section 4.5), which are generally very easy to identify. A party dealing on its own standard terms can only rely on an exclusion clause if that clause is reasonable.

Provisions (b) and (c) are however rather more obscure. Although they are clearly aimed at the use by a party of standard terms to undermine his contractual obligations, they can be difficult to apply. If for example the terms of sale used by the wine wholesaling company in our example in section 5.3.9 state that the company is under no obligation to supply any wine at all, that term is covered by both (b) and (c). It is also clearly unreasonable and therefore ineffective. But what if, as is more likely, the company's terms of sale state that, where the wine ordered is unavailable, the company has the right to supply wine of comparable quality at its list price? This term is probably not covered by (c), but is it covered by (b)? And, if so, is it reasonable?

On the other hand, some types of terms are clearly not covered at all. Most notably these include terms which, instead of excluding the liability or undermining the obligations of the party whose terms they are, impose obligations on or increase the liabilities of the other party. So for example the following terms, all of which are common in standard terms of sale, are not covered:

■ Price increase provisions.

- Provisions for high interest rates on late payments.
- Retention of title clauses (discussed in section 9.2.5).
- Indemnities imposed on the buyer.*

5.4.3 Negotiations over standard terms

The Unfair Contract Terms Act 1977 raises one further conundrum which may have important practical consequences, and that is: when do a party's standard terms cease to be his standard terms? Let us try to illustrate.

Imagine a small company which sells office equipment and which does not have its own terms and conditions of purchase. This company is contacted by a new supplier offering to supply word processors at a lower price than its current supplier. The proprietor of the company, who understands both the principles of standard terms and the Unfair Contract Terms Act 1977, looks closely at the terms and conditions of sale used by this new supplier. He ignores those provisions which he knows are covered by the Act but takes issue with two provisions which are not (or may not be) covered and are of particular importance to him. These are the provisions stating that any agreed delivery date is an estimate only (which may or may not be covered by (b) above) and that the seller has the right to increase the agreed price if the manufacturer's prices rise prior to delivery (which is not covered). He tells the new supplier that he will only place an order on the express understanding that these two provisions will not apply, since he needs to be sure about both delivery dates and prices. The supplier agrees, so a contract of sale is entered into which expressly incorporates the supplier's terms and conditions of sale except for those two provisions.

Unfortunately however, as we saw in section 5.4.1, the Unfair Contract Terms Act 1977 applies where one party is dealing 'on *his own* written standard terms of business' but not where the parties have negotiated a set of terms and conditions. So, in our example, is the supplier dealing on his own standard terms of sale (in which case the Act applies) or is he dealing on a negotiated set of terms (in which case it does not)? It may be that in negotiating over those standard terms the buyer has deprived himself of the protection of the Act altogether. The only safe advice is that if you negotiate over any part of the other party's standard terms you must go the whole way and not rely on the Act at all.

---

* An indemnity is covered by the Act and subjected to the test of reasonableness where the party giving the indemnity is a consumer – see section 4.6.2.

The complexity of the Act, its patchy coverage and the numerous uncertainties surrounding it lead us to the conclusion that it is an inadequate answer to the problems raised by the use of standard terms. We do however have the impression that over the last 10 years or so standard terms of business have become less one-sided, and it may be that the Act is slowly forcing the users of standard terms to moderate them.

Since 1 July 1995 the consumer has enjoyed additional protection against unfair standard terms as a result of legislation enacted by the European Union. For consumers this may well prove to be an altogether more potent weapon.

5.5 THE UNFAIR TERMS IN CONSUMER CONTRACTS REGULATIONS 1994

5.5.1 Background

In April 1993 the European Union issued a directive on unfair terms in consumer contracts, which was required to be enacted by each member state of the Union by the end of 1994. In the United Kingdom (including Scotland and Northern Ireland) it was enacted by the Unfair Terms in Consumer Contracts Regulations 1994, which came into force on 1 July 1995.

The purpose of these Regulations is to protect the consumer against unfair standard terms used by a business. This of course is also one of the main purposes of the Unfair Contract Terms Act, and an unfair standard term imposed on a consumer may fall foul of both the Act and the Regulations. The Regulations are however more comprehensive than the Act in that they apply to any standard term which is unfair to the consumer except the price and the terms which define the main subject matter of the contract. The Regulations do not however use the phrase 'standard terms', but refer instead to terms which 'have not been individually negotiated'. Although the meaning is the same, this formulation neatly avoids the problem raised by the Unfair Contract Terms Act 1977, discussed in the previous section, of exactly what constitutes a standard term.

5.5.2 Outline of the Regulations

In substance the Regulations provide that, when a business contracts to supply goods or services to a consumer, any term which has not been individually negotiated and which is unfair is not binding on the consumer. Any such term is therefore completely ineffective, and the contract is applied as if that term does not exist.

An unfair term is defined as 'any term which contrary to the requirement of good faith causes a significant imbalance in the parties' rights and obligations under the contract to the detriment of the consumer'. This gives the court a very broad scope to strike down any standard term which it considers unfair. The courts of the United Kingdom may however have difficulty with the words 'contrary to the requirement of good faith'. The requirement of good faith is a concept familiar to continental lawyers, but in the United Kingdom there is no general requirement that the parties to a contract act in good faith. There are two other features of these Regulations which are worth considering. The first is that a business which is dealing with a consumer is placed under a general obligation to ensure that any written term of the contract between them is expressed in plain, intelligible language. Perhaps surprisingly, this is the first time that the requirement of plain language has ever been introduced into any part of the English law of contract.

Secondly, where the standard terms used by a business are unfair, the Regulations allow a complaint to be made to the Director General of Fair Trading, who can prevent the continued use of those unfair terms. It is not necessary that you have contracted on those terms before you can make such a complaint.

So, for example, it is now possible for a rail passenger or a consumer association (or for that matter anyone else) to have British Rail's Conditions of Carriage reviewed to establish whether any of those Conditions are unfair and, if so, to prohibit British Rail from using them.

5.5.3 Conclusions

These Regulations apply only to standard form contracts with consumers. They do not apply to standard form contracts between businesses, so they have no bearing on the battle of forms. But in relation to standard form contracts with consumers the Regulations may well have far reaching effects.

The broad definition of what is meant by an 'unfair term', coupled with the mechanism which enables a business to be prohibited from using unfair standard terms, appear to open the way for a root and branch attack on unfair standard terms deployed against the consumer. For consumers, the notorious 'small print' may well become a thing of the past.

CHAPTER 6

The interpretation of a contract

6.1 ABOUT INTERPRETATION

6.1.1 The importance of interpretation

The contractual process has two sides. First, a contract is entered into, which is a matter of negotiating and agreeing a form of words to define the parties' contractual rights and obligations. Second, a contract has to be performed, which necessarily involves the interpretation of the words used to define those rights and obligations. With a large business these two functions are usually separated: for example a company whose business is selling goods will probably have a sales department which is responsible for the first and a distribution department which is responsible for the second. With a small business the same individuals may be responsible for both. But, whichever side of the contractual process an individual is engaged in, he is primarily concerned not with the rules of contract law but with the use and meaning of words, and he needs to understand how the words of a contract are interpreted. In practical terms therefore this chapter is the most important in the book.

6.1.2 Different forms of contract

The principles of interpretation which we shall be discussing apply to every contract irrespective of what form that contract is in. But where a contract is made orally or by an exchange of letters or telexes the parties usually express themselves in a direct and comprehensible way, so understanding what they meant is not usually a problem. An oral contract in particular is much more likely to give rise to a dispute about what the parties said than what they meant, and we considered in section 4.1.2 how such a dispute is resolved. Where on the other hand a contract is in writing, it is easy to identify what the terms of the contract are but it can be very difficult to work out what they mean. So our emphasis in this chapter will be on formal written agreements, and we must start by recognising and trying to explain the peculiar difficulties involved in interpreting contracts of this type.

6.1.3 The problem with formal written agreements

Formal written contracts are notoriously hard to understand. In our experience an individual who is not used to dealing with such contracts will often abandon the attempt, baffled by long and tortuous sentences, numerous cross-references and unfamiliar words and usage. Having spent much of our careers with our heads wrapped in a proverbial cold towel, trying to understand what particular contracts are supposed to mean, we have every sympathy with him. Although this impenetrability is perhaps excusable where the ideas being expressed are themselves complex, it is inexcusable where (as is all too often the case) the ideas being expressed are simple. The main reason for it is, unfortunately, the involvement of lawyers.

Most substantial commercial agreements (or at least the standard forms from which they are derived) will have been drafted by a lawyer. If not actually a lawyer he will be a contracts draftsman who has through long exposure come to think like one. Lawyers use certain words in a specialised legal sense which you need to recognise if you are to understand a formal contract. We have already encountered the most common of these (e.g. person, warranty, title, etc) in this book. Lawyers also tend, largely for convenience, to use certain archaic words and phrases (e.g. herein, notwithstanding, aforesaid, etc). Most people understand these terms even if they do not themselves use them. But the core of the problem lies not so much in the use of specialised or archaic words as in the culture of the legal world.

For most lawyers 'good drafting' is an arrangement of words from which another lawyer can distil a single unambiguous meaning. Legal culture does not demand either brevity, clarity or style. Indeed the fact of being a lawyer seems to exempt someone from all these considerations, and some lawyers seem actually to take pride in the complexity of their drafting. In extreme cases they become incapable of expressing a simple idea simply even when it is in their interests to do so. It is this legal culture which explains why the 'gobbledegook' category of the annual Plain English Awards is regularly won by a legal document, and why commercial contracts can be so hard to decipher.

It should also be said that sometimes this impenetrability is deliberate, a calculated attempt to get the other party to commit itself to terms which it has not really understood. We should in fairness add that at least as many businessmen as lawyers appear to engage in this highly disreputable practice.

6.2 PRINCIPLES OF INTERPRETATION

6.2.1 Statement of principles

The principles of interpretation hardly deserve such a grand title. They can be simply stated as follows:

> The interpretation of any contract is a matter of working out, from the terms of that contract, what the parties meant at the time the contract was made. To do so you must assume that the words of the contract are used in their ordinary and natural sense but you must also consider the contract as a whole.

6.2.2 Objective meaning

It is very important to note that the starting point is the terms of the contract. Although as we have seen the court will hear evidence from the parties if this is necessary to establish what the terms of the contract are, once those terms are established the issue is the objective one of what those terms mean rather than the subjective one of what the parties thought they meant. What the parties thought the contract meant is irrelevant and of no consequence.

This distinction was dramatically illustrated in a case widely reported in the press in January 1991 concerning the rent review clause in a commercial lease. It is common practice in commercial leases for the rent to be increased periodically in line with some indexation factor such as the Retail Prices Index (or RPI). These periodic increases are known as 'rent reviews'. The lease in question provided for a rent review every three years, and at each rent review the rent was to be increased as follows:

The review rent to take effect from the date of review shall be the rent payable hereunder prior to the date of review (whether such rent is itself a reviewed rent or the Basic Rent) and in addition such sum as shall be equal to the Basic Rent multiplied by the variable factor (hereinafter collectively called 'the index linked rent').

When the tenant entered into the lease, both he and his solicitor reportedly thought this meant that the rent would simply be increased in line with the 'variable factor', which was in fact the Retail Prices Index. But if they had read the clause carefully they would have seen that the clause does not say that at all. It actually says that at each rent review the existing rent is increased by *adding* a sum equal to the original rent multiplied by the variable factor. So at the first rent review, assuming an annual inflation rate of 5 per cent, the original annual rent of £7,500 increased not to £8,682 but to £16,182. After 18 years, assuming 5 per cent inflation, the rent would be £84,118.

It was reported that a number of tenants had entered into commercial leases containing this form of rent review clause, so this particular case was a test case to see if the courts would apply this clause in accordance with its objective meaning. Unfortunately for the tenants the clause is, on a close examination, perfectly clear and unambiguous, and the court was prepared to enforce it. A number of these tenants were reportedly facing bankruptcy as a result.

As we saw in Chapter 5, this search for the objective meaning of a contract can reach logical absurdity with a contract incorporating one party's standard terms. Even where the other party has not read those standard terms, the court will still analyse the contract to see what the parties meant. In this situation 'the parties' intention' is of course entirely notional.

The other point to note is that what matters is what the parties meant *at the time the contract was made*. So the meaning of the words they used must be judged by reference to the circumstances at that time and not by reference to subsequent circumstances or events. The meaning of a contract cannot be altered by subsequent events.

The practical implications of this objective approach are so obvious that we need not labour them. When working out what a contract means it is necessary to start without preconceptions and to see what the contract actually says. Scanning the document quickly is seldom enough to reveal its true meaning: it is all too easy to see what you expect to see rather than what the contract really says. In our rent review example both the tenant and his solicitor made that costly mistake. Equally, when you receive a draft contract (whether drafted by someone on your side of the negotiation or the other side) for your comment or approval, it is not enough that it 'broadly reflects' what you discussed, and it is a serious (though common) mistake to say to yourself that 'we both know what we meant' and then enter into a contract which says something else.

In our experience this is especially likely to happen when the individuals on each side have a good personal relationship. The temptation is to think that that personal relationship will enable you to resolve any problems which may arise if the terms of the contract do not reflect your true intentions. While good personal relationships do enable many contractual disputes to be resolved amicably at an early stage, if something goes seriously wrong lawyers will soon become involved. They will be interested in the terms of the contract rather than the understanding and goodwill existing between the parties; and in our experience when one party asserts its legal rights, goodwill disappears very rapidly indeed. Personal relationships are the first casualties of litigation.

6.2.3 The ordinary and natural meaning of words

The legal maxim that 'the parties to a contract must be taken to have used words in their ordinary and natural sense' may give a certain wry amusement. After all, as we discussed in section 6.1.3, lawyers are the worst culprits both for using words in a specialised sense and for using archaic words. But perhaps it is this very fact which elevates a statement of the obvious into a maxim of interpretation. In order to understand someone at all it is of course necessary to assume that he is using words in their ordinary and natural sense, that when he refers to a 'motor car' he means a motor car and not a bus, train or aeroplane, and that when he says he 'will' do something he means that he will do it and not that he may do it or will try to do it or will do it if it suits him.

But the implications of this maxim are striking. Lawyers have no monopoly in either the use or meaning of words, and legal training involves no direct study of either. So a lawyer's view of what the words of a contract mean is not necessarily any better than anyone else's view, and there is no reason in principle why a businessman cannot negotiate and draft a contract just as effectively as a lawyer can.

The reality is however that most lawyers are good with words. The profession attracts individuals with an affinity for language, and then gives them a great deal of practice in using it. A lawyer who combines a flair for words with commercial experience and acumen (and there are many) is a powerful business resource. His value goes far beyond the avoidance of legal problems: his involvement should make it more likely not only that a deal is reached but also that the deal is a good one.

If there is doubt about the ordinary and natural sense of a word, the best place to start is of course a dictionary. Judges themselves do so when there is a dispute about the meaning of a word. But the dictionary definition is not necessarily conclusive. It may be that a particular word or phrase in a contract is being used in a different way.

6.2.4   Defined terms

It is of course open to the parties themselves to define what they mean by a particular word or phrase. Any formal agreement is likely to contain a number of these defined terms, and when a particular term is defined then it must be understood in that sense rather than its ordinary sense. Defined terms are usually (but not always) indicated by capital first letters and are often alphabetically listed in a definitions clause at the beginning or end of the agreement. The clause quoted in our rent review example in section 6.2.2 contains three defined terms: 'Basic Rent', 'variable factor' and 'index linked rent'. You will note that capital first letters are used only in the first of these terms, and that the definition of the last term is buried inside the clause itself, a practice which can make the definition difficult to find and dangerously easy to overlook.

Since the object of the exercise is (or should be) to make the contract as easy to understand as possible, our view is that defined terms used in a contract should always be listed (if appropriate merely referring to the clause in which the definition appears) and indicated by capital first letters. When used properly defined terms can be very helpful not only in making the contract clear but also in keeping it short, since the definition need not be repeated each time the term is used.

6.2.5   Customary usage

There is another situation in which a word or phrase may be used other than in its ordinary sense, and this is where customarily used in the trade or industry concerned in a specialised way. Every trade and industry tends to develop its own specialised vocabulary. To take just one example, in the oil and gas industry the word 'mud' is used to refer to the mixture of chemicals which is pumped down a well to control the pressure in the well, lubricate the drill bit and return the cuttings to the surface. In the oil business this is the ordinary meaning of the word, so when it is used in a drilling contract it has to be understood in this sense. Everyone in the business knows that 'mud' does not mean a mixture of earth and water.

'Custom of the trade', the importance of which we have already discussed in relation to the formation of a contract (section 3.3.2) and implied terms (section 4.7.3), is therefore also important in relation to the interpretation of a contract. Where appropriate the court will hear evidence from experts in that trade or industry about its customs. This means that you can safely use specialised words in a contract provided that they do have a meaning which is universally recognised in that trade or industry.

Unfortunately however it sometimes happens that trade jargon, even jargon which is hallowed by centuries of use, proves to have no discernible meaning. In this event the court will not guess at or invent a meaning since that would be to impose obligations on the parties which they had not voluntarily undertaken.

The case of the *Andreas Lemos* 1983 is a fine example. This was a dispute over the interpretation of a contract of marine insurance, under which the hull and machinery of the *Andreas Lemos* was insured on the terms of the standard form of English marine policy. These terms, which in their essentials have been in use in England for over three hundred years, provide cover for loss caused by (among other things) 'pirates' and 'rovers'. While the ship was anchored off Bangladesh, a gang armed with knives secretly boarded it and stole some of the ship's equipment. At that point they were seen by the crew and made their escape. The judge's analysis was that, although the gang had threatened the crew with knives in order to escape, the actual theft was committed without violence and did not therefore constitute piracy. This left the question of whether the gang were 'rovers' within the meaning of the policy. The judge declined to answer that question, saying: 'I am by no means clear what are rovers.... Its only current and popular meaning is, I suppose, a species of motor car, such as a Ford or a Vauxhall.' It followed that the loss was not covered by the policy.

This case is a good illustration of what a colleague and friend refers to as the 'hallowed nonsense' principle. When a lawyer or draftsman prepares a draft agreement, he seldom starts with a clean sheet of paper; he starts with a draft run off a word processor, which is based on the text of other similar contracts. Often therefore the draft incorporates provisions which have not been carefully thought out in the context of that transaction but are included simply because they have been used before. When you find provisions like this and you ask the party which produced the draft to explain what they are intended to achieve, often there is no satisfactory explanation. The argument for their inclusion (if it can be called an argument) is that 'we don't really understand them but all our contracts include these provisions' – the hallowed nonsense principle. This is not a sufficient basis for including those provisions. If the parties themselves, at the time the contract is entered into, do not understand what certain of its provisions are intended to achieve, it is folly to expect a court to guess what they meant.

6.2.6 Legal usage

Before leaving the subject of the ordinary and natural sense of words, we need to say a little about the specialised legal usage of words, which we noted in section 6.1.3. All the terms which are commonly used in contracts by lawyers in a specialised legal sense are covered in this book. We want to add only two things. First, nobody should be intimidated by this specialised usage. The meaning of most of these terms is very straightforward and anyone dealing with formal contracts very quickly becomes familiar with them. Second, do not feel obliged to use them when negotiating or drafting a contract yourself. Nearly all of these terms can readily be substituted by more familiar expressions.* For example, lawyers tend to use the words 'title' or 'property' rather than the more familiar word 'ownership'. But they all mean the same thing, and it does not matter whether a contract says 'title to the goods shall pass when ...' or 'property in the goods shall pass when ...' or 'the buyer shall become owner of the goods when ...'. All that matters is that you express your meaning clearly.

---

* The one exception is the phrase 'subject to contract', the use and meaning of which we discussed at length in section 1.4.7.

6.2.7 Considering the contract as a whole

The final part of our statement of the principles of interpretation is that the contract must be considered as a whole. This point can be simply illustrated.

Imagine that you are looking through a formal agreement in order to advise your board of directors of the price payable for the goods or services to be supplied under it. You find a sentence in the agreement which says 'the price shall be £250,000'. You may however be making a mistake if at that point you return the agreement to your files and advise the board that the price is £250,000. That statement of the price may be qualified, altered or superseded by other provisions of the agreement. Those other provisions may be located in the same clause (e.g. 'provided however that the price shall be increased in the event that …') or in a completely different part of the agreement (e.g. 'the price stated in clause 5 shall be reduced in the event that …'). And in the latter case, while there may be a reference in clause 5 to alert you to the other relevant provisions (e.g. 'subject to clause 18 the price shall be £250,000'), equally there may be no such reference. So in order to be sure about even a relatively straightforward matter such as price, you must first locate all the provisions which have anything to do with price and then work out how these provisions fit together. Overlooking a relevant provision is the easiest, most common and potentially the most dangerous mistake to make when interpreting a formal agreement.

6.2.8 The structure of formal agreements

What makes it so easy to overlook a relevant provision in a formal agreement is the size and complexity of most such agreements. Most formal agreements have the same basic structure, so let us briefly consider the structure of a typical one. It begins by recording for reference purposes the date of the agreement and then sets out the identities and addresses of the parties. Then comes the 'preamble' or 'recitals', also known as the 'whereas clauses' because they nearly always begin with the word 'whereas'. The preamble sets out the circumstances which led the parties to enter into the agreement. This sets the scene and is a very useful starting point in understanding why the agreement came to be entered into. Strictly speaking however the preamble is not part of the agreement, so it should not contain any part of the parties' contractual rights and obligations. The agreement itself starts after the preamble and is introduced by a formal statement such as 'Now therefore it is hereby agreed between us as follows'.* The main operative provisions (or 'main body') of the agreement now follow, divided into numbered clauses (or 'articles'), with headings and sub-headings.

While the headings and sub-headings usually provide an accurate summary of the contents of the clause, this cannot be relied on. Headings are not strictly part of the agreement and cannot affect the interpretation of the clauses, and most formal agreements include a provision which expressly embodies this principle along the following lines: 'In this Agreement headings are used for convenience only and shall not be taken into account in the interpretation of the operative provisions hereof.'

After the main body of the agreement there will probably be a number of appendices (also commonly called 'schedules', 'attachments' or 'exhibits') containing such things as technical descriptions and drawings, payment schedules, accounting matters, draft parent company guarantees, and so on. The parties' signatures or seals are generally found at the end of the main body of the agreement or else right at the end after the appendices.

6.2.9   Priority between different provisions

There are a number of misconceptions about how the different parts of an agreement relate to each other. The first is that priority derives from the numerical order of the clauses so that the contents of clause 5 take priority over the contents of clause 18 but are subordinate to those of clause 3. The second misconception is that the main body of the agreement necessarily takes priority over the appendices. The third misconception is that, where an agreement incorporates standard terms in small print, the large print must take priority over the small.

The relationship between different provisions in an agreement cannot however be judged by their position in the agreement or the size of the print; it can only be judged by the words and meanings of the different provisions. For example, there is no difficulty in seeing how the following provisions fit together:

* This formal statement often incorporates a pointless and ineffective reference to the consideration provided by the parties, e.g. 'Now in consideration of the mutual covenants and promises hereinafter appearing it is hereby agreed as follows'. This is pointless since, as we saw in section 3.2, if one party provides no consideration for the agreement then there is no contract. The defect cannot be cured by a reference to non-existent consideration.

The price shall be £250,000.

The price shall be increased in line with any increase in the price of raw materials between the date of this agreement and the date when the seller purchases them for the purposes of this agreement.

The price shall be reduced by 1% for each day by which the seller fails to meet the Delivery Date.*

These three provisions are not actually inconsistent and so the question of priority does not arise. Priority between provisions which are (or are potentially) inconsistent is usually indicated by the phrases 'provided that', 'subject to' or 'notwithstanding'. As we saw in section 5.3.9, a party seeking to incorporate its standard terms almost invariably does so with the words 'subject to the terms and conditions ...'. This has the intended effect of giving those standard terms priority over the terms negotiated between the parties. Similarly a clause in a formal agreement limiting the total liability of one of the parties under the contract will usually begin 'notwithstanding any other provision of this agreement ...', indicating that all the contractual obligations of that party are subject to that overall limitation.

In order to determine the relationship between the main body of an agreement and an appendix you need to find that part of the main body which refers to that appendix and see what it says. With for example a contract for the sale of land, it is common for the land to be described in the main body of the agreement and for a plan of it to be included as an appendix. If the words in the agreement referring to the plan say 'the land to be sold is for the purposes of identification only marked on the plan attached hereto', then it is clear that the plan is only illustrative and that the description of the land in the agreement takes priority. But if the wording is 'the land to be sold is more particularly delineated on the plan attached hereto', then it is clear that the plan takes priority over the description.

Large commercial agreements often contain a provision which expressly gives the main body priority over the appendices, for example: 'In the event of any inconsistency between the main body of this agreement and any of the appendices, the provisions of the main body shall prevail.' A well drafted contract will of course contain no such inconsistency, but the inclusion of this provision

---

* *This provision is a liquidated damages clause. Such clauses are discussed in section 7.2.6.*

is a tacit admission by the draftsman of how difficult it is to be sure that no inconsistency exists. But unless this provision is included you cannot take it for granted that the main body of the agreement takes priority over the appendices. Sometimes the reverse is the case.

6.3 SPECIALISED RULES OF INTERPRETATION

Now that we have concluded our discussion of the central principles of interpretation, we need to mention two specialised rules. They are much less important than the central principles and we will deal with them briefly.

6.3.1 The interpretation of exclusion clauses

The first of these rules, which we have already encountered in section 4.5.6, concerns the interpretation of exclusion clauses. If there is any ambiguity in an exclusion clause, that ambiguity is resolved against the party seeking to rely on the clause. Let us consider an example to illustrate this rule.

Suppose that a contract for the sale of goods provides that 'the seller shall not be liable for any loss suffered by the buyer as a result of any defect in the goods'. Suppose that a defect in the goods causes them to explode while on the buyer's premises, injuring one of his employees. That employee sues the buyer, as his employer, for failing to provide a safe place of work and wins substantial damages. The buyer sues the seller to recover these damages and his own legal costs of the first action. The seller relies on the exclusion clause. The court will probably conclude that the phrase 'any loss' is not sufficiently clear and unambiguous to cover damages payable by the buyer to a third party or the costs of defending the action, in which case the buyer will win his action against the seller.

This rule of interpretation, which is known as the *contra proferentem* rule (meaning 'against the person relying'), is the main reason why exclusion clauses have become so expanded as draftsmen attempt to remove any conceivable ambiguity. You are unlikely in practice to encounter quite such a simple exclusion clause as the one in our example. That clause is more likely to read:

the seller shall not be liable for any loss, damage, injury, claims, costs, expenses or other liabilities whatsoever, including without limitation loss of trade, loss of profit and consequential loss, suffered by the buyer as a result of any fault or defect of any kind whatsoever, whether latent or patent and whether resulting from the seller's negligence or otherwise, in the goods, their components or their packaging.

But even this exclusion clause is restrained by comparison to some you may encounter in standard terms and conditions of sale.

6.3.2 Lists of words

The second specialised rule of interpretation concerns lists of words. Suppose that a contract requires one party to notify the other, if a certain event occurs, 'by telephone, telex, facsimile or other means'. The principle is that the meaning of the general phrase 'other means' must be construed in the light of the specific words preceding it. The common link between telephone, telex and facsimile communications is that receipt is instantaneous, so 'other means' must refer only to other means where reception is instantaneous; so a face-to-face notification would count as 'other means' but a postal notification would not. This rule is known as the *eiusdem generis* rule (meaning 'of the same type'). Its effect is that a list of words cannot be made inclusive by the addition of a catch-all phrase at the end of the list.

There are two types of provisions which are especially likely to contain a list of words, and both are concerned with the mitigation of contractual liabilities. The first is a simple exclusion clause, and the example in the previous section included such a list ('any loss, damage, injury, claims, costs, expenses or other liabilities whatsoever'). The *eiusdem generis* rule means that the final phrase 'or other liabilities whatsoever' probably adds nothing to the list which precedes it. The second is a *force majeure* clause (discussed in section 7.2.8), which protects one or both parties from liability for events which are outside his control, e.g. 'neither party shall be liable for any failure to perform its obligations hereunder due to Acts of God, Acts of war, Acts of Governments, floods, hurricanes, earthquakes ...'. As a result of the *eiusdem generis* rule, such lists of words have expanded relentlessly as draftsmen try to cover every conceivable contingency.

6.4 SUBSTANTIAL WRITTEN AGREEMENTS

6.4.1 The importance of interpretation

We have now covered the whole spectrum of commercial contracts, from an oral contract for the retail sale of a chocolate bar through to substantial written agreements between large businesses which are of high value and often long duration. Although the principles of interpretation are applied right across this spectrum, irrespective of the form or value of a contract, we need to say more about substantial written agreements because with contracts of this kind issues of interpretation are all-important.

Many of the legal issues with which we have been concerned up until now simply do not arise with a substantial agreement of this type. Neither party is a consumer and neither is attempting to incorporate its standard terms. Very little of the legislation we have considered applies to that agreement, and such of it as does apply can generally be excluded if the parties so choose. The agreement will be freely negotiated between the parties, each of which will have all the appropriate commercial, technical, legal, tax and insurance advice. The agreement itself will be in writing and signed on behalf of each party by a senior executive who will have the express authority of his board of directors to do so; no problems of authority, offer and acceptance or consideration are likely to arise. The agreement is without doubt intended to be legally binding, and it is highly unlikely that its validity will ever be called into question. The agreement will be inclusive, leaving very little room for claims of misrepresentation or reliance on implied terms. If the agreement does end up being considered by a court, the overwhelming probability is that the question will be one of interpretation.

With an agreement of this kind the function of the courts is not to protect either of the parties from the other but simply to enforce the agreement in accordance with their express intentions. The parties will have negotiated the text of the agreement with great care and a close attention to detail, and commercially speaking it is very important that the court takes a strict objective approach when interpreting it. For example, in our discussion of the contract for the supply of a gas turbine in section 4.4.2, we saw that the agreement will typically include cross-indemnities in relation to claims by the parties' personnel, so that each party undertakes to meet any claim arising out of the death or personal injury of its employees even if that death or injury was the fault of the other party. (You will note incidentally that Section 2(1) of the Unfair Contract Terms Act 1977 does apply to this contract and prevents either party from excluding its liability for death or personal injury caused by its negligence, but the Act does not prevent the parties from indemnifying each other in respect of such liability since neither party is a consumer.)

The rationale for these cross-indemnities is that each party will have insurance to cover such claims by its employees, so if an employee claims against the other party the indemnity passes that claim back to the employer and ultimately to his insurers. If a court takes the view that the indemnity is unfair and therefore interprets it in such a way as to deprive it of its intended effect, the consequence will be that the liability falls on the party which is not insured against it.

The courts of England and Wales, and the commercial courts in particular, are well aware of the need to interpret the provisions of such agreements strictly; this is one of the major reasons for the popularity of the English courts as a forum for international commercial disputes, many of which (as we shall see in section 12.2.5) have no connection with England at all.

6.4.2 The negotiation of a written agreement

The negotiation of any substantial written agreement usually follows the same basic pattern. Initially contact is made between senior commercial representatives of each party to see whether there are the makings of a deal, and if so to establish its basic commercial terms. These discussions will usually involve the release of sensitive technical and commercial information, in which case the parties will first have protected the confidentiality of that information by means of a confidentiality agreement, which prohibits the recipient from disclosing it to third parties or using it for any purpose other than the evaluation of the proposed transaction. When the basic commercial terms are established they will often be recorded in a document such as a heads of agreement. As we saw in section 1.4.5, this document will not usually be intended to be legally binding, but in any event it will form the framework for the negotiation of the full agreement which follows.*

---

* The other possibility is that the contract is put out to tender, in which case as we saw in section 3.5.3 the negotiation will be on the basis of the contract terms and conditions included in the tender documents.

The negotiation will centre on a draft agreement, and one of the first issues which needs to be decided is which party will be responsible for producing the draft. Often this question will be decided on the basis of convention: for example with contracts for the sale of a business the convention is that the buyer produces the draft whilst with contracts for the sale of land the convention is that the seller produces the draft. Equally however there may be no such convention, in which case both parties may lay claim to the drafting. Sometimes the desire to do the drafting has a cynical motive: the party concerned intends to produce a document which is slanted steeply in his favour. In this situation however there is little advantage to be gained by producing a one-sided draft, because no substantial and well advised business will be coerced or manipulated into accepting such a document; at best this tactic serves only to generate ill-will and prolong the negotiation, and at worst the other party will refuse to proceed on the basis of your document and counter with a draft of its own.

A comprehensive and even-handed first draft will set the agenda for the negotiation, and there lies the real advantage in doing the drafting. In order to produce the draft you will have to think the transaction through carefully, and having produced the draft you will be more familiar with its structure and detail than the other party is. So unless the other party is disciplined enough to think the transaction through for itself and to make itself thoroughly familiar with your draft, you will have a double advantage in the negotiation.

A good first draft will greatly simplify the negotiating process, and it is well worth the time and effort required to get it right. Although most draftsmen start with a standard form from a word processor, every large transaction is in some respects unique and the draft will have to be tailored to the circumstances. Unless you have a similar transaction to use as a precedent, it is often better to start with a blank sheet and to think carefully about the important issues in the transaction and how they should be dealt with. In any event drafting is best done alone. A group of people round a table all calling out different forms of words can never produce a satisfactory draft: as the old adage has it, a camel is a horse designed by a committee.

A good draft is as short and as clear as the circumstances permit; it deals even-handedly with the issues raised by the transaction and takes account of matters such as tax which affect its structure and content; it is internally consistent and contains no extraneous material. The measure of a good draft is that it enables the parties readily to identify the real differences between them.

The negotiation proceeds with a series of meetings between the parties' negotiators, and the text of the document is refined through successive drafts until there is complete agreement. Behind the scenes the negotiators on each side will be referring each draft for specialist advice on matters such as the technical, tax and insurance aspects of the transaction. The input required from these various specialists is very specific. Is the wording of the current draft acceptable? Should different wording be proposed? Does the draft need to cover other matters which have been overlooked? However, the value which can be added by such advisers is not restricted to the sphere of their professional expertise; they will have their own view on what the words of the draft mean, and it often happens that they read a particular provision in a completely different way from the main players in the negotiation. Dangerous ambiguities can be brought to light in this way.

For the negotiators themselves, one of the most valuable attributes is a keen sense of priorities. Some issues are more important than others, and some are more important to one party than to the other. Contrary to the view of some negotiators, it is not possible to win on every issue. With some types of issue a head-on confrontation cannot be avoided, the most obvious example being price. But with many issues a drafting solution acceptable to both parties can be found, although it is a mistake to resort to wording which is either patently ambiguous or else so vague as to be meaningless. With those issues for which no drafting solution can be found, the art is to trade those issues which are less important to you for those which are more important.

6.4.3 Danger in the period before signature

It is of course always possible that the negotiators will fail to reach agreement on the terms of the contract, but equally the transaction may fail for some reason not connected with the negotiation of its terms. A change in market conditions may have made the proposed transaction less attractive to one of the parties (although of course this will have made it correspondingly more attractive to the other). One party may have found a better means of meeting its objectives. Its parent company may have refused to authorise the transaction or its bankers may have declined to finance it. Sometimes a party simply has second thoughts and decides not to proceed. When one party pulls out of the transaction the other may feel aggrieved, and may well consult its lawyers to see if it has any legal redress.

If the terms of the contract have actually been finalised, this is an extremely dangerous situation for the party which pulls out. The lawyers will conduct a minute examination of the correspondence between the parties since those terms were finalised, and they will be particularly interested in any communication which uses the language of contractual intention and does not include the words 'subject to contract'. Once the draft is finalised the negotiators will probably be thinking of the deal as finished, so the lawyers may well find a letter from the party which subsequently pulled out saying 'we enclose a copy of the final draft which is now agreed between us' or 'we are delighted that agreement has now been reached'. On this basis the aggrieved party has a respectable claim that a contract already exists, saying in effect that signature of the documents would merely have been evidence of that contract rather than the formation of it. The party which did not want to proceed may now be forced to sign the agreement rather than face a massive claim for damages for breach of contract.

One way to ensure that such a dispute cannot arise is to ensure that all correspondence to the other party, and especially correspondence which is sent after the text of the agreement is finalised, is marked 'subject to contract'. There may however be a great volume of correspondence, in which case it can be difficult to ensure that every communication is marked in this way. So a better solution is to say specifically what your intentions are, for example 'we are delighted that agreement has now been reached, but to avoid any misunderstanding we must make clear that no contractual commitment is intended on our part until the documents are signed'. This only needs to be said once. Either method will of course prevent you, if it is the other party which pulls out, from claiming that a contract already exists, but you cannot have it both ways.

6.4.4 Providing for the unforeseen

Although the terms and meaning of a contract are fixed at the moment it is entered into, its purpose is to govern the future relations of the parties. A substantial written agreement will usually govern those relations over a period of several years or sometimes decades.

Some provisions of the agreement deal with events which are certain to happen. With a long term supply contract, the provisions dealing with the nomination of quantities will have to be referred to regularly by both parties. In our example of the contract for the supply of a gas turbine, the technical specification of the turbine will of course be absolutely central for the purposes of the performance of the contract. As already noted earlier, substantial parts of that contract provide for future events which may not arise: all the liability, indemnity and insurance provisions fall into this category.

One of the most difficult things in drafting and negotiating a contract like this is to know how far to go in providing for events which may not happen. While there is little point in dealing with extremely remote contingencies, it can be very awkward if something does happen which the contract does not provide for. So substantial written agreements routinely provide for future events which, although not certain to happen, are at least reasonably foreseeable, such as changes in the cost of raw materials, changes in the rate or scope of existing taxes, the imposition of new taxes, the enactment of new legislation (and especially these days new environmental measures), mechanical failures, the departure or death of key personnel, strikes, the outbreak of war, natural disasters and other such contingencies which can have a material effect on the rights and obligations of the parties under the contract.

In spite of this, it is remarkable how often the provisions of an agreement do not quite fit the events which happen. Often this is because the draftsman and negotiators were working with unspoken (and often unconscious) assumptions which are betrayed by events. We can illustrate this by reference to the price provisions in a long term supply contract, which we touched on in section 4.2.3, under which the agreed initial price is escalated in accordance with the Producer Prices Index. Sometimes these provisions neglect to say whether or not the price can actually go down, in which case a fall in the PPI may well precipitate a dispute involving large sums of money. The seller will rely on the word 'escalation' to support his contention that the price can only go up; the buyer will point out that on a strict application of the formula in the contract the price should fall in line with the PPI. A slightly different interpretation may also be possible, namely that the price can fall with the PPI but cannot fall below the agreed initial price.

6.4.5 Negotiation and interpretation

Although the negotiation of the wording of an agreement and the subsequent interpretation of that wording are two sides of the same coin, they take place in very different circumstances.

When you sit down late at night to read the fifth redraft of a two hundred page document, it is difficult to read it objectively. Apart from those issues on which the parties actively disagree (and, incidentally, if the draftsman has not marked the draft to highlight all the changes from the previous one you should insist that he does) the rest of the document will be thoroughly familiar. It is easy to become word-blind and just turn the pages without really focusing on their content or meaning, and it is very hard to see what has been overlooked.

It was reported in 1997 that Toyota was obliged to halt car production because of a fire at a supplier's factory, an event that served to highlight the dangers of the just-in-time supply arrangements pioneered by Japanese businesses. Should this sort of event happen to you, and you reach for the agreement to see what it has to say about this situation, you will be in a quite different frame of mind. The chances are that only a handful of the provisions in the agreement will be remotely relevant, but these will require very close scrutiny. You may depend upon it that the other party is looking at the very same provisions. In this sort of situation you are well advised to take legal advice, not because a lawyer's opinion of the meaning of the agreement is necessarily better than yours, but because the matter may well end up in court. Although the immediate question is what are your rights under the contract, the secondary question of how you can enforce those rights is not far behind.

Of course nobody ever sits down to read and interpret a contract for the fun of it. The purpose in doing so is to identify the obligations of the parties under that contract, either to see prospectively what each party is required to do to perform the contract, or else to see retrospectively whether they have in fact performed it. Performance is the subject of the next chapter.

CHAPTER 7

Performance and non-performance

7.1 STRICT LIABILITY

7.1.1 Principle of strict liability

From the moment a contract is entered into, the parties are committed. Each party has to perform its obligations under that contract exactly and in full, and anything less than exact and full performance is a breach of the contract by that party.

Imagine then a simple contract for the sale of goods, where the seller agrees to deliver a certain quantity of a certain type of goods on a certain date and the buyer agrees to pay the price in cash when the goods are delivered. If the seller fails to deliver the goods on that date or if he delivers the wrong type of goods or if he delivers a short quantity, then he will be in breach of the contract. Similarly if the buyer refuses to take delivery (an obligation which if not express will be implied) or fails to pay the purchase price in cash when the goods are delivered, then he will be in breach of the contract.

It is of course fundamental that neither party can back out of the contract on the grounds that he had not fully appreciated what it involved or that he has had second thoughts. But neither can a party justify any failure to perform on the grounds that the contract was or had become disadvantageous to him or that the failure was not his fault. So in our example the seller cannot justify his failure to deliver the goods on the grounds that the market price of the goods had risen since the contract was made, or that he had been unable despite his best efforts to obtain the goods from his wholesaler, or that his delivery truck had broken down. And similarly the buyer cannot justify his failure to take delivery on the grounds that he had found a cheaper supplier or that the order he was seeking to meet had failed to materialise or that because of a mistake by his bank he did not have enough money to pay the purchase price.

The legal expression of this principle is that contractual liability is strict. The commercial expression of it is that a deal is a deal.

7.1.2 *De minimis*

The requirement that a contract is performed exactly is not however taken to its ultimate extreme. If for example a seller contracts to supply 500,000 barrels of Brent blend oil but his actual delivery is one barrel short, that discrepancy would be said to be *de minimis*, meaning too small to amount to a breach of the contract. But a shortfall large enough to be significant in the context of the transaction would be a breach of the contract.

7.2 QUALIFIED OBLIGATIONS

7.2.1 The two types of qualified obligation

In our sale of goods example the parties' obligations under the contract were absolute: they gave unqualified undertakings to achieve particular results, the seller to deliver and the buyer to pay. This is the case with many simple contracts, including for example my contract with the newsagent for the sale of a Mars bar. It is however common for a contractual obligation to be qualified in some manner, and broadly speaking there are two ways in which this can be done. The first is to make the obligation less than absolute, and the second is to mitigate the consequences which would otherwise follow from a failure to perform it.

7.2.2 Reasonable and best endeavours obligations

A common example of a qualification of the first type is where a party, rather than undertaking to achieve a particular result, undertakes only to try to achieve it. It would for example be foolish for a party to give an unqualified undertaking to obtain planning permission for the development of a building plot, since the grant of planning permission is a decision for the local planning authority and is outside that party's control. If a party undertakes to try to obtain planning permission, then he is not in breach of the contract if he fails to obtain it but only if he fails to try.

In formal agreements obligations to try to do something are commonly expressed in terms of 'endeavours', usually either 'best endeavours' or 'reasonable endeavours'. You often hear such obligations referred to in a distinctly cavalier way ('we're only under a reasonable endeavours obligation'), and it is of course much easier to prove that someone failed to achieve something than that they failed to try. But such obligations do need to be taken seriously, since the party concerned may ultimately have to explain in court what steps he took to perform that obligation.

A best endeavours obligation requires that party to do everything within his power, irrespective of the effort or expense involved, to achieve the required result. For example, a best endeavours obligation to obtain planning permission might well require him to appeal against a refusal of planning permission. By contrast a reasonable endeavours obligation does not require unlimited effort and expense but only such effort and expense as is reasonable in the circumstances. Anyone involved in the negotiation of formal contracts will be familiar with debates about whether a particular obligation should be absolute or qualified, and if qualified whether reasonable endeavours or best endeavours is the appropriate standard of performance.

7.2.3 Conditional obligations

Another common qualification of the first type is where the obligation is conditional. In section 1.4.6 we discussed conditional contracts, that is where the contract itself is conditional upon the occurrence of a certain event. The same principle is often applied to a particular obligation under a contract rather than the contract itself, in which case the party on whom the obligation is placed only has to perform it if the condition is satisfied. So a seller's obligation to deliver the goods on a particular day may be made conditional upon repairs to his delivery truck having been completed before then. His obligation to deliver on that day arises only if those repairs have been completed.

Sometimes the obligation to make payment is itself conditional, and the terms on which recruitment agents do business are an example. The usual arrangement is that if the recruitment agent finds a suitable candidate who accepts the job, he is paid a percentage of the annual salary of the candidate. This means that it is unnecessary to define the standard of performance required from the recruitment agent. While he will not give an unqualified undertaking to find a suitable candidate, it does not matter whether his obligation is to use best endeavours, reasonable endeavours or merely to try; the fact that his payment is conditional upon achieving a particular result will provide all the incentive he needs to perform.

The mirror image of a conditional obligation is an obligation the performance of which is excused if a certain event occurs. It is for example common for construction contracts to require the construction to be completed by a certain date but to allow the builder more time if work is delayed by severe weather conditions or strikes. All the standard form building and engineering contracts contain such provisions.

7.2.4 Termination provisions

Finally in this first category we need to mention termination clauses. A party only has the right to terminate a contract in two situations; the first, which is discussed in section 8.2, is where the other party has committed a serious breach of the contract, and the second is where the terms of the contract give him that right. A clause giving a party that right is known as a termination clause.

While a simple contract for the supply of goods or services is unlikely to contain such a clause, a contract where the parties' obligations are continuing (whether for a stated period or indefinitely) often will. In for example a contract of employment, where the parties' obligations are usually (though not necessarily) of indefinite duration, each party will generally be given the right to terminate the contract at any time by giving the other party a certain period of advance notice. The continuing obligations of each party are therefore qualified: neither the employer nor the employee can at any time be sure of the contract continuing any longer than the notice period.

In a contract for a stated period, such as a lease, one party may be given the right to terminate the contract before the end of that period. For example a lease may be for a term of twelve years, but with the tenant having the right to terminate after six years (known as a 'break clause'), and the landlord having the right to terminate at any time if the tenant breaches any term of the lease. Here the landlord cannot be sure that the lease will continue for more than six years, and the tenant is constantly at risk of his tenancy being terminated if he does not scrupulously observe all the terms of the lease (although the landlord and tenant legislation protects most types of tenant against the arbitrary exercise of a right of termination by the landlord).

A contractual right to terminate can of course only be exercised in accordance with its terms. So if the contract allows one party to terminate by written notice to the other, an oral notice of termination will be ineffective. Similarly if the contract allows a party to terminate only at a particular time or only in specified circumstances, that party can only terminate the contract at that time or in those specified circumstances. Provided the right of termination is exercised in accordance with its terms the contract terminates on the expiry of the notice period (if any), with the result that no new obligations arise under the contract after that point. A right to terminate is obviously valuable to a party if the contract has become disadvantageous to him or if he knows that he will not be able to perform it.

In the negotiation of a commercial contract such as a long term supply contract, a joint venture agreement or a contract which, like the contract for the supply of a gas turbine, will take some time to perform, the termination provisions are likely to be a contentious issue. If a party has to concede any right of termination, he will want it to be as narrow and specific as possible in order to minimise the uncertainty which such a right introduces. So the seller of the gas turbine may have to concede a right for the buyer to terminate the contract if the necessary approvals for his power generation project are not received by a certain date (and if so the seller will want the clause to provide that he is not only paid for work done but also receives a profit element), but he will be most unwilling to give the buyer a more general right which would allow him to terminate if, for example, he had discovered that he could obtain the turbine more cheaply elsewhere.

It will however come as no surprise that a party's standard terms and conditions of business often give that party a general right to terminate the contract at any time if he so chooses.

7.2.5 Exclusion clauses

These examples are all common ways of making contractual obligations less than absolute, and all of them are perfectly consistent with the principle that each party has to perform its contractual obligations exactly and in full. That principle is however rather more difficult to reconcile with the second way of qualifying a contractual obligation, which is by mitigating the consequences which would otherwise follow from a failure to perform it.

The most common example of this second type of qualification is the exclusion clause, discussed at length in section 4.5. The effect of an exclusion clause is not to reduce a party's obligations but to exclude or limit his liability if he fails to perform them. But where a contract imposes an obligation on a party and at the same time totally excludes his liability if he fails to perform it, that obligation is completely undermined and that party can ignore it with impunity.* So an exclusion clause does in a sense qualify the obligations of the parties under the contract.

7.2.6 Liquidated damages provisions

Another common provision of this second type is the liquidated damages clause. A liquidated damages clause actually specifies the liability that a party will incur if he fails to meet a particular obligation.

Suppose for example that I contract with a builder to build me a house, which he undertakes to complete by 1 November. The contract provides for liquidated damages of £100 for every day that completion of the house is delayed after that date. So if as things turn out the house is not completed until 11 November, the builder will owe me £1,000 which, under the principle of set-off discussed in section 9.4.6, I am entitled to deduct from any sums due to him under the contract. The usual rule, which would allow me to recover any loss I actually suffer as a result of his failure to meet the completion date, is completely superseded by the liquidated damages clause. He cannot refuse to pay me the £1,000 on the grounds that my actual loss is lower, and I cannot demand more than £1,000 on the grounds that my actual loss is higher. So although strictly speaking the builder is under an obligation to complete by 1 November and there is an incentive upon him to do so, he knows exactly what the consequences of failing to meet that obligation will be. He can ignore it at a cost to him of £100 per day. So if during September he is also building an office block where the liquidated damages for delay are £1,000 per day, and he is behind schedule on both projects, he will understandably give that contract priority over mine.

---

* But, as we shall see in section 8.4.4, an exclusion of liability may make it more likely that the court will order the party to perform the obligation.

7.2.7 Liquidated damages distinguished from a penalty

A liquidated damages clause must however be distinguished from a penalty. A liquidated damages clause is valid provided that the amount of the liquidated damages is a genuine pre-estimate of the loss that the innocent party would suffer as a result of a breach of the contract. But if the clause is used simply to provide an incentive to perform and bears no relation to anticipated losses, then it is what is known as a penalty. The law does not regard a penalty as an acceptable way of ensuring that a contract is performed, and a penalty is void and therefore unenforceable. This does not however affect the validity of the rest of the agreement; the offending clause is simply ignored, and the innocent party can recover such loss as he actually suffers as a result of the breach.

In our example of the contract for the building of a house, liquidated damages of £100 per day broadly correspond to the cost of keeping me and my family in a hotel, so the court would accept this as a genuine pre-estimate of my loss and give effect to that clause. But if the liquidated damages were £1,000 per day, a figure which is higher than any loss I could reasonably expect to suffer, that clause would be void as a penalty. So if the builder is late in completing the house I could not recover liquidated damages although I could recover any actual loss which results from his breach of the contract.

The fact that a particular provision is called a liquidated damages clause does not of course prevent a court from concluding that it is in reality a penalty. Sometimes however a contract actually refers to such payments as penalty payments. This is profoundly unhelpful if it becomes necessary to enforce those payments through the courts. Because of its legal connotations the word penalty should never be used in a contract.

7.2.8 *Force majeure* provisions

As we have seen, a party is liable for breach of a contract even if that breach occurs through circumstances beyond his control. The harshness of this principle is often mitigated in commercial contracts by means of a *force majeure* clause, the purpose of which is to relieve a party of liability in such circumstances. *Force majeure* clauses are especially common in contracts where problems can be expected although the precise nature of the problems cannot be foreseen. For example, a contract for the development over five years of a new radar system for an aircraft might be expected to involve all kinds of unforeseen technical, commercial, legal and regulatory problems, and is therefore likely to contain a *force majeure* clause. Contracts involving the uncertainties of the sea, such as contracts for the carriage of goods by sea, also usually include such a clause.

The protection given by that clause will usually extend to both the parties even if most of the obligations under the contract are on one party: it is of course hard for a party to argue that his obligations should be subject to *force majeure* relief while those of the other party should not.* However, obligations to pay sums of money are nearly always excluded from *force majeure* relief, since it is obviously undesirable for a party to be entitled to refuse to make payment on the grounds that, due to circumstances beyond his control, he has no money.

A *force majeure* clause can operate in either of two ways. The first is to suspend the obligations of any party for as long as he is unable to perform them due to circumstances outside his control. The second is to exclude the liability of any party for breach of any obligation resulting from circumstances outside his control. The first type of *force majeure* clause makes the parties' obligations less than absolute, while the second is a kind of exclusion clause. Both have the same effect, but the advantage of the first type of clause is that it avoids the problems associated with exclusion clauses.

The phrase '*force majeure*' has no settled legal meaning, so a provision that 'neither party will be liable in the event of *force majeure*' will not have any effect. To be effective a *force majeure* clause must set out the circumstances in which relief is to be granted, which can be done in a general way ('due to circumstances outside that party's control'), or by means of a specific list ('due to acts of God, acts of government, strikes, war[†] ...'), or by an amalgamation of the two.

In our experience the parties to a contractual negotiation often

---

* A force majeure *clause is also sometimes included in a party's standard terms and conditions, and here (predictably) the protection given by that clause generally extends only to that party's obligations.*
[†] *The word 'war' is potentially ambiguous: must war actually have been declared before relief is granted, or is relief available in the event of hostilities where war is not formally declared? There was no formal declaration of war in either the Falklands conflict of 1982 or the conflict with Iraq in 1991, and both conflicts led to a considerable number of disputes on precisely this question. The ambiguity can be avoided by using words like 'hostilities between states (whether war is declared or not)'.*

agree to include a *force majeure* clause on the basis that it is only fair and reasonable to do so, as if strict liability under the contract is as unacceptable in these enlightened times as beating school-boys. They then accept whatever *force majeure* clause the draftsman produces for them, as if it does not really matter what the clause says because it is just legal boilerplate. But the effect of the clause may be more harmful to one of the parties than he had supposed.

Imagine that the contract in question is the contract for the supply of a gas turbine considered in section 4.4.2, and that the parties agree a broad clause granting relief for any failure due to circumstances outside a party's control. Now the buyer has over-looked the fact that, as is the case with nearly all contracts for the supply of goods or services, most of the significant obligations under the contract fall on the seller. He will be responsible for the manufacture of the turbine, for meeting completion deadlines and for demonstrating that it meets the performance criteria, and he will be required to give undertakings of some description as to its quality and performance. While the buyer will be under a variety of less significant obligations such as approving the design, attending progress meetings and performance tests, and so on, his most significant obligations involve payment of the purchase price, and as we have seen payment obligations will almost certainly be excluded from *force majeure* relief.

But whenever the seller fails to meet a significant obligation he will almost automatically claim *force majeure* and, having consulted his lawyers, explain why, due to illness among his key staff or having been let down by a subcontractor or some other plausible excuse, that failure was not really his fault. The buyer will find explanations of that kind very difficult to refute, and he may well be left not only without the performance he contracted for but also without any remedy against the seller for his failure to perform.

The moral is that neither a *force majeure* nor any other clause is intrinsically either fair or unfair: every clause has to be judged in the context of that particular transaction and the obligations of the parties under it.

7.3 FRUSTRATION

Suppose that a party is under a contractual obligation from which the terms of the contract provide no means of escape, and he is unable to perform it. In one very narrow situation the law will excuse his failure to perform, and this is where the circumstances are such as to frustrate the contract altogether. If the circumstances do not amount to a frustration, then there is only one other way in which he can escape liability for breach of contract, and this is where the other party (or parties) agree to terminate or vary the contract or else waive his obligation to perform it. Variation, termination and waiver are discussed in section 7.4.

7.3.1 The principle of frustration

The law will regard a contract as having been frustrated if a drastic and unforeseen change in circumstances since the contract was entered into has made its performance impossible, illegal or pointless.

There are three important points to note about this statement of the doctrine of frustration. First, there must have been a change in circumstances since the contract was entered into; if a party undertakes to do what is or turns out to be impossible, then he cannot claim that the contract has been frustrated. Second, that change in circumstances must have been of a drastic and unforeseen character; ordinary events such as increases in the price of raw materials, even if those price increases are dramatic and unexpected, can never frustrate a contract. Third, that change in circumstances must have made performance of the contract impossible, illegal or pointless; it is not enough that the change in circumstances merely made performance more difficult or more expensive.

Let us take three simple examples to give the flavour of a frustrating event. A contract for the sale of a specific car would be frustrated if the car is accidentally destroyed prior to delivery; a contract to export goods to a particular country would be frustrated by a subsequent government order prohibiting exports to that country; and a contract of employment would be frustrated by the death of the employee. In these three examples it would be nonsense to require performance of the contract, and in most instances of frustration it is obvious to all the parties that the contract cannot proceed. But the narrowness of the doctrine means that it is unlikely to assist a party who in reality is looking for a way out of a disadvantageous contract. So while instances of frustration may be relatively common, instances of a successful frustration claim which is disputed by the other party are very rare.

The case of *Tsakiroglou & Co Ltd* v *Noblee and Thorl GmbH* 1962 is a good illustration of the difficulty in making out such a claim.

The case involved a contract for the sale of a cargo of ground nuts cif. (Under a cif contract the seller is responsible not only for supplying the goods but also for shipping them and insuring them *en route*, so the price paid by the buyer includes cost, insurance and freight – hence cif. The opposite arrangement where the buyer is responsible for shipping and insuring the goods is known as an fob contract, standing for free on board.) Although no route was specified in the contract, the defendant intended to ship the goods through the Suez canal which was the obvious and shortest route. After the contract was made but before the voyage, the Suez crisis closed the canal to shipping. The seller failed to ship the cargo and claimed that the contract had been frustrated, but the House of Lords decided that he was in breach of the contract because he could still have shipped the cargo round the Cape of Good Hope, a voyage of three times the length of his intended route. If the contract had specified shipment through the Suez canal, it would have been an obvious case of frustration.

7.3.2 Effects of frustration

Where a contract is frustrated, the effect is to release the parties automatically from all future obligations, that is from all obligations arising under the contract after the events which frustrated it. Historically the parties remained liable to perform all obligations which arose under the contract before the events which frustrated it, but while this rule appears logical it sometimes had unfair results. For example a purchaser who had paid cash in advance for a particular car could not recover his money if the contract of sale was frustrated by the accidental destruction of the car before delivery; and a party who had received a valuable benefit under a contract was not obliged to pay anything for it if the contract was frustrated before any contractual payments were due. The rule was therefore changed by the Law Reform (Frustrated Contracts) Act 1943.

In outline this Act provides that, when a contract has been frustrated, money paid before the frustrating event can be recovered and a party who has received a valuable benefit under the contract must pay a just amount for it. We will not examine the Act in any further detail, partly because instances where a commercial contract is frustrated are too rare to justify it, but also because when an important contract is (or may have been) frustrated the prudent course for both parties is to seek legal advice.

7.4   VARIATION, TERMINATION AND WAIVER

If one party is unwilling or unable to perform the contract or a particular obligation under it, he is always free to ask the other party (or parties) to allow him not to perform. The other party may be prepared to agree to this, and if so three outcomes are possible. First, the parties may agree to vary the terms of the contract so that it can be performed in its varied form. Second, the parties may agree to terminate the contract altogether, in which case they may or may not agree a new contract to replace it. Third, the other party, while not agreeing to vary or terminate the contract, may indicate that he will not insist on performance of it or a particular obligation under it, in which case the obligation or obligations in question would be said to have been waived. Although the effect in each case is to release the first party from his original obligation or obligations, the principles applicable to a variation or termination are different from those applicable to a waiver, and the two need to be discussed separately.

7.4.1   Variation or termination by agreement

The parties are free at any time to agree to vary or terminate a contract. The important point is that any such agreement is itself a contract to which all the principles discussed in this book (including the requirement that each party provides consideration for the agreement) apply. So, just as the original contract only comes into existence if all the parties agree, equally it can only be varied or terminated if all the parties so agree. By unanimous agreement the parties can vary the contract as they see fit or terminate it altogether, but if one party does not agree then the original contract continues unaltered.*

Suppose then that a company has taken a 12 year lease of an office block at a rent of £100,000 per year, and that the terms of the lease give the tenant no right to terminate it or to sublet any part of the office block. After two years the company's workforce has shrunk and it no longer needs so much space. All it can do is to ask the landlord to agree to terminate the lease or vary it so that the

---

* *We are not concerned here with contractual terms which provide for the variation or termination of the contract by less than unanimous agreement. Terms allowing one party to vary the contract are discussed in section 7.4.2, and termination clauses in section 7.2.4.*

tenant occupies fewer than all the floors of the block.* The land-lord's response will depend on the state of the market for office premises in that area. If he can relet the space at a higher rent, he will agree to terminate or vary the lease. If not, he will either refuse outright or else demand a cash payment as the price of his agree-ment; if the market for office premises is very bad, his price for agreeing to terminate may well approach £1 million, being the future rent which termination of the lease will deprive him of. If the tenant cannot reach agreement with the landlord, the lease will continue. So a lease is not necessarily an asset but can, depending on the rent, the terms of the lease and the state of the market, be a huge liability.

An agreement for the variation or termination of a contract may, as with any other contract, be in whatever form the parties choose. So an oral agreement to vary or terminate a contract is effective notwithstanding that the original contract is in writing. This means that it is always possible for a formal signed agreement to be (or for a party to claim that it has been) varied or even terminated by a subsequent oral agreement between the parties.†

Suppose for example that the seller under a long term supply agreement demands payment on the first of the month as required by the signed agreement, but the buyer claims that the seller's accounts manager had agreed that the buyer need not pay until the end of the month. That claim raises the very problems which the parties originally tried to avoid by signing a formal agreement, and it also of course raises the issue of whether the individual concerned had the authority to vary the contract by making that concession. Formal agreements often contain a provision designed to prevent such problems arising, for example: 'This agreement may only be varied or amended by a formal written agreement signed by the duly authorised representatives of each party.' But the effectiveness of such a provision is open to question. While the court will give due weight to the parties' express intention that no oral variation should be effective, that express intention would in our view have to give way in the face of clear evidence of an oral variation agreed by individuals who plainly had both the authority and the intention to make it. The requirements of such a provision should of course be observed if this is possible: that way you will

---

* *The other possibility, which is for him to assign the lease to a third party, also presents problems which are discussed in section 11.1.4.*
† *This is not true with a deed. A deed can only be varied by means of a further deed.*

not have to pay lawyers to find the answer to this potentially important (and, so far as we know, untested) conundrum.

7.4.2 Provisions for unilateral variation

Where one party has sufficient bargaining power to impose terms on the other, he may include a provision giving him the right to vary the terms of the contract unilaterally. Banks often include such a provision in the terms governing the use of credit cards, and it can also be found in the terms used by utilities and sometimes in contracts of employment. The validity of such provisions has never so far as we know been challenged, which suggests that the power to vary the contract is generally exercised with restraint, but an arbitrary or unreasonable variation may well be open to attack.

Depending on the circumstances, the other party may be able to argue that the provision is ineffective under the Unfair Contract Terms Act 1977 (see section 4.6), or else that there is an implied term that the power to vary will not be exercised unreasonably (see section 4.7), or else that the provision, or perhaps even the whole contract, is void for uncertainty (see section 4.2). In any event it seems most unlikely that the court would be prepared to uphold an arbitrary or unreasonable unilateral variation. In a contract negotiated between two businesses however, the right to vary the contract unilaterally should never in any circumstances be conceded.

7.4.3 Waiver

In the commercial world it is very common for a contractual obligation to be waived. Suppose for example that a contract obliges the parties to attend a progress meeting on a certain day, but one party is unable to attend on that day. He will simply ask for the meeting to be rescheduled, and the other party is unlikely to object since this will serve no purpose. In rescheduling the meeting that other party will have waived the first party's obligation to attend the meeting on the stipulated day. More significant obligations such as an obligation to deliver goods at a particular time are also commonly waived when the time of delivery is not of any practical importance.

The legal principle involved can be expressed as follows. Where one party leads the other by clear words or conduct to believe that he will not insist on the performance of a contractual obligation owed to him, then neither party can subsequently insist on the performance of that obligation.

It is important to note the requirement of clear words or conduct: mere failure by a party to insist on the performance of an obligation does not amount to a waiver of it. Problems can however arise with repeated failures to meet a recurring obligation. Suppose for example that the buyer under a long term supply contract is required to pay on the first day of the month but always pays late. If the seller allows this to continue without protest, the buyer may ultimately claim that the seller's acquiescence amounted to a waiver of his obligation to pay on the first. Although the court is unlikely to accept such a claim in the absence of some positive indication of a waiver by the seller, a sensible seller will prevent that claim ever being made simply by reminding the buyer (preferably at an early stage and in writing) that payment is due on the first. This makes clear that his patience is not to be interpreted as a waiver.

There is a clear legal distinction between a variation, which is a contractual agreement, and a waiver, which is not. In practice however it can be very difficult to tell whether you are dealing with a variation or a waiver. Suppose that a buyer of goods contacts the seller and asks for more time to pay for them, and the seller agrees. If this agreement is a variation it is ineffective since the buyer has provided no consideration for it, but if it is a waiver it is binding on both parties since no consideration is required. The courts have yet to provide a satisfactory statement on how to distinguish the two.

One final technicality needs to be mentioned, and this concerns the waiver of a joint obligation. In section 2.3.3 we illustrated a joint obligation using the example of a contract where party A is owed £100 jointly by a group comprising B, C, D and E, and we noted that legally this is a single obligation. One consequence is that if A waives B's obligation this not only releases B from the obligation but also releases C, D and E. So if you are owed money by a partnership and one partner pleading poverty and friendship asks you to waive his obligation to pay, if you do so you will release all the partners and extinguish the obligation altogether. This legal technicality can therefore have important and expensive practical consequences. This problem does not however arise with several obligations or joint and several obligations, since these are not legally a single obligation.

We have now exhausted the excuses available to a party who fails to perform. If the terms of the contract do not excuse that failure, and the circumstances do not amount to a frustration of the contract, and the other party refuses to vary or terminate the contract or waive the obligation, then that party is in breach of the contract and must face the consequences. Those consequences are the subject of Chapter 8.

Legal remedies for breach of contract

Under the laws of ancient Rome, if someone failed to pay you a sum of money due under a contract, you were entitled to drag him in chains round the market place on three successive market days, and then if the debt was still unpaid you were entitled to cut him into small pieces. The remedies available to you today are (to the lasting regret of credit controllers) less drastic and also no doubt less effective.

8.1 PRELIMINARY MATTERS

8.1.1 About legal remedies

Today the ultimate threat against the party in breach is not to cut him into small pieces but to take him to court. In this chapter we will be considering the legal remedies available for breach of contract. This is not to say that all contractual disputes end up in court, nor that the first thing to do when someone breaks a contract with you is to sue him. The emphasis in this book is on how to avoid having to go to court, and our discussion of legal remedies is not intended to detract from this in any way.

The question of what can be achieved by going to court is important because it defines the legal rights of the parties. A legal right is a right which can be enforced by court action, so any discussion of legal rights is a discussion about what would happen if the issue went to court. And the perception of what is likely to happen if the case does go to court defines the position of each party and dictates the outcome in the great majority of disputes which are settled without going to court.

In the light of our discussion of legal remedies, we will return in the next chapter to the practical issues of how to avoid problems arising in the first place and how, when they do arise, to resolve them without going to court.

8.1.2 Two things to remember

There are two things to remember in considering legal remedies for breach of contract:

1. It is not a crime to break a contract, and a party cannot be fined or imprisoned for doing so.* So it is no use trying to get the police interested unless the breach involves some criminal element such as fraud. Even then they will be much more interested in prosecuting the offender than in helping you solve your contractual problems.
2. The legal remedies we shall be discussing are only available to a party against a party, since as we saw in section 1.5.1 a contract cannot confer rights or impose obligations on anyone who is not a party to it. So even where a third party stands to benefit from the proper performance of a contract, or else may be damaged by the breach of it, he has no contractual remedies at all against a party who breaks it. Similarly the remedies of the wronged party can be exercised only against the party in breach and not for example against that party's parent company.

8.2 THE RIGHT TO TERMINATE

8.2.1 Outline of remedy

A serious breach of contract gives the wronged party the right to terminate that contract. Where the wronged party has the right to terminate he can exercise it without going to court, which as we shall see is both the attraction and the danger of the remedy. This is why, although it is not as important in practice as the right to damages, we are discussing it first.

The principles involved are best illustrated in the context of a fixed term contract for services. Suppose for example that an

---

* *But as we shall see in section 8.4.1 a party can be fined or imprisoned for ignoring a court order.*

engineering company enters into a three year contract with a specialist computer company for the maintenance of all its computer systems, and the contract contains no provision for either party to terminate before the end of that period. If during the contract the engineering company discovers that the computer company has committed a flagrant breach of the contract, such as stealing commercial secrets or submitting inflated invoices, the engineering company can terminate the contract forthwith.

There are a number of points to note about the right to terminate:

1. The breach does not automatically terminate the contract: it merely gives the wronged party the right to do so. In our example it is entirely up to the engineering company whether to terminate the contract or to allow it to continue.
2. The wronged party can terminate the contract by notifying the party in breach that it is doing so. The form of that notification does not matter, but once given it cannot be retracted.
3. If the wronged party does not exercise its right of termination within a reasonable time after it becomes aware of the breach, that right lapses and the contract continues.
4. If the wronged party exercises that right the contract terminates at that moment and the future obligations of both parties cease. Prior obligations are unaffected, so in our example the engineering company will have to pay for the computer maintenance which has been carried out.
5. Whether the wronged party terminates the contract or not does not affect his right to damages for the breach. Either way the engineering company can still sue for compensation for any loss caused by the breach.

8.2.2 Meaning of a serious breach

While a serious breach gives the wronged party the right to terminate, a minor breach does not. The crucial question is therefore what is meant by a serious breach: how in practice can a serious breach be distinguished from a minor one? Unfortunately the numerous reported cases do not provide a simple or satisfactory answer to this question. The traditional approach is to consider the term which was broken and to decide whether it is a 'condition' (breach of which always allows the wronged party to terminate), a 'warranty' (breach of which never allows the wronged party to terminate), or an 'innominate term' (where the question depends on the circumstances and consequences of the breach). Other cases suggest that the wronged party has the right to terminate if the breach 'goes to the root of the contract', or else if the breach deprives him of the whole or a significant part of the benefit he would have gained from performance.

Although these various approaches make this a favourite academic topic, none really adds much to the phrase 'a serious breach'. Each particular case must be considered on its own facts, including the relative importance of the term which is broken, the nature of the breach, and the severity of the consequences for the wronged party. The question cannot be approached in a mechanical way and very often the answer is not clear cut.

The breaches used as illustrations in the previous section both involved dishonesty and probably also constituted criminal offences. The victim of this kind of breach can be fairly confident that he is justified in terminating the contract. But in practice incompetence is much more common than dishonesty, and if your complaint is that the other party is not performing his obligations very well you are well advised to seek legal advice before you terminate, especially if the contract is a substantial one.

8.2.3 Contracts for the sale of goods

Very similar principles apply to contracts for the sale of goods. When the buyer takes delivery of the goods, he has a reasonable time in which to examine them and to satisfy himself that they conform to the requirements of the contract. If in any significant respect the goods do not conform to the contract, the buyer has the right to reject them. If the buyer exercises that right the contract terminates: title to the goods reverts to the seller, and if the goods have been paid for the buyer is entitled to the return of the price. Whether he terminates or not the buyer is still entitled to compensation for any loss he suffers as a result of the seller's breach of the contract.

The buyer's right of rejection is essentially the same as the right to terminate, and the same principles apply. The difference is that with contracts for the sale of goods the question of how serious the breach is does not arise; the question is whether the goods conform to the contract. The seller must deliver the quantity and quality which he contracted to supply. In a sale by description the goods must conform to their description, and in a sale by sample they must conform to the sample. Any significant discrepancy will allow the buyer to reject them. Assuming that the seller is acting in the course of a business, the contract will include the statutory implied terms that the goods will be of satisfactory quality and fit for their purpose (section 4.8.1), so any significant defect in the goods will constitute a breach of one or both of those implied terms which will allow the buyer to reject them.

There is a popular misconception that a customer who buys goods from a shop always has the right to change his mind and return the goods for a refund. Strictly however, unless the terms of the contract give him that right (e.g. 'your money back if not completely satisfied'), the customer has no right to return the goods unless they fail in some way to conform to the contract.

8.2.4 Wrongful termination

What happens where one party terminates the contract on the basis of a breach by the other, but that breach was not in fact serious enough to give him the right to terminate? Here the termination is itself a breach of the contract which is classified as a 'repudiation' (discussed in section 8.5). So the victim of the original breach has himself broken the contract and the other party may now sue him for failing to perform it.

This is the great limitation of the right to terminate. If you are the victim of a flagrant breach such as fraud you can be confident that you have the right to terminate, but with a less extreme breach it will be impossible for you or your lawyers to be sure. So if you do decide to terminate there is a risk that the other party will take you to court, and that the court will ultimately decide that your termination was wrongful. Although you can still recover damages for loss caused by the original breach, the chances are that the damages you will have to pay as a result of your wrongful termination will be far greater.

In principle the position is the same where the buyer of goods wrongfully rejects them: the seller can sue him for failing to take delivery of the goods (an obligation which if not express will be implied) or to pay for them. In practice however, because the question is whether the goods conform to the contract rather than whether the breach is serious, that question is more likely to yield a clear-cut answer.

8.2.5 Value and limitations of remedy

Whether or not the right to terminate the contract is of any value to the wronged party depends on the circumstances. In some situations this will be the only remedy he needs. If you find yourself tied to a fixed term contract with a grossly incompetent contractor, as long as his incompetence has not actually caused you significant financial loss you will want nothing more than to be rid of him. And with a contract for the sale of goods, the threat to reject the goods will usually be sufficient to persuade the seller to replace them with goods which do conform to the contract.

In other situations however the right to terminate the contract is of very little value to the wronged party. To begin with, if the contract is advantageous to him he will not want to terminate it. In this situation what he wants is proper performance, and the existence of the right to terminate will not help him to get it. Similarly neither terminating the contract nor threatening to do so will help the wronged party to recover compensation for loss or damage caused by the breach. To achieve that he may well have to sue.

The reported cases which deal with this topic reveal the commercial reality behind most of these disputes. The usual situation is that the contract has for some reason become disadvantageous to one of the parties. He is therefore looking for a way out of it, and he takes advantage of some breach by the other party and terminates the contract. This commercial reality inevitably colours the determination of the legal issue, which is whether the breach was such as to allow the wronged party to terminate. This largely explains the complexity of the law on this issue.

It is perfectly legitimate to take advantage of a breach by the other party to free yourself from a disadvantageous contract provided that the breach is sufficiently serious to give you the right to terminate. If the contract is disadvantageous to you it will be correspondingly advantageous to the other party, which makes it more likely if you do terminate that he will take you to court. But the difficulty in determining whether the breach is sufficiently serious, and the consequences if the court ultimately determines that it was not, can make this a dangerous game to play. When the real reason for wishing to terminate the contract is that it is disadvantageous, it is doubly important to seek legal advice before you do so.

8.2.6 Delay in performance

Finally we need to consider delay in performance. Most substantial commercial contracts provide for the parties to perform their obligations within a specified time. If no time is specified for the performance of a particular obligation, the law will imply a term that it is to be performed within a reasonable time. What then is the position if a party fails to perform within the time explicitly or implicitly provided? Does that failure give the wronged party the right to terminate?

If the contract stipulates that performance within the time specified is essential (considered below), then any delay, no matter how short, will allow the wronged party to terminate. If however there is no stipulation that time is essential, then we are in the grey area and the wronged party can only terminate if in all the circumstances the delay amounts to a serious breach.

Suppose then that a contract for the sale of goods provides for the seller to deliver them by 23 July, and the market price of those goods has fallen since the contract was made. The contract has therefore become disadvantageous to the buyer, and he would ideally like to free himself of it so that he can buy the goods elsewhere at the current market price. If 23 July comes and goes without the seller delivering the goods, the buyer is in a dilemma. The failure to deliver is a continuing breach of the contract, and the longer it lasts the more serious that breach becomes. So the longer the buyer waits before terminating the greater the chance that his termination is justified. But the risk if he waits too long is that the seller will deliver the goods, and he cannot afford to terminate at that point because it will be self-evident that the late delivery was not the real reason for the termination.

Where the time for performance is crucial, the way to indicate this is to make time of the essence. Suppose that in our example the contract had said that the seller was to deliver the goods by 23 July 'and time shall be of the essence'. That phrase gives the buyer the right to terminate immediately if the goods are not delivered by the 23rd: the question of how serious the breach is simply does not arise. In effect therefore the phrase is a shorthand termination provision.

If you are the victim of a delay in performance and the contract does not say that time is of the essence, it is still possible to make time of the essence. You can do this by serving a notice on the party in breach giving him a reasonable time in which to perform. For practical reasons that notice should be in writing, and it should specify the final date by which performance is required. Provided that you have given him a reasonable time in which to perform (and if the contract is a substantial one you should take legal advice on what constitutes a reasonable time before you send the notice), then you can terminate if the party in breach has not performed by the final date stated in the notice.

8.3 THE RIGHT TO DAMAGES

8.3.1 The primary remedy

A breach of contract entitles the wronged party to damages, that is to compensation from the party in breach for any loss or damage which the wronged party suffers as a result of the breach. Damages are said to be 'the primary remedy', and the significance of this description is twofold.

First, damages are an automatic right. As we saw in section 8.2, the wronged party only has the right to terminate the contract if the breach is a serious one, and the court orders discussed in section 8.4 are in the court's discretion and are seldom in fact granted, but a breach of contract always entitles the wronged party to damages unless the contract itself provides otherwise.

Second, damages are the primary remedy in the sense that they are the court's preferred remedy: as we shall see, an injunction or an order for specific performance will not be granted at all if the wronged party's loss or damage can be compensated by an award of damages. The great majority of actions for breach of contract are in fact claims for compensation.

To say therefore that an agreement is 'enforceable', a phrase which we touched on in section 1.4.1 and have since used freely, is rather misleading. It does not mean that the court will necessarily order the agreement to be performed. It means only that the agreement is binding, or to put it another way is a valid contract. The only thing which necessarily follows is that the parties will be entitled to compensation if the agreement is broken.

8.3.2 The compensatory principle

The object of awarding damages to the wronged party is to put him in the position he would have been in if the contract had been performed. The purpose is therefore to compensate the wronged party and not in any sense to punish the party in breach. It follows that a party can break a contract without fear of being taken to court if he compensates the other party for the loss or damage he suffers as a result. Such breaches are in fact commonplace.

Suppose for example that an employer no longer requires the services of a particular employee. The contract of employment requires the employer to give three months' notice of termination, but the employer tells him to leave immediately and pays him three months' salary in lieu of notice. The employer is in fact breaking the contract by not giving the required notice period, and the three months' salary is the sum which the employee could recover in damages for that breach, being the salary he would have received if the employer had observed those notice requirements. Pay in lieu of notice can be seen as a damages payment.*

You may think that merely having to compensate the other party for his loss or damage provides little incentive to perform, but a very different example will demonstrate that it does. This example involves a dispute between two imaginary limited companies, which we will call Purity plc and Filters Ltd.

Purity plc, a profitable company which extracts, bottles and sells natural mineral water, is taking a rising share of an increasing market. Purity replaces the filters in its bottling plant with new ones bought from Filters Ltd, and the purchase contract includes the statutory implied term that the filters will be fit for their purpose, which is to remove impurities from the water. Unfortunately they are not. The first sign that something is wrong comes with complaints from consumers about stomach upsets. Purity sends samples for analysis which discovers impurities in them, so Purity closes its bottling plant and recalls all prior production. Because of adverse publicity all Purity's major customers terminate their existing contracts for the water and decide no longer to stock it. When Purity has identified the problem and solved it by replacing the filters, nobody wants to buy: its market has collapsed.

Purity is entitled to damages from Filters to put it in the position it would have been in if the filters had been fit for their purpose. Purity can therefore claim:

1. All the costs of analysis and identifying the problem;
2. All the costs of buying and fitting replacement filters;
3. All the costs of recalling prior production;
4. All Purity's lost profit on its cancelled contracts;
5. The difference between Purity's future profit if the filters had been fit for their purpose and the profit (or loss) it can now expect to make; and
6. All compensation paid by Purity to consumers, whether as a result of negligence claims made directly against Purity or else

---

* The employee may also have a right to a redundancy payment or the right to bring a claim for unfair dismissal to the industrial tribunal. Both are statutory rather than contractual rights.

damages paid by Purity to its customers to reimburse claims against them,* and its legal costs.

The total damages figure will clearly be huge, and all of it flows from defective filters which may have cost only a few hundred pounds. It is easy to understand the attraction of an exclusion clause limiting or excluding a party's potential liabilities under the contract. But since damages are purely compensatory, an exclusion clause preventing Purity from recovering its loss from Filters means that Purity, the innocent party, will have to bear that loss itself.

8.3.3 Claims passing up the chain of supply

In our example, Purity's claim against Filters is not necessarily the end of the story. If the defective filters were not manufactured by Filters Limited but were purchased by Filters from somebody else, then Filters may be able to sue the supplier and recover from him the damages it has to pay to Purity. It is common for a claim to be passed up the chain of supply in this way, and it is worth taking a closer look at this situation.

Suppose that certain goods which have a manufacturing defect are sold by the manufacturer to a wholesaler, who sells them on to a retailer, who in turn sells them on to a customer. At this point the defect in the goods becomes apparent and causes loss or damage to the customer. Since the manufacturer, wholesaler and retailer are each selling the goods in the course of a business, each contract of sale will (unless that contract provides otherwise) include the statutory implied terms that the goods are of satisfactory quality and are fit for their purpose. The customer is party to the contract with the retailer but is not party to the other two contracts, so he has no contractual rights against the wholesaler or the manufacturer. He must therefore recover compensation for the loss or damage he has suffered from the retailer on the basis of the retailer's breach of the implied terms.

* *If Purity sold the water direct to the customers they will be able to sue Purity for breach of contract, but whether they bought directly from Purity or not they will be able to sue Purity under the Consumer Protection Act 1987. That Act makes the manufacturer of a product strictly liable for death, personal injury or property damage suffered by a consumer as a result of a defect in that product, whether or not there is a contract between the manufacturer and the consumer. The Act was introduced to implement a directive from the European Union.*

Although the retailer is not responsible for the defect in the goods, the principle of strict liability means that he cannot resist the customer's claim for damages by pointing the finger at the manufacturer. He will have to meet the customer's claim and recover that loss in damages from the wholesaler on the basis of the wholesaler's breach of the implied terms. In our experience some retailers try to avoid complaints and claims from their customers by saying that it is a manufacturing defect and should be referred to the manufacturer, although most members of the public recognise that this is a wholly erroneous proposition.

The wholesaler will have to meet the retailer's claim for damages and will in turn have to recover that loss in damages from the manufacturer on the basis of the manufacturer's breach of the implied terms.

The claim will in fact inflate as it is passed up the chain of supply. For example, the retailer will want compensation not only for the damages which he has had to pay to the customer but also for the costs he has incurred in dealing with that claim. If the customer has announced that in future he will obtain his goods elsewhere, the retailer's claim against the wholesaler will include a claim for loss of future profit, being the profit which the retailer could have expected from future sales to that customer if it had not been for the wholesaler's breach of contract.

In theory therefore the totality of the losses should ultimately be borne by the manufacturer, who was responsible for the defect in the goods and so cannot pass the claim on to anyone else. In practice however things may not work out quite so neatly. It does not necessarily follow that, because the retailer has to pay damages to the customer, he can recover those damages from the wholesaler. The position as between the wholesaler and the retailer depends on the terms of the contract between them: this contract is of course entirely separate from the contract between the retailer and the customer, and may be on completely different terms.

For example, the wholesaler may seek to rely on his standard terms of sale, which may purport to exclude the statutory implied terms, or exclude his liability under the contract, or both. Both types of exclusion are ineffective under the Unfair Contract Terms Act 1977 unless the clause is reasonable, and so the wholesaler will have to show not only that his standard terms of sale were incorporated into the contract, but also that the clause was reasonable in the circumstances. But if he can cross both these hurdles this will prevent the claim being passed any further up the chain of supply.

In practice therefore it is by no means certain that the claim will be passed all the way up the chain to the manufacturer.

With contracts for goods which will have to be obtained from a third party supplier, it is common for the seller to stipulate that he will pass on the benefit of any warranty he receives from his supplier in respect of the goods, but that he does not warrant the goods beyond that. In this way the seller tries to ensure that he does not incur any liability in respect of the goods which he cannot pass on to his supplier. The contract for the sale of the gas turbine in our example in section 4.4.2 may well contain such a provision. It also appears occasionally in standard terms of sale.

8.3.4 Liquidated and unliquidated claims

There is an important distinction between liquidated and unliquidated claims for damages. A failure to pay a sum of money due under a contract gives rise to a liquidated claim, that is to a claim for that specific sum. So a claim for the unpaid purchase price of goods or for the overdue repayment of a loan or for any other unpaid debt is a liquidated claim.*

Any breach of contract other than a failure to pay a sum of money gives rise to an unliquidated claim, that is to a claim for damages the amount of which will have to be quantified. The claim by Purity plc in our example is an example of an unliquidated claim, and as we shall see the quantification of some elements of that claim will itself be a highly contentious issue. The quantification of that claim, either by agreement between the parties or else as a result of a damages award by the court, will convert it into a liquidated claim.

The fact that a liquidated claim is already quantified has two beneficial consequences for the party pursuing it. First, as we shall see in section 8.7.1, the court procedure for a liquidated claim is simpler and very much quicker than for an unliquidated claim. Second, as we shall see in sections 9.4.6 and 9.4.7, there are two ways of pursuing a liquidated claim without suing for it which are not possible with an unliquidated claim. One of the attractions of a liquidated damages provision (discussed in section 7.2.6), is that, as its name suggests, it converts an unliquidated claim into a liquidated one, making it very much easier to pursue.

The fact that a party claiming a liquidated sum may also be claiming interest on that sum does not make that claim an unliquidated one. Claims for interest are discussed in section 8.3.9.

We now need to consider the quantification of unliquidated claims (section 8.3.5) and three situations in which a party with an unliquidated claim cannot recover all of his loss (sections 8.3.6 to 8.3.8). In the next four sections therefore we are concerned only with unliquidated claims.

8.3.5 Quantifying an unliquidated claim

Any unliquidated claim has to be quantified, which is a matter of putting a financial value on the loss or damage suffered by the wronged party as a result of the breach.

Sometimes this is a matter of simple arithmetic. Suppose for example that I contract to buy an ounce of gold bullion for $350, but the seller fails to supply it. My loss is a function of the market price of gold bullion at the time delivery should have taken place. If the market price at that time is $400 an ounce, my claim (assuming I have suffered no other loss or damage) is for the then sterling equivalent of $50.* If the market price is less than the contract price I have no claim because I have suffered no loss.

Some types of claim are however very much more difficult to quantify. The claim by Purity plc for lost future profit (item number 5 in section 8.3.2) is an example. Putting a financial value on that element of the claim involves speculating not only on the company's future profits or losses but also on what its future profits would have been if the contract had not been broken. If the parties cannot negotiate a settlement the court will put a value on that claim, on the basis of the evidence presented to it, as part of a single overall damages award. Once the court has done so neither party will be able to reopen the matter if the court's expectations of the company's future performance prove to be incorrect.

8.3.6 Problems of causation

The wronged party can only recover compensation from the party in breach for loss or damage caused by the breach. The issue of causation can however be a difficult one, and this can be illustrated from the example of the defective filters.

One of the arguments open to Filters Ltd runs as follows. If Purity had been properly monitoring its water quality then it would have discovered the impurities at an early stage, and could have solved the problem simply by changing the filters. In other words most of

* I do in fact have the option to claim in dollars if I wish.

Purity's loss was caused not by the breach but by the inadequacies of its own quality control system. This argument will only succeed if the court thinks that Purity's monitoring system was so inadequate that it only has itself to blame for what followed, in which case Filters will only be liable for the costs of changing the filters and a certain amount of lost production.

So questions of causation are not judged in a metaphysical way but as a matter of common sense: what was the real cause of the wronged party's loss?

8.3.7 Remoteness of damage

Sometimes the wronged party may be unable to recover particular items of loss or damage even though they were caused by the breach. This is where the party in breach could not reasonably have foreseen, at the time the contract was entered into, that particular loss or damage was liable to result from his breach of it. In this situation that particular loss or damage is said to be 'too remote' to be recoverable.

The principle of remoteness is well illustrated by *Hadley* v *Baxendale* 1854, a case so famous that even the most idle law student cannot fail to have heard of it. Hadley owned a mill in Gloucester which was brought to a standstill when the crankshaft broke. Baxendale contracted to take the broken crankshaft to its makers in Greenwich to serve as the pattern for a new one, and promised to deliver it there on the following day. Unfortunately it was delayed in transit, and Hadley sued for damages for loss of profit caused by the delay. He failed because the carrier was not aware, when the contract was entered into, that Hadley had no spare crankshaft and that the mill would therefore be idle until the new one arrived. The claim for loss of profit was too remote to be recoverable.

As always the crucial question is the state of mind of the parties when the contract is entered into. Hadley would have won his case if he had told the carrier, before the contract was made, that his mill would be inoperative until the new crankshaft arrived. But it was no use giving the carrier that information after the contract had been formed.

Although remoteness is a favourite legal topic, in our experience the issue seldom arises in commercial disputes. We do not therefore propose to say more other than to make two practical points. First, if you are involved in a claim where questions of remoteness do arise you should seek legal advice. Second, where your purpose in entering into a contract is an unusual one, or where you will for some reason be peculiarly vulnerable if the contract is broken, you should make that fact clear to the other party and you should do so before the contract is entered into.

8.3.8 The duty to mitigate

The wronged party is under a duty to mitigate his loss, which means he must take such steps as a reasonable person in his position would take to minimise the loss or damage he suffers as a result of the breach. If he fails to do so, and in consequence his loss or damage is greater than it need have been, he cannot recover that additional loss or damage from the party in breach. He has brought it on himself.

This principle, despite its grand name, is only a matter of common sense. Someone in the position of Purity plc in our example will be very anxious indeed to minimise the damage to his business, and provided he acts reasonably in doing so he will be complying with his legal duty to mitigate his loss.

If Purity's claim comes to court, Filters' lawyers will probably conduct a minute examination of Purity's actions following the breach in an effort to reduce the damages claim by showing that it failed to mitigate its loss. The court will however take a robust view. Purity's damages will not be reduced simply because, with hindsight, it could have handled the matter better than it did: they will only be reduced if the court finds that Purity inflated its loss by acting in an unreasonable way.

8.3.9 Interest on damages

Whether his claim is liquidated or unliquidated, a party who has a right to damages for breach of contract should in principle be entitled to interest on those damages to compensate him for the time he has been deprived of his money. Historically, however, there was no automatic entitlement to interest unless the contract provides for interest to be paid.

This remains the position with an unliquidated claim, and with any liquidated claim arising under a contract where one or more of the parties is a consumer. With contracts between businesses however, a statutory right to interest on unpaid debts is being introduced by the Late Payment of Commercial Debts (Interest) Act 1998. We will begin by setting out the historical position, and then we will turn to consider the effect of the 1998 Act.

Historically a party pursuing a damages claim cannot demand interest as well unless the contract provides for interest to be paid. If in the absence of such a provision the wronged party takes his claim to court and is awarded damages, he can generally expect to be awarded interest as well. The court's usual practice, with both liquidated and unliquidated claims, is to award interest running from the date the claim arose at a rate close to bank base lending rates, but that award is entirely discretionary: the court may decide to award interest from some later date or at a different rate, or not to award interest at all.

As a result of the unsatisfactory state of the law on this subject, substantial commercial contracts routinely provide for interest on late payments. When negotiating such a contract, the party who will be responsible for the payments cannot realistically argue that he should have an interest-free ride if he pays late, so the argument is usually restricted to what the interest rate should be. Typically the parties will settle on a figure equal to or slightly higher than the base rate quoted by one of the major banks or the London inter-bank offer rate (LIBOR). Standard terms and conditions of supply also routinely provide for interest if the price is not paid on the due date, but often a very much higher rate is specified. A supplier who specifies an excessive rate runs the risk that the whole provision is void as a penalty (see section 7.2.7).

Where the wronged party has a contractual right to interest, this completely displaces the court's discretion on the matter. The wronged party can demand, and if necessary sue for, not only the unpaid sum but also the interest payable under the contract. If the payment is made late but without interest, the wronged party can in principle sue for the interest owed to him. In practice however the sum involved will have to be very large if the interest figure itself is to be large enough to justify legal action to recover it.

A party claiming interest on the basis of his standard terms of supply will usually face a further practical problem. The buyer will usually insist that the contract incorporates his own standard terms of purchase, which do not of course provide for interest on late payments, and as discussed in section 5.3.11 that argument is itself unlikely to be resolved without going to court. The buyer knows that, if he withholds payment for a couple of months and then pays without interest, his supplier is most unlikely to take him to court just for the interest. So provisions for interest in standard terms of supply provide little incentive in practice for the buyer to pay on time.

We now turn to consider the effect of the Late Payment of Commercial Debts (Interest) Act 1998, which introduces a statutory right to interest on unpaid debts arising under a contract between businesses for the supply of goods or services.

It is still open to the parties to agree a contractual right to interest, and provided that the interest is sufficient to compensate the supplier for late payment and is fair and reasonable, this contractual right replaces the statutory right to interest. Where the contract does not contain such a provision, the supplier has the statutory right to interest on outstanding sums at the surprisingly high rate of bank base rate plus 8 per cent (a rate that would, if agreed between the parties, run the risk of being void as a penalty). Interest runs from the due date for payment agreed between the parties or, if no such date has been agreed, 30 days from the date on which the goods or services were supplied or 30 days from the date on which the invoice was rendered, whichever is later.

This statutory right to interest is, however, being introduced in three phases, in order to protect small businesses from adverse cash flow effects. As from 1 November 1998, small businesses have the right to interest on unpaid debts due from all large enterprises (including public sector organisations). As from 1 November 2000, small businesses will have the right to interest on unpaid debts due from any other business. Finally, as from 1 November 2002, all businesses and all public sector organisations will have the right to interest on unpaid debts due from any other business. (For this purpose, a business is 'small' if it has no more than 50 full-time employees or part-time equivalents.)

It is too early to predict whether this legislation will solve the problem of late payment, or what its side effects may be. In any event, the Act does not address the secondary problem that it is uneconomic to sue for small amounts of interest.

8.3.10 Enforcing a damages award

When the court makes a damages award there is also a mechanism for the enforcement of that award if it is not met promptly. This involves an official appointed by the court arriving at the defendant's premises and carrying off his assets. The official will then sell those assets and apply the proceeds to meeting the damages award, returning any surplus to the defendant. There is also a series of treaties between most of the world's trading nations enabling a damages award in one jurisdiction to be enforced in another, so in principle it is possible to enforce an English damages award against a foreign defendant even if he has no assets in the jurisdiction.

In practice however enforcement proceedings seldom produce the desired result, even where the defendant is within the jurisdiction. The chances are that a defendant who refuses to pay is simply unable to do so, and it is unlikely that such a defendant has valuable assets to seize. Even if he does have such assets there is a strong probability that they will have been charged to his bank, which means that the court official will not be able to sell them. You cannot get blood from a stone and equally you cannot get money from a person who has none.

8.4 INJUNCTIONS AND ORDERS FOR SPECIFIC PERFORMANCE

8.4.1 Outline of remedies

As we have seen, the court's preferred remedy for the breach of a contractual obligation is to make a damages award. The court does however have the power to prohibit the party in breach from breaking the obligation ('an injunction') or to order him to perform it ('an order for specific performance'). When these orders are granted they are highly effective. If the party in breach ignores such an order, the court will regard that as a serious matter and has the power to (and usually will) fine or imprison him for contempt of court. Where the party in breach is a company, the directors and officers of that company are themselves liable to be fined or imprisoned for contempt.

The attraction of these orders to the wronged party as a means of solving his problems is therefore considerable. In practice however their usefulness is restricted because there are only very limited situations in which the court is likely to make such an order.

8.4.2 Discretionary nature of remedies

Injunctions and orders for specific performance are, unlike the right to damages, discretionary remedies: the court will only grant them if it thinks the circumstances make it appropriate. With many kinds of breach, and the breach by Filters Ltd in section 8.3.2 is an example, there is no point at all in prohibiting the breach or ordering performance. An injunction is only appropriate where the breach consists of a failure to comply with a continuing contractual obligation not to do something, and an order for specific performance is only appropriate when what the wronged party wants is proper performance. But even here the court will only grant the order if the wronged party's loss or damage cannot be adequately compensated by a damages award.

8.4.3 Appropriate circumstances for an injunction

Let us take two examples of the kind of situation where the court may grant an injunction:

1. A contract for the sale of a business prohibits the seller from running a similar business in the area, but the seller nevertheless does so.*
2. A party is disclosing sensitive information to third parties in breach of a contractual confidentiality obligation.

The distinctive feature of both situations is that the damage which will be suffered by the wronged party if the breach continues will be impossible to quantify in financial terms, so the court may be persuaded to grant an injunction prohibiting any further breach. In both cases the wronged party will probably apply for an interim injunction, that is a temporary injunction prohibiting any further breach pending the outcome of the full court hearing of the action. In an appropriate case an interim injunction can be obtained in a matter of days, and often the wronged party's sole object in commencing legal action is to get an interim injunction which is as often as not the end of the matter. So an injunction can be a very powerful remedy in situations of this type.

8.4.4 Appropriate circumstances for specific performance

Specific performance is the most disappointing of the remedies. When your supplier's failure to deliver is putting you in breach of your commitments to your customers, who are all terminating their contracts and threatening to sue you, an order for specific performance against your supplier may appear to be just the remedy you

---

Such provisions are common in contracts for the sale of a business in order to prevent the business acquired by the buyer from being undermined by the continuing activities of the seller. If the provision is too widely drawn it is void as being 'in restraint of trade' – discussed in section 10.4.5.

need. Unfortunately in this type of situation you have no chance of obtaining such an order. First, since there is no such thing as an interim order for specific performance, it will probably take you two years to obtain a full court hearing to consider the matter. Second, even if you could get the matter to court quickly, the court would refuse to grant the order on the grounds that your mushrooming losses could ultimately be compensated adequately by a damages award against your supplier.*

There is only one situation in which orders for specific performance are at all common, and this is where the owner of land contracts to sell it but fails to convey it to the buyer. The law considers that each plot of land is unique: although damages would enable the buyer to acquire a similar plot, this is an inadequate remedy since the seller contracted for that particular plot. So generally, provided of course that the seller has not conveyed the land to a third party in the meantime, the court will order him to convey it to the buyer. It is perhaps surprising that the law does not consider a work of art or a vintage car to have the same unique character.

By contrast, there are two particular types of contract which the court will never order to be performed. These are contracts for personal services (which include contracts of employment, partnership, apprenticeship and agency) and contracts which would require constant supervision by the court.

With the vast majority of commercial contracts, although specific performance is available in principle, the remedy is of little practical value for the reasons we have discussed.

When you want the other party to perform and to perform now, you will have to find another means of persuading him to do so. The other means available to you are discussed in section 9.4.

8.5 REPUDIATION

Sometimes a party indicates before the time for performance arrives that he is not going to perform. He may do so directly, for instance by ringing to cancel his order, or else he may do so indirectly, for instance by selling the specific goods which he has contracted to sell to B to C instead. Where a party indicates that he is not going to perform he is said to have 'repudiated' the contract,

---

* *If your right to damages is restricted by an exclusion clause this can ironically increase your chance of obtaining an order for specific performance.*

and this is itself a breach of the contract known as an 'anticipatory breach'.* The wronged party does not have to wait until the time for performance arrives before taking action. A repudiation gives him the immediate right to terminate the contract if he so wishes and the immediate right to sue for damages or, where appropriate, an injunction or an order for specific performance.

8.6 TIME LIMITS

The rights which a breach confers on the wronged party do not last indefinitely. As we saw in section 8.2.1, if the breach gives the wronged party the right to terminate the contract he must exercise that right within a reasonable time after the breach.

The wronged party's right to sue for damages can be extinguished in either of two ways. First, that right is extinguished if he negotiates and agrees a settlement of his claim with the party in breach, which means that once a damages claim has been settled it cannot be resurrected. Second, if that claim is not settled the Limitation Act 1980 bars him from commencing legal action later than six years after the date of the breach which gave rise to it, or twelve years if the contract is under seal. His claim is effectively extinguished at that time if he has not commenced legal action.†

If the wronged party wants an injunction or an order for specific performance, the position is less clear cut. Since these remedies are discretionary the court will refuse to grant them if the wronged party does not commence and pursue his action with reasonable diligence, and what counts as 'reasonable diligence' depends on the circumstances of the case.

8.7 ABOUT LITIGATION

8.7.1 Conclusions on legal remedies

The conclusion must be that the legal remedies seldom provide a ready solution for a business involved in a contractual dispute. The main reason for this is the law's emphasis on damages rather

---

* As we saw in section 8.2.4, when a party terminates a contract on the basis of a breach which is not serious enough to give him the right to terminate, his termination is itself a repudiation of the contract.
† These time limits may be extended in certain circumstances by the Latent Damages Act 1986.

than enforcement: in many circumstances the only legal remedy available to the wronged party is to sue for damages. If the wronged party could obtain and enforce his damages award quickly and cheaply, it could be argued that this situation is not in itself unsatisfactory. But the reality is that litigation, as well as being notoriously costly and hazardous, takes a very long time by business standards.

A party with a liquidated claim will take a minimum of two or three weeks from the commencement of proceedings to obtain a damages award even if the claim is undisputed. So a debtor can safely ignore the payment date stipulated in the contract, knowing that it will be several weeks before he is sued and several weeks after that before he can be forced to pay up. Many businesses habitually and deliberately withhold payments in order to improve their cash flow position.

An unliquidated claim is much more likely to be disputed, and even if the party in breach admits liability he is almost certain to dispute the amount of that liability. So a party with an unliquidated claim may well take two or three years from the commencement of proceedings to obtain his damages award. Again this is a situation which a party can use to his commercial advantage. Suppose for example that the supplier of the gas turbine under the contract discussed in section 4.4.2 refuses, without any contractual justification, to deliver the turbine unless the buyer agrees to increase the contract price. If this threatens to delay the buyer's power generation project he is in a very difficult position. In principle, and provided the contract does not limit the supplier's liability, the buyer can recover all the losses caused by the delay in damages from the supplier. In practice of course this remedy is useless to someone in the buyer's position. He does not want the prospect of large damages in three years' time: he wants his power station to be operational in three months, and to achieve this he may have to submit to the supplier's demands. The best way for the buyer to prevent this situation from arising is to require a performance bond, discussed in section 9.3.4.

8.7.2 The hazards of litigation

Most businessmen regard litigation as alien, expensive, time-consuming, destructive of business relationships, uncertain in its outcome and most unlikely to yield swift results. Generally, and with the exception of the two situations referred to in section 8.7.3, this is a correct assessment.

This is not entirely the fault of lawyers and the legal system: our discussion of Purity's claim against Filters demonstrates some of the genuine complexities and uncertainties involved in such a dispute. But whether lawyers are to blame or not, the practical conclusion is that litigation is the last resort; while it can be an effective threat, legal action should only be commenced when every other avenue is closed. In particular it is a mistake to commence litigation in anger, on a point of principle, to teach the other party a lesson, or in the belief that a claim form will make him see sense. The decision to litigate should be taken on the same basis as any other business decision where there is a lot of money at stake: coolly, rationally and on the basis of the best obtainable information and advice.

One of the authors was recently involved in a dispute over a construction contract, in which the contractor claimed that he was entitled under the contract to extra payment for extra work performed. Although it was clear that he was entitled to some extra payment, it was far from clear that he was entitled to the huge sums he was claiming. The parties were locked in negotiation over the amounts due to him when without warning he issued a writ for the full amount of his claim. This was presumably done in the belief that it would strengthen his position in the negotiation, but the strategy backfired badly. The writ brought the discussions between the parties to an abrupt end, and the contractor had to withdraw the writ in order to resurrect the negotiation. His advisers should have known that a writ is a declaration of war and should never be used as a bargaining ploy.

8.7.3 Two situations where litigation is effective

Despite the conclusion in the previous section, there are two types of problem to which legal action can provide a swift, effective and relatively inexpensive solution. The first is the kind of situation discussed in section 8.4.3, where an interim injunction can effectively end the problem. The second is where you are pursuing a liquidated claim which is not genuinely disputed or else the subject of a counter claim (discussed in section 9.4.6) by the other party. Here a damages award can generally be obtained quickly and cheaply, which makes this the only situation in which it is economic to sue for a small sum. In this situation it is likely that the other party is close to insolvency, in which case the sooner you commence legal action the greater your chances of recovering your money.

8.7.4   The necessity of winning

Litigation cannot always be avoided. Sometimes all else will fail and there will be no other course open to you, and sometimes the other party will commence legal proceedings against you. Only a tiny percentage of legal actions ever result in a final judgment by the court; most result in an agreed settlement, usually long before the court hearing. But where there is a final judgment one party will win and the other will lose. The consequences for the loser can be catastrophic, not least because he will usually have to pay the winner's legal costs in addition to his own.

A litigant cannot afford to assume that his case will be one of the majority which are settled, and he cannot afford to fight the case and lose it. So when you become involved in litigation your aim from the outset must be to win. Litigation is like any other kind of battle: few cases are so strong that they cannot fail, and few are so weak that they cannot succeed. So, while victory can never be certain, the chances of success can be maximised by meticulous planning and preparation. You must therefore be prepared to put in as much time, money and effort as is required to build a winning case, and that in turn will maximise your chances of achieving a favourable settlement out of court. To achieve all this you will need to find the right solicitor.

8.7.5   Finding the right solicitor

Most firms of solicitors will be prepared to conduct litigation for you, and substantial firms generally have a specialised litigation department. Finding a firm with a good reputation for litigation is therefore the first step, and this will not necessarily be the firm you usually go to for legal services and advice. But of greater importance than the reputation of the firm is the character of the individual solicitor who will actually conduct your case; you want an individual who not only litigates regularly but also wins regularly. So before instructing a firm, make sure that you meet the individual who will conduct your case and get a preliminary assessment of it, together with an explanation of the firm's fees. The right individual will be aware of the unpredictability of litigation but will also be aware of the absolute necessity of winning. So beware of someone who appears uninterested, who tells you that it is all terribly difficult, who tells you too readily that you cannot lose or cannot win, or that it all depends on the barrister you select or the judge who hears the case. You are looking for someone who will dedicate himself or herself to the business of winning your case.

Whether or not you have found such an individual should become clear very quickly. The right solicitor will want to explore the strengths and weaknesses of your case and will want every available scrap of information about it: you will be bombarded with questions and requests for documents, explanations and meetings. Within about a month he should be in a position to give a full assessment of your case and advise on the tactics you should adopt. If you hear nothing within that time you should cut your losses and find someone else.

8.8 INSOLVENCY

8.8.1 The problem of insolvency

Our discussion of legal remedies in general and of claims for damages in particular has been haunted by an obvious and important fact to which we have so far paid little attention: a claim for damages is worthless if the party in breach has no money or assets to pay it from. While this commercial fact of life cannot be blamed on the law, the risk that the insolvency of the party in breach will leave the wronged party with no remedy at all is compounded by two of the factors we have mentioned.

The first is the law's emphasis on damages rather than enforcement. The court will not order the performance of a contract or prohibit the breach of it if damages would in principle be an adequate remedy: the fact that the party in breach may have no money to meet a damages award is not part of the equation and does not generally enhance the wronged party's chances of obtaining such an order. The second compounding factor is the length of time it can take to obtain a damages award, particularly with an unliquidated claim or a liquidated claim which is genuinely disputed or the subject of a counter claim. Events tend to move much faster in the business world than the legal, and the financial position of a business can deteriorate in weeks rather than years. If he is close to insolvency, the party in breach will be all the more reluctant to settle outstanding claims against him.

8.8.2 Consequences of insolvency

A person is insolvent if he has insufficient funds to meet his liabilities as they become due, but this fact does not in itself stop him from carrying on his business. That only happens when he is put into receivership or liquidation (in the case of a company) or when he is declared bankrupt (in the case of an individual).

In section 11.4 we will return to consider the effect of receivership, liquidation or bankruptcy on a party's outstanding contracts, but we will not spend any time on a detailed consideration of their effect on outstanding claims. The reality is that a person with an outstanding claim against him will not recover a penny unless he has some form of security, a subject discussed in the next chapter.

CHAPTER 9

The shadow of litigation and insolvency

The twin problems of litigation and insolvency discussed in the previous chapter cast a very long shadow over the commercial world. No business wants to find itself in the position of having to go to court to enforce its contractual rights, and in particular no business wants to find itself with a damages claim, whether liquidated or unliquidated, that the other party cannot meet. The best way to avoid the first problem is to deal only with persons you know to be reliable, and the best way to avoid the second is to deal only with persons who are financially secure.

Of course the commercial reality is that it is not always possible to be so choosy, and even when it is there is always a risk that a person who has in the past been reliable and solvent will cease to be so. In this chapter we are concerned with various means by which a party can protect himself against these risks.

The first line of defence is to contract on terms which either reduce the risk of your having to litigate, or else provide protection against the other party's insolvency, or both. Contractual devices of this nature fall into two categories: terms relating to the timing of payments (section 9.1), and devices which provide some form of security against a breach by the other party. Devices which provide security again fall into two categories: those giving security against an asset (section 9.2) and those where security is given by a third party (section 9.3). Some of these various devices reduce the chance that the other party will fail to perform by providing some form of incentive* (see footnote on page 185), while others do not. What they all have in common is that they enhance the position of one party to the other party's detriment. So whether or not you can use them in a particular transaction depends on the relative strength of your bargaining position.

No matter how much contractual protection you have, it is always possible that the other party will fail to perform. When this happens your aim must be to settle the dispute without going to court, either by persuading him to perform or else by persuading him to compensate you for the breach. This subject is discussed in section 9.4. In section 9.5 we go on to consider a number of alternative ways of resolving a dispute without going to court.

9.1 CONTRACTUAL DEVICES

9.1.1 Payment in advance

The ideal position for a party contracting to supply goods or services is to require payment before he supplies them. As often as not payment will be the buyer's only obligation, in which case the seller is completely protected against the insolvency of the buyer. This does not of course mean that there will be no dispute under the contract, but it does mean that if there is a dispute it will be the buyer and not the seller who has to enforce his rights by legal action. In this way the hazards of litigation and the reluctance to start it work in favour of the seller rather than against him. This device is commonly used by businesses supplying goods or services to the public such as for instance package tour companies. But where you are supplying another business you are unlikely to be able to use it: if you will not give your customers credit your competitors almost certainly will.

9.1.2 Deposits

A deposit is a more limited version of the same device. When you order a new car you will probably have to pay a percentage of the purchase price as a deposit at the time the contract is made. The idea is of course that you will forfeit the deposit if you fail to go through with the transaction. If you fail to take delivery the seller is most unlikely to sue you (although he could): he will just keep the deposit.

---

* *The most obvious way of providing an incentive to perform, that is by imposing a financial penalty on the other party if he does not, is legally ineffective because penalty provisions are, as noted in section 7.2.7, void.*

Deposits are very common indeed with contracts for the sale of land, which is particularly revealing since the intricacies of land law and conveyancing make such contracts the almost exclusive territory of lawyers. So the deposit is the lawyer's favoured solution to the problems we have been discussing.

Conceptually it is difficult to see much difference between a deposit and a penalty (discussed in section 7.2.7). A deposit is effectively a financial penalty on a party who fails to perform, and the amount of the deposit may bear no relation to the loss which the other party may suffer as a result of that failure. Until quite recently however there was no suggestion that the legal rules on penalties might also apply to deposits, but that link was made in the case of *Jobson* v *Johnson* 1989.

In that case Johnson contracted to buy Jobson's shares in Southend United football club for £351,688, payable in instalments. The agreement provided that if Johnson defaulted on the payment of any instalment he would retransfer all the shares to Jobson for £40,000. Having paid a total of £140,000 Johnson did default on the payment of an instalment and Jobson demanded the retransfer of the shares. The Court of Appeal held that this provision was in the nature of a penalty, there being no distinction between a penalty which requires the payment of money and a penalty which requires the forfeiture of property, and so Jobson could not enforce the retransfer of the shares.

This line of reasoning suggests that a party who forfeits a deposit may be able to recover it if he can show that the provision is in the nature of a penalty, or in other words that the amount of the deposit bears no relation to the loss which the other party might be expected to incur as a result of his breach. *Jobson* v *Johnson* is a good example of how the law is constantly developing from case to case, and demonstrates why law books are always having to be updated.

9.1.3 Retention money

The same device can of course be used in reverse to protect the buyer's position. Construction contracts often provide for a certain percentage of the price to be retained for a period after construction is complete. The circumstances in which the client has to release that sum to the builder, and the circumstances in which he can apply it to make good defects in the construction, are usually provided for in some detail. The practicality is however that if the client refuses to release it the builder will ultimately either have to sue for it or else write it off. So retention money gives the builder a considerable incentive to perform and gives the client considerable leverage over him.

9.1.4   Default under loan agreements

We have done well to get this far into the subject of protective devices without mentioning banks, whose mastery of self-protection against their commercial and domestic customers makes their record of huge unprotected loans to third world governments and insolvent entrepreneurs all the more remarkable. Commercial loan agreements generally provide that any default by the borrower makes the entire outstanding amount of the loan immediately repayable. 'Default' is generally defined to include not only a failure by the borrower to repay any instalment of the loan or to meet any other obligation under that loan agreement, but also any default under any of his other loans, whether from that bank or some other lender. This arrangement enables the bank to pursue a liquidated claim for the whole outstanding amount of the loan at the first sign that the borrower is in financial difficulties.

Where the borrower is a registered company, the definition of 'default' is generally even further extended to cover any default by any other company in the same group. This is known as a 'cross-default' arrangement, and it means that the bank can call in its loan if another company in the group gets into difficulties, even though the borrower itself is meeting all its obligations under the loan agreement. Although in principle companies in the same group are entirely separate legal entities, and one member is not obliged to meet the liabilities of another, a cross-default arrangement effectively ties them all together, so that the failure of one company will generally bring down the whole group.

9.2   SECURITY AGAINST AN ASSET

9.2.1   Pawn

To say that a party has security against an asset means that, in addition to a damages claim, he has a claim against that asset if the other party fails to meet his obligations under the contract.

A familiar example of a party who has security against an asset is the pawnbroker, who lends money against the security of an asset owned by the borrower which he takes into his possession. This is an arrangement known as a 'pawn' or a 'pledge'. If the borrower fails to repay the loan, the pawnbroker is entitled to sell the asset and recoup the loan from the proceeds. As long as the value of the asset exceeds the value of the loan, the pawnbroker does not care whether the borrower repays the loan or not, although he is obliged to return the excess after deducting his costs. If the asset realises less than the value of the loan, the pawnbroker can (if he can find him) pursue the borrower for the difference.

9.2.2 Charges

Of greater commercial importance is a device known as a charge, which is also most commonly used to provide security for a loan. There are many different types of charge, and the law relating to them is extremely complex, especially where an asset is charged more than once. In essence however a charge is very similar to a pledge except that the lender does not take possession of the asset. The parties identify an asset belonging to the borrower which will stand as security for the loan. If the borrower defaults, the lender is then entitled to take possession of the asset, sell it and recoup the loan from the proceeds. For his part the borrower undertakes to inform the lender if he at any time proposes to sell the asset and to apply the proceeds of sale to the repayment of the loan. If the borrower goes into bankruptcy or liquidation, the lender's claim to the asset by virtue of the charge takes priority over the claims of any of the unsecured creditors.

Any asset, whether a tangible asset such as a car or a painting or an intangible asset such as shares in a company or a contractual right to payment, can be made the subject of a charge. In practice however the lender is unlikely to be content with security in the form of a charge over any of these particular assets. The reason for this is that the charge does not give him physical control of the asset: there is nothing to prevent the borrower selling it to a third party without telling the lender, and pocketing the proceeds. Unless the purchaser was or should have been aware of the existence of the charge, he takes free of it, meaning that the lender cannot pursue his claim against the asset in the hands of the purchaser. He is left only with a claim for damages against the borrower for breach of contract, which is precisely the situation he was trying to avoid by taking the charge in the first place.

In practice therefore the lender will require a charge over some kind of asset where there is some means of notifying prospective purchasers of the existence of the charge. For example, the existence of a charge over a ship or aircraft is recorded in a central register. A prospective purchaser of the ship or aircraft will inspect the register, see the charge, and make arrangements to pay the necessary part of the purchase price to the lender in order to extinguish the charge. If he buys the ship or aircraft without inspecting the register, the lender's charge will remain in existence because the purchaser should have been aware of it.

A charge over an aircraft or a ship is often referred to as an aircraft mortgage or a ship mortgage. The most familiar type of charge, which is also referred to as a mortgage, is a charge over land. The existence of all charges over land is recorded in the land charges register kept at the Land Registry, and from the lender's point of view land has the additional attraction of being immovable. A ship or aircraft may be stolen or disappear but land cannot. A charge over land is therefore the best of all forms of security against an asset, with a decline in the value of the land being the lender's only real exposure. Generally however the lender is required to obtain a court order before he can repossess the land.

9.2.3 Fixed and floating charges

A more complex but equally common arrangement, where the borrower is a registered company, is a fixed and floating charge. The existence of any charge over a company's assets is recorded in the records kept by the Registrar of Companies (see section 2.1.8). A fixed and floating charge involves the lender taking a charge over the company's fixed assets such as its premises and plant (the fixed charge), and in addition a floating charge over its other assets such as its stocks of raw materials, work-in-progress and finished products and its cash-in-hand and book debts.

While the company's power to sell its fixed assets is restricted by the fixed charge, the floating charge imposes no such restriction in relation to its other assets. Only if the company defaults and the bank calls in the loan will the floating charge crystallise on the assets owned by the company at the time. In that event the bank will appoint a receiver to sell all the assets charged on the most favourable basis, whether that is to sell the business as a going concern or to sell the assets piecemeal. The existence of a fixed and floating charge almost always means that, if the company fails, its unsecured creditors will see none of the money owed to them.

We have discussed charges in the context of security for a loan, but in principle a charge can be used to secure the performance of any kind of contractual obligation. The reason why in practice charges are seldom encountered in any other context is twofold. First, the subject is highly complex, and if you are proposing to contract on terms which give you a charge you will need the services of a lawyer to ensure that the charge is enforceable and to handle such matters as registration. Second, the banks will almost always have got there before you. The existence of a prior charge does not prevent the asset from being charged a second time (although often the consent of the holder of the first charge will be required), but the first charge will take priority. Only when the first charge has been paid off in full will the second have any value.

9.2.4 Liens

The third important form of security against an asset is the lien. A party who is in possession of goods is said to have a lien if he has the right to retain possession of them until the other party has performed his contractual obligations.

Although a lien may, like a charge, be created by express agreement between the parties, in two very common situations one party has a lien as a matter of law unless the parties have agreed otherwise. The first concerns contracts for the sale of goods where, unless otherwise agreed, the seller has a lien over the goods until the buyer has paid for them. This is known as an unpaid vendor's lien. With most commercial contracts for the sale of goods the parties do agree otherwise in that the goods are supplied on credit, which means that the seller forfeits the lien he would otherwise have had.

The second situation where a lien arises as a matter of law is where one party takes possession of goods belonging to the other in order to provide services in respect of those goods. So when a customer leaves his car at a garage for service or repair, the garage proprietor can refuse to hand it back until the bill has been paid. Again the proprietor will have no lien if he has agreed to give the customer credit.

9.2.5 Retention of title

Another relatively recent contractual device which gives security against an asset is the retention of title clause, which is used mainly in standard terms and conditions of sale. As discussed in section 4.9.2, when goods are sold title and risk generally pass to the buyer at the latest when the goods are delivered. If the goods are supplied on credit and the buyer fails to pay for them, the seller cannot reclaim the goods because title has passed to the buyer. The parties are however free to make a different arrangement as to the passing of title and risk if they so choose, and a retention of title clause does just that.

In essence a retention of title clause provides that the seller retains title to (but not risk in) the goods until the buyer has paid for them or, in a more extreme version of the clause, until the buyer has paid all the outstanding sums which he owes the seller. If the buyer fails to pay, the seller can reclaim the goods on the basis that they still belong to him. His preferred means of doing so will be physically to seize possession of the goods from the buyer's premises, although this can easily lead to a fight with the buyer's employees or security guards, who are unlikely to be familiar with or interested in the provisions of the Sale of Goods Act 1979. A seller who attempts this is well advised to have his lawyers with him.

If the seller cannot seize the goods he can go to court for a declaration that the goods belong to him and if necessary an order that they are delivered up to him. By this time however the probability is that the buyer will have had a receiver or liquidator appointed. The receiver or liquidator will want to sell those goods for the benefit of other creditors, and so he will resist the seller's action if he can find a basis to do so. If (as is usually the case) the seller is claiming that he owns the goods on the basis of a retention of title clause contained in his standard terms and conditions of sale, the receiver or liquidator will of course resist the seller's action on the basis that the contract did not include those standard terms.

The other weakness of a retention of title clause is that the buyer will not have bought the goods in order to leave them sitting indefinitely in his warehouse. He will be intending either to use the goods himself or else to resell them, and in either case this will destroy the seller's title. If the goods have been used, for example either burnt for fuel or incorporated in some manufacturing process, nothing will remain which the seller can recognise and claim as his. If the goods have been resold to a third party, that third party does in fact get title to the goods even though the buyer himself does not have title. As we saw in section 4.8.1, the general rule is that a person selling goods cannot pass title if he does not have title himself, but there are a number of exceptions to this rule. One of these exceptions, contained in Section 25(1) of the Sale of Goods Act 1979, is that where a buyer has bought or agreed to buy goods and is in possession of them with the consent of the seller, the buyer can pass title if he resells them to a third party (provided of course that the third party is not aware of the original seller's rights in those goods). The acquisition of title by the third party necessarily destroys the title of the original seller.

9.3 SECURITY FROM A THIRD PARTY

9.3.1 Principles

The other main way for a party to protect himself is to require some form of security from a third party, the objective being to ensure that the contractual liabilities of the other party will be met. Since a contract can never impose obligations on a third party, such security requires a second contract between the third party providing the security and one of the parties to the first. There are many different kinds of third party security, but we will discuss only four common and important ones. These are guarantees, insurance, performance bonds and letters of credit.

9.3.2 Third party guarantees

A guarantee is a contractual undertaking by a third party in favour of one party to the main contract to meet the liabilities of the other party under that contract if he fails to meet them himself. In section 1.2.5 we saw that the liability of the third party guarantor is secondary; the primary obligation to perform the main contract, or else to pay damages for his failure to do so, remains with the party whose liabilities are guaranteed. Only if he fails to meet those liabilities can the party to whom the guarantee is given pursue his claim for damages against the guarantor.

A guarantee is however a very effective way for one party to protect himself against the insolvency of the other, and guarantees are commonly used when there is doubt about the ability of a party to a major contract to meet his potential liabilities under it. So if you put a substantial construction or engineering contract out to tender and the most competitive tender comes from a company which is believed to be in financial difficulties, you might decide to award the contract to that company on condition that it procures a guarantee in your favour from a financially secure third party.

Obviously a third party will not voluntarily undertake a secondary liability for another person's breach of contract unless he perceives some advantage to him in doing so which outweighs the risks of liability under the guarantee. Two categories of third party may perceive such an advantage. The first is someone whose connection with the party whose liabilities are to be guaranteed gives him a vested interest in that party securing the contract, such as for example that party's parent company. When a small private company seeks a bank loan the bank will often demand personal guarantees from the individuals behind the company, which effectively deprives them of the advantages of trading with limited liability which we discussed in section 2.1.4. But even a third party with a vested interest will avoid giving a guarantee if he can: he will only do so if the contract is sufficiently important and there is no other way of securing it. So you will not get a guarantee from a connected third party unless he believes that without it you can and will award the contract to someone else.

The second category of third party who may be prepared to give a guarantee is a commercial entity which makes money out of assuming financial risks, such as a bank. A bank's incentive to give a guarantee is quite different from that of a connected third party: a bank has no vested interest and stands to gain only the fee it will charge for providing the guarantee. A bank's decision whether to provide a guarantee, and if so the size of its fee, will involve a hard-headed analysis of the contractual obligations of the party whose liabilities are to be guaranteed, the size of those potential liabilities and the risk that he will not be able to meet them.

If you require the other party to procure a bank guarantee, this raises the subsidiary question of who will pay for it: you will need to be in a very strong position indeed to require the other party to pay to protect you against his insolvency. If your bargaining position is not that strong there is a different way of approaching the matter: tell the other party that you require a bank guarantee which you will pay for. Since it will cost him nothing it will be difficult for him to refuse. If he cannot find a bank to provide a guarantee, or else the bank's fee is prohibitive, this will confirm your concerns about his financial position and you should place the contract with someone else.

If the other party agrees to procure a third party guarantee in your favour, you need to ensure that the guarantee is in writing and signed by or on behalf of the person giving it. This avoids any question of the guarantee being unenforceable under the Statute of Frauds 1677, discussed in section 1.2.5. As a general rule you should also insist that the guarantee is under seal because, if it is not, it may be unenforceable for lack of consideration. The problem is that the obligations under the contract of guarantee are all one way: the guarantor is undertaking a secondary liability to you, but unless you are paying for the guarantee you are probably not undertaking to do anything in return. If the guarantee is entered into before or at the same time as the main contract, it may be that the obligations which you undertake under the main contract will also serve as your consideration for the contract of guarantee. But if the guarantee is entered into at some later time, your existing obligations under the main contract cannot serve as your consideration for the guarantee. Obviously you cannot afford to have the security given by the guarantee hanging on technical arguments about consideration. If you have the bargaining power to insist on a guarantee you also have the power to insist that it is under seal.

9.3.3 Insurance requirements

We noted in section 4.5.4 that a party can if he so wishes insure against his potential liabilities under a contract. By requiring him to take out such insurance the other party can make certain that funds will be available if those potential liabilities arise, and it is fairly common for commercial contracts to contain an insurance requirement. For example, the standard terms used by television and video rental companies not only make the hirer liable for loss of or damage to the equipment due to fire, flood or theft but generally also require him to insure against those risks. The protection which that insurance gives to the hire company is indirect. The hire company is not a party to the contract of insurance and so cannot sue the insurer directly, but it can safely assume that if for example the equipment is stolen the hirer will pass the claim to his insurer.

In this example the potential liability in question is owed by one party to the other, and in this situation the requirement of insurance has essentially the same effect as requiring a third party guarantee of that liability (although, as we have seen, third party guarantees generally cover all one party's potential liabilities to the other and not just a particular one). The fact that the protection afforded by the contract of insurance extends to persons who are not parties to that contract means however that an insurance requirement can, unlike a guarantee, be used to secure the position of third party claimants. So an indemnity from one party to the other against third party claims (discussed in section 6.4.1) is often accompanied by a requirement that the party giving the indemnity has an appropriate level of insurance against such claims.

On a practical level nobody gets any protection at all if the party who is required to take out insurance fails to do so, and since the other party is a stranger to the contract of insurance he may not become aware of that failure until it is too late. So he is well advised to impose the additional requirement that he is supplied with a copy of the insurance policy.

9.3.4 Performance bonds

From the viewpoint of the party requiring security, the problem is that neither a guarantor nor an insurer will pay out unless it is satisfied that the other party really is liable, and it may be necessary to go to court to show that he is. This problem can be circumvented by means of an on-demand performance bond, a device which is commonly encountered with major construction and engineering contracts.

The party awarding the contract requires the successful bidder to arrange for a third party, usually a bank, to provide a performance bond. This is an irrevocable undertaking by the bank to pay that party on demand a specified sum of money. The bank will of course make appropriate arrangements to enable it to recover that sum from the other party if the bond is called. The party to whom the bond is payable can therefore demand the specified sum from the bank at any time without having to show that the other party is liable to him under the contract. If he does so it is then up to the other party to recover the amount by which that sum exceeds his liability under the contract. A performance bond gives enormous commercial leverage against the other party as well as protection against his insolvency.

9.3.5 Letters of credit

The difficulties which a seller may have in recovering the purchase price are greatly increased with an export sale: if the buyer fails to pay it will be necessary to pursue him through the courts in the country where he resides. With a substantial export sale therefore it is common for the seller to require payment by means of a letter of credit, which is essentially a written promise to pay, and this generally involves not one bank but two.

The buyer arranges for a bank in his country ('the issuing bank') to issue an irrevocable and unconditional letter of credit for the purchase price which is then sent to a bank in the seller's country ('the correspondent bank'). Provided that the correspondent bank is satisfied that it will be reimbursed by the issuing bank, it confirms the letter of credit and issues it to the seller. With this arrangement the purchase price is paid by the correspondent bank under the letter of credit, and only if that bank collapses will the seller have to pursue the buyer for the price.

9.4 NEGOTIATION AND SETTLEMENT

9.4.1 Legal constraints

The commercial reality is that, in many of the deals you enter into, you will simply not be in a position to demand extravagant contractual protection. Even when you are, there is no completely certain way to ensure that the other party will perform, a proposition borne out by the bad debt records of all the major banks. So whatever business you are in, you are certain from time to time to be the victim of a breach of contract, and we must now turn to the practical issue of what you can do about it short of taking the party in breach to court. If you are to settle the matter without legal action, you need to find some means of persuading the other party to give you what you want.

Although this subject is not strictly a legal one, the law comes into it in two distinct ways. First, as we noted in section 8.1.1 your rights against the party in breach are in an important sense defined by the legal remedies available if you do have to go to court. For this reason it may be worth taking advice on your legal remedies from your usual solicitor before you approach the other party, although this will depend on the circumstances and nature of the breach. Second, the fact that the other party is in breach of contract does not exempt you from the law of the land and it is important not to resort to illegal means to rectify the situation. If for example the other party has failed to pay a sum due under the contract, you are not entitled to take the money from him or seize his possessions: that would be theft or, if violence is used, robbery. Nor does the other party's breach justify you in retaliating by breaking other contracts between you. But within these two legal parameters you can be as demanding and persuasive as the situation requires or your imagination permits.

9.4.2 Deciding what you want

Merely complaining to the party in breach may make you feel better but is unlikely to achieve anything else. You need to have a clear idea of what you want from him, and this will depend on the circumstances and the nature of the breach. If that breach is a failure to pay a sum due under the contract, then what you want is performance. With any other kind of breach you may want performance (or some variation of it), or compensation, or both. If you want compensation you will need an itemised and substantiated statement of your losses before any sensible discussions with the party in breach can begin; a damages claim which is unsupported or uses figures plucked from the air will not be taken seriously. But if you want performance the more swiftly you act the better, so if you want compensation as well it is best to leave that issue on one side while you try to persuade the other party to perform.*

Suppose then that you have purchased some goods which prove to have serious defects. While you will certainly want compensation if you have suffered loss as a result, that issue can wait until later. Although strictly speaking it is too late to insist on performance as such, your immediate decision is between the following four options:

1. Terminate the contract and demand a refund, which leaves you with a liquidated but unsecured claim for the purchase price;
2. Require the seller to replace the goods, which is a variation on performance;
3. Require the seller to repair the goods, which is another variation on performance; or
4. Have the goods repaired by a third party, which leaves you with an unliquidated and unsecured claim for the cost of the repairs.

In a contract of this type the court will not order the seller to repair or replace the goods, so if you cannot persuade him to do so you will ultimately have to make a second choice between options 1 and 4.

9.4.3 The personal approach

Every individual develops his own negotiating style, and the best is the one which works for him. We propose therefore to give only a brief outline of the personal approach which we ourselves find most effective.

In our experience threatening letters addressed to 'Dear Sirs' seldom have much effect. Even when the party in breach is a company, you are not trying to persuade a fictitious legal entity but

* *Note however the two pitfalls discussed in section 9.4.5.*

the real people who make decisions on its behalf. The personal approach is a matter of finding out who has the decision-making power and making personal contact with him, preferably face-to-face. If you already have a business relationship with that individual, then so much the better. If not, develop one. At this stage it is generally better not to have lawyers present, even if you have taken legal advice: the best solution is a swift and amicable one which minimises your losses and leaves business relationships intact. This approach does however require you to be flexible. You may for example be prepared to waive your right to damages if the defective goods are promptly replaced, or to write off the more speculative items of your claim if the others are paid promptly and in full.

9.4.4 Legitimate threats

The threat of legal action is best played down, at least to begin with. The individual you are dealing with will probably be just as keen to avoid litigation as you are, and will also generally recognise a moral obligation to help you solve the problems created by the breach. If he is not prepared to help you, other threats can be just as persuasive as the threat to litigate.

The threat to give the other party no further business is perfectly legitimate and can be even more effective. Suppose for example that you are claiming damages for breach of a construction contract by a construction company, which is stalling and refusing to admit any liability to you. It comes to your attention that a different company in the same group wishes to bid for another very much larger contract which you are about to put out to tender. Although you cannot pursue any legal remedy against that affiliate company, a telephone call making clear that the affiliate will not be invited to tender unless the outstanding dispute has been resolved may well result in a swift and satisfactory settlement offer.

The threat of adverse publicity can also be effective, and this also is legitimate provided that your publication of the breach is not defamatory. In the case of *Bestobel Paints* v *Bigg* 1975, a firm of painters and decorators painted the exterior of a house with brown paint manufactured by Bestobel Paints and marketed under the name of 'Carsons'. Six months later the paint had turned a hideous green colour, but Bestobel refused to accept that the paint was defective or to pay compensation. The house happened to be situated on the busy South Circular Road in London, so Bigg displayed a large notice on the wall of the house which read: 'This house is painted with CARSONS paint.' Bestobel sued for an injunction to prevent Bigg from displaying the notice, but they failed because the statement was true.

If all else fails and you do have to resort to the threat of legal action, it is vital that the threat is credible. One way of achieving this is to make that threat formally by means of a letter before action from your solicitor. A more sophisticated stratagem is to send the party in breach a photocopy of a completed but unissued claim form prepared by your lawyers and detailing your claim. Since the claim form needs only to be stamped by the court in order formally to commence the action, this will usually convince the party in breach of your intention to sue if no compromise can be reached.* If you do have to commence proceedings negotiations for a compromise can of course still continue. By that stage however lawyers will be involved on both sides, and those negotiations will normally be conducted between them.

9.4.5 Settling a dispute

When the parties agree to compromise (or, in legal phraseology, to 'settle') their dispute, that agreement is itself a contract. In essence the wronged party agrees, usually although not necessarily in return for a damages payment, not to commence legal action or, as the case may be, not to proceed with it. This means that the wronged party cannot subsequently pursue his legal remedies for the breach of the original contract: all his rights in respect of that breach are effectively extinguished by the settlement. Lawyers signify this complete extinction of the rights of the wronged party by the phrase full and final settlement, for example 'the wronged party agrees to accept damages of £100,000 in full and final settlement of all claims arising out of the breach'.

When you are negotiating with the party in breach and lawyers are not involved, there are two pitfalls to beware of. First, you must ensure that a partial solution such as the repair or replacement of defective goods cannot subsequently be interpreted as a full and final settlement of your claims, unless of course that is what you

---

* *This technique is especially effective when the individuals acting for the party in breach are either stone-walling and refusing to speak to you or else are going through the motions with no genuine intention of resolving the matter. Such ostrich behaviour generally indicates that those individuals are frightened, hoping against hope that you and your problem will go away. They need to be convinced that you will not.*

intend. If in this situation you wish to reserve the right to sue for loss caused by the breach you must make this clear. Second, you must ensure that any settlement offer you make does not prejudice your position if that offer is rejected. Suppose in our defective goods example that you are prepared to forget about the loss you have suffered if the seller agrees to replace the goods. The seller rejects this settlement offer but subsequently claims that it amounted to a waiver of your right to sue for that loss. This danger can be avoided by ensuring that any settlement offer is made 'without prejudice', meaning without prejudice to your legal rights and remedies if the offer is rejected. This is why written settlement offers prepared by lawyers are always headed 'without prejudice'.

9.4.6 Set-off and counter claim

Where two persons owe each other liquidated sums they are always entitled to set one sum off against the other. There is no requirement that the transactions giving rise to those separate liabilities are in any way related. So, where you have a liquidated claim against someone, you can exercise your right of set-off and recover your money by simply subtracting the sum owed to you from any other sum which you owe him, leaving you to claim or to pay the difference.

This general right of set-off does not however apply to unliquidated claims. An unliquidated claim can only be set off against a debt which arose from the same transaction. If therefore you purchase goods on credit and they prove to be defective, you are entitled to withhold the purchase price until the damages due to you from the seller have been quantified, either by agreement between the parties or, failing that, by a court judgment. At that point the two claims can be set off and the difference paid. You can therefore resist any claim by the seller for the purchase price on the basis of your counter claim for damages for his breach of the contract.

9.4.7 Winding-up petition

Where you have a liquidated claim exceeding £750 against a registered company, and you have reason to believe that the company has failed to pay because it is in financial difficulties, there is another way of pursuing the claim. This is to apply or threaten to apply to the court to wind the company up. To understand how this works we need to say a little about corporate insolvency.

The court will order a company to be wound up (or, to put it another way, put a company into liquidation) if the company is unable to pay its debts. Under Section 123 of the Insolvency Act 1986, a company is deemed to be unable to pay its debts if a creditor who is owed more than £750 sends a written demand for the sum due to the company's registered office, and that sum is not paid within three weeks of receipt of that demand. The procedure is therefore to send the company a statutory demand for the sum in question. The form of the statutory demand is set out in the Insolvency (Amendment) Rules 1987: essentially the demand gives the name and address of the company and of the creditor and sets out the amount of the debt and the particulars of how the debt arose.

The demand is best sent to the company's registered office by registered post addressed to the Company Secretary, partly because every company has a secretary and partly because he is more likely than anyone else to understand its significance. If after 21 days you have still not been paid, you can then instruct your solicitor to present a winding-up petition against that company, a procedure which is relatively quick and inexpensive. There are only two ways for the debtor company to avoid being put into liquidation. The first is to convince the court that the debt is genuinely disputed or the subject of a genuine counter claim, and the second is to pay it. The procedure is therefore very effective when the company concerned is in financial difficulties and is delaying all payments until the last possible minute.

Statutory demands have become increasingly common over the last 10 years, and it would appear that some businesses are using a statutory demand followed by a winding-up petition as a routine means of collecting debts. Although this bears witness to the efficacy of the technique, a note of caution needs to be added. The service of a winding-up petition leads to the freezing of the company's bank accounts, and will usually constitute a default by that company under its loan agreements. So, if the company is solvent, it may well suffer substantial loss and expense as a result of the service of the petition. If the creditor had no grounds for believing that the company was insolvent, he is liable to compensate the company for that loss and expense. A winding-up petition is therefore a powerful weapon which it is dangerous to use indiscriminately.

9.5 ALTERNATIVES TO LITIGATION

9.5.1 Arbitration

The length, expense and uncertainty of litigation has led to a number of attempts to find a quicker, cheaper and more predictable alternative. The most common and important of these is arbitration, where the parties seek an adjudication of their dispute not from the court but from one or more specialist arbitrators appointed for the purpose. There are two ways in which this can happen. The first is where the contract itself stipulates that disputes under it, or specified kinds of disputes under it, are to be referred to arbitration rather than to the courts. Such a provision is known as an arbitration clause. The second way is where, although the contract does not contain an arbitration clause, the parties nevertheless agree to submit a particular dispute to arbitration. Arbitration proceedings are governed by the Arbitration Act 1996. The idea is that the arbitrator's award should bind the parties just as if it had been made by the court. In principle an appeal to the court is only possible if the arbitrators have made an error of law and not if they have made errors of fact.

We do not think that the original vision of arbitration as a more efficient way of solving commercial disputes has been fulfilled. Arbitration proceedings tend to be just as lengthy, complicated and unpredictable as court proceedings, and it is as unwise to represent yourself in an arbitration as it is to do so in court. In our experience arbitration is if anything more expensive: at least with litigation the parties do not have to pay the judge or to pay for the room in which he hears the case. The other problem is that the loser can in practice almost always allege some error of law by the arbitrators, so substantial arbitrations tend to end up in court anyway on appeal from the arbitrators' award.

Arbitration does however retain one significant advantage over court proceedings, and this is that arbitration proceedings are held in private. Unlike court proceedings, members of the public and the press are not entitled to attend an arbitration, and arbitrators' awards are not published. Although arbitration clauses remain common, especially with international transactions such as shipping contracts, we generally advise our clients against including arbitration clauses in their contracts unless there are reasons for keeping any potential dispute confidential. It is always open to the parties to agree to go to arbitration if they think it appropriate. The best time to consider the question is after the dispute has arisen rather than before the contract is made.

9.5.2 Technical experts

Where the dispute is technical in nature, it is common for the parties to refer it to a technical expert rather than to a court or an arbitrator. As with arbitration, the reference to an expert can either be provided for in the contract or else it can be agreed by the parties after the dispute has arisen. In either case it is usually agreed in advance that the expert's opinion will be binding on both parties, although as with arbitration it is not unusual for a party which disagrees with the expert's opinion to challenge it in court.

Reference to an expert is only appropriate where the dispute turns on a highly technical question: so a dispute over the quality of a metal might usefully be referred to a metallurgist, or a dispute over a computer program to a computer specialist. Although the individual selected will be an expert in his field, he is not likely to have been trained as a judge or arbitrator or to be experienced in contract law and disputes. So it is important that his terms of reference identify precisely the technical question on which his expert opinion is required: you are not asking him to adjudicate on the commercial or contractual implications of his technical opinion.

9.5.3 Loss adjusters

A different approach which can be both effective and time-saving is to engage a third party to try to negotiate a settlement on your behalf. A lawyer, who may seem to be the obvious choice, is not the best person for the task unless the dispute is already on the brink of litigation. Professional etiquette prevents a lawyer from dealing directly with the other party unless his lawyer is also present, and when lawyers are instructed on both sides the parties' respective positions can rapidly become entrenched. A better candidate is a loss adjuster, who is a professional valuer of claims. Insurance companies, who have more experience than most businesses of the costs and risks of litigation, routinely appoint a loss adjuster when they receive a substantial insurance claim. In our experience however, a loss adjuster will be equally happy to act directly for either party to a dispute (but not for both) even where no insurance is in place. Engaging a loss adjuster has the additional advantage of minimising the rancour between you and the other party.

Your loss adjuster will not commit you to a settlement unless you authorise him to: his brief usually is to negotiate a settlement with the other party (or the other party's loss adjuster) which he can recommend to you. You are free to reject his recommendation, but you should think carefully before doing so since litigation may well be the only option left.

9.5.4 Alternative dispute resolution

We should also mention a procedure known as alternative dispute resolution or ADR, which has become a standard part of court procedure in the United States and has recently begun to be used in the UK.

The parties refer the dispute on an entirely informal basis to an independent third party, whose function is not to adjudicate on the dispute but to mediate between them. This can be done at any stage of the dispute, whether or not lawyers are involved and whether or not legal action has been commenced, and the procedure seldom lasts longer than one day. The mediator hears a summary of each party's case separately and in confidence, and then tries to find a basis for settlement which is acceptable to both. The settlement rate is reportedly high, and generally the parties would seem to have little to lose by pursuing a settlement in this way. ADR proceedings can be arranged through the Centre for Dispute Resolution, a non-profit-making body which operates from the headquarters of the CBI in London. It remains to be seen however whether ADR will become an established part of British court procedure.

CHAPTER 10

Invalid contracts

10.1 INVALIDITY AND ITS CONSEQUENCES

10.1.1 Practical significance of invalidity

In this chapter we shall be discussing the various factors which can make a contract, or a particular provision in a contract, invalid. The subject of invalidity is a lawyers' paradise, and every contract law textbook has substantial sections devoted to it. It is however important not to get a false impression of the practical importance of the subject. In practice it is very unusual indeed, especially with the kinds of contract we have been dealing with in this book, for the validity of a contract ever to be questioned. The parties proceed on the assumption that their contract is valid which, in the vast majority of cases, it is.

The question of validity tends to arise only when a party who is unwilling or unable to perform, or who has failed to perform, seeks advice on his legal position. As discussed in section 7.1.1, the principle of strict liability often leaves little room for manoeuvre. But if the lawyer finds that the contract is invalid (or, failing that, finds a respectable basis on which to argue that it is) then that is the legal equivalent of a golfer's hole-in-one: if the contract is invalid his client cannot be held liable for breaking it. In the case mentioned in section 2.2.4, the lawyers acting for the London Borough of Hammersmith and Fulham scored a hole-in-one when they realised that their client's lack of contractual capacity enabled it to walk away from interest rate swap agreements worth £6 billion. So while invalidity is an important legal subject, the businessman needs only a sufficient knowledge of it to enable him to avoid entering into an invalid contract.

10.1.2 Types of invalidity

A contract may be void, voidable or unenforceable, and we need to understand the difference between these three terms:

1. *Void contract:* A void contract is neither valid nor enforceable. In the eyes of the law, and no matter what the parties may have thought, there never was a contract in the first place. It follows that neither party is bound to perform his obligations under that contract and no legal action can be maintained against him if he fails to do so. An extreme and obvious example of a void contract is an underworld 'contract', that is an agreement to kill.
2. *Voidable contract:* A voidable contract is a valid and enforceable contract which one party has the right to nullify (or, in legal language, 'avoid'). If he exercises that right the contract is then void with retrospective effect, as if it had never existed. If he does not exercise that right the contract remains valid and enforceable. We noted in section 2.2.2 that, with certain exceptions, a contract entered into by a minor is voidable at his option.
3. *Unenforceable contract:* Normally if a contract is unenforceable then neither party can maintain a legal action against the other if he fails to perform it. Although in legal theory an unenforceable contract is valid, both parties can ignore their obligations under it with impunity. There is therefore no practical distinction between a contract which is void and a contract which is merely unenforceable. An example of an unenforceable contract is an agreement to marry, which has been unenforceable since 1971 by Section 1(1) of the Law Reform (Miscellaneous Provisions) Act 1970. Another example, as we saw in section 1.2.5, is an oral guarantee.

10.1.3 Consequences of invalidity

When the parties have performed or partially performed a contract which is invalid, a secondary question can arise: can the parties take legal action to recover money paid, goods supplied or recompense for services rendered under that invalid contract? There is no universal answer to this question. It depends on the specific reason for the invalidity of the contract. Generally speaking the courts are more likely to entertain such a claim where the contract is invalid for a technical reason than where it is invalid for a moral one, but the behaviour and state of mind of the claimant in a particular case also enter the equation. Although we will deal with this secondary question in the context of our discussion of each of the various reasons for invalidity, we will do so very briefly. It is better and easier to keep your ship off the rocks in the first place than it is to try to salvage something from the wreckage.

10.1.4 Severance

Sometimes the legal objection is to a particular provision in a contract rather than to the contract itself. In this situation the invalid provision is in effect deleted and treated as if it was not there at all, a process known as 'severance'. Provided that the remainder of the contract makes sense without the severed provision, then its validity is not affected. In section 7.2.7 we encountered an example of a provision which can be severed: a penalty provision is void and the court will simply ignore it, but that does not affect the validity of the remainder of the contract. Whether or not severance is possible again depends on the specific reason for the invalidity, and we will note the position in the context of our discussion of each of those various reasons.

10.1.5 Outline of chapter

For the purposes of our discussion we have divided the factors which result in invalidity into three: invalidity due to a defect in the formation of the contract (section 10.2), statutory invalidity (section 10.3), and invalidity due to the repugnance of the contract (section 10.4). This division is made only for convenience and there is no distinction of substance between the three categories. In all cases we are dealing with contracts which, for one reason or another, the law is not prepared to enforce.

10.2 FORMATIVE DEFECTS

10.2.1 Formative defects already covered

One of the difficulties in studying contract law is that one idea can be expressed in a variety of different ways. We have already encountered a number of factors which can make a contract invalid, but we have not always expressed it in that way. In our discussions of the requirement of consideration (section 3.2) and the requirement of certainty of terms (section 4.2), we stated that no contract comes into existence if those requirements are not met. We could equally well have said that these are formative defects which make a contract void, since the law considers that a void contract never was a contract in the first place. Similarly in section 4.3.2 we noted that where a party is induced to enter into a contract by a misrepresentation of fact, that party can generally 'rescind' the contract. Again we could equally well have said that the contract is voidable at that party's option. By contrast lack of contractual capacity, another formative defect discussed in section 2.2, is said to result in the formation of a contract which is void or voidable.

We must now consider a number of other factors which can, if operative at the time agreement is reached, result in the formation of an invalid contract. These are fraud, duress, undue influence and (in relation to contracts of insurance) non-disclosure.

10.2.2   Fraud, duress and undue influence

Where one party induces the other to enter into a contract by means of fraud or duress or by the exercise of undue influence over him, then that contract is voidable at the option of the other party. Fraud means active and intentional dishonesty; duress means violence or threats of violence; and the exercise of undue influence means the abuse of an abnormal degree of power over the other party.

Suppose then that I persuade an elderly widow to sign a contract to sell me her mansion in Kensington for £10,000 either (i) by telling her that it is a contract for the maintenance of her gardens, or (ii) by threatening to hit her if she does not, or (iii) by telling her as her trusted legal adviser that is the best deal she is going to get. In all three situations she can avoid the contract and, if the mansion has been conveyed to me, take legal action to force me to reconvey it to her. In that case of course I would want my £10,000 back. Whether or not I am legally entitled to its return is not entirely clear from the reported cases, which is perhaps a reflection of the understandable distaste which the courts have for such claims.

We do not intend to go any further into these topics since they hardly ever arise with business contracts. A business which unwittingly accepts the other party's standard terms, even if they are wholly one-sided and unreasonable, stands no chance of succeeding with a claim of fraud. Similarly a business which is forced to agree highly disadvantageous terms because of the weakness of its bargaining position stands no chance of succeeding with a claim of undue influence. And, in the only instance either of us knows of one businessman hitting another, both worked for the same company.

10.2.3 Non-disclosure in contracts of insurance

In section 3.4.4 we noted that contracts of the utmost good faith (or contracts *uberrimae fidei*) are an exception to the general principle that there is no obligation to disclose relevant facts. The most important example of a contract of the utmost good faith is a contract of insurance. Here the party wanting insurance is obliged to disclose to the insurer, before the contract is entered into, all material facts of which he is aware. A material fact is any fact which would influence the insurer in deciding whether to accept the risk or in setting the premium. If the insured has failed to disclose a material fact then the contract is voidable at the insurer's option. The insurer will of course only avoid the contract if and when a claim is made under it, and he is entitled to do so even if the claim is not in any way related to the undisclosed fact.

It is therefore very unwise when taking out insurance to conceal relevant information, since that enables the insurer to walk away from the contract just when you need it. The same warning applies when you are renewing your insurance, since legally a renewal is not an extension of the old contract but a completely new one.

10.3 STATUTORY INVALIDITY

10.3.1 Statutes already covered

There are many examples of Acts of Parliament and other legislation which make particular types of contract, or particular types of contractual provision, invalid. We have already dealt with a number of them. In section 1.2.5 we discussed statutes which require particular types of contract to be in a specified form, and such contracts are generally invalid if these formal requirements are not met. In section 2.2 we considered the restrictions on a person's contractual capacity, which affect the validity of contracts entered into by him, and some of these restrictions are themselves statutory. In section 4.6 we considered at length a variety of contractual provisions which are made ineffective by the Unfair Contract Terms Act 1977. Finally we mentioned earlier in this chapter that agreements to marry were made unenforceable by statute in 1971.

We will now deal briefly with wagering contracts before turning to the important subject of competition legislation.

10.3.2 Wagering contracts

Section 18 of the Gaming Act 1845 makes all gaming or wagering contracts void, which betrays an interesting legislative value-judgement. Gambling is of course perfectly legal and some kinds of betting are subject to a special betting tax. But while the state is prepared to raise revenue from betting transactions, it is not prepared to enforce them through the courts. So for example a bookmaker cannot sue a customer for his stake money, and a customer cannot sue the bookmaker for his winnings. No doubt this often results in gambling debts being collected by less savoury means.

10.3.3 Competition legislation

The capitalist world considers competition between businesses to be both beneficial and necessary, and most industrialised western countries have some form of rules prohibiting anti-competitive arrangements such as price-fixing or market-sharing. In England and Wales these rules are currently contained in the Restrictive Trade Practices Act 1976 and the Resale Prices Act 1976. In addition however the competition rules of the European Union also have the force of law in the United Kingdom by virtue of the European Communities Act 1971.

The difficulty with any such legislation is to define satisfactorily what arrangements are to be prohibited as anti-competitive. Both the English and European approach is to draw the prohibition very broadly indeed and to provide a mechanism to exempt arrangements (or classes of arrangements) which, although falling within the prohibition, are not considered to be anti-competitive. This piecemeal approach has two unfortunate consequences. First, it can be very difficult to predict, and it can take a long time to find out, whether a particular arrangement within the prohibition will be exempted or not. Second, a very complex body of law builds up as exemptions are granted or refused in particular cases.

So businesses in England and Wales have to reckon with two entirely separate sets of competition rules, both of which are wide-ranging, complex and constantly evolving. We can attempt only the barest outline of these highly specialised subjects, but we need to do so because one of the sanctions when a contract infringes

English or European competition rules is to make that contract, or the offending provisions in it, void.

The current English competition rules will be replaced from 1 March 2000 by the new rules contained in the Competition Act 1998. These rules are based on, and are similar to, the European competition legislation. We will therefore consider the current English rules in the following two sections, then consider the European rules in section 10.3.6, and finally return in section 10.3.7 to consider in outline the new English rules which will take effect in March 2000.

10.3.4 The Restrictive Trade Practices Act 1976

The Restrictive Trade Practices Act 1976 requires certain agreements (defined to include any agreement or arrangement, whether intended to be legally enforceable or not) to be registered with the Director General of Fair Trading. An agreement is registrable when two or more parties carrying on business within the United Kingdom in the production, supply or processing of goods or the supply of services accept restrictions as to:

1. The prices to be charged for goods or services;
2. The terms or conditions of supply; or
3. The persons or areas to be supplied.*

Certain categories of agreements within this definition are exempted from the requirement of registration by the Act itself or by subsequent legislation. These include:

1. Agreements under which the restrictions relate exclusively to the supply of goods or services outside the United Kingdom.
2. Agreements under which the only restrictions relate to the supply of professional services.
3. Most sole agency agreements.
4. Most bilateral contracts of sale.
5. Agreements for the supply of insurance services.

Any agreement which is required to be registered must be notified to the Director General of Fair Trading within three months after it

---

* Agreements under which such parties merely agree to exchange information about their prices or terms and conditions of supply (known as 'information agreements') are also registrable.

is entered into. The Director General then refers the agreement to the Restrictive Practices Court, which determines whether or not the restrictions in it are contrary to the public interest. If so those restrictions are void, and the court may issue an injunction to prohibit the parties from operating them. In fact very few restrictions considered by the Restrictive Practices Court have survived the public interest test.

If an agreement which is required to be registered is not registered within the three months allowed, the restrictions contained in it are void, and the Court may issue an injunction to prohibit the parties from operating them. In addition a party who operates such a restriction in an unregistered agreement can be sued for damages by anyone who suffers loss as a result of it.

Under the European competition rules, huge fines can be levied on businesses guilty of anti-competitive behaviour, and in the United States the executives responsible can be sent to prison for it. It must be said that, by comparison, the threat of being taken to the Restrictive Practices Court and being told not to do it again is not a particularly effective sanction.

10.3.5 The Resale Prices Act 1976

It used to be common for suppliers of goods to set a minimum resale price for those goods. This was usually achieved by a term in the contract of sale prohibiting the buyer from reselling the goods for less than the minimum resale price, and it was common for suppliers to withhold supplies from buyers who undercut that price. All this was effectively ended by statutory provisions now contained in the Resale Prices Act 1976, which are for once relatively straightforward.

The Resale Prices Act prohibits the maintenance of minimum resale prices by contract or agreement, and renders any such contractual requirement void. It also prohibits the maintenance of minimum resale prices by withholding supplies or other discriminatory conduct against buyers. Any supplier contravening these prohibitions can be sued for damages by anyone who suffers loss as a result.

Applications for particular classes of goods to be exempted from the operation of the Act can be made to the Restrictive Practices Court, which essentially will only grant an exemption if this is in the public interest. In fact only two such exemptions have ever been granted, in respect of books (the controversial 'net book agreement', which was finally abandoned in September 1995) and medicaments. This is why suppliers of all other classes of goods are careful to set only 'recommended' resale prices. It is however perfectly legitimate to set maximum resale prices.

10.3.6 European competition law

The central pillar of European competition law is Article 85(1) of the Treaty of Rome 1957, which reads as follows:

> The following shall be prohibited as incompatible with the common market: all agreements between undertakings, decisions by associations of undertakings and concerted practices which may affect trade between Member States and which have as their object or effect the prevention, restriction or distortion of competition within the common market, and in particular those which:
>
> (a) directly or indirectly fix purchase or selling prices or any other trading conditions;
> (b) limit or control production, markets, technical development, or investment;
> (c) share markets or sources of supply;
> (d) apply dissimilar conditions to equivalent transactions with other trading parties, thereby placing them at a competitive disadvantage;
> (e) make the conclusion of contracts subject to acceptance by the other parties of supplementary obligations which, by their nature or according to commercial usage, have no connection with the subject of such contracts.

Anyone accustomed to the pedantic precision of English legislation is likely to find the broad-brush European style rather obscure. Sir Teddy Taylor MP engagingly refers to this as 'Eurowaffle', but since the maximum fine for a business which infringes Article 85(1) is 10 per cent of its annual worldwide group turnover, this particular piece of Eurowaffle needs to be taken very seriously indeed.

Clearly the main thrust is against the familiar targets of price-fixing and market-sharing, but the words 'in particular' indicate that the five sub-paragraphs are subservient to the main paragraph and are not an exhaustive list of the prohibited arrangements. The central prohibition of 'agreements ... decisions ... and concerted practices ... which have as their object or effect the prevention, restriction or distortion of competition within the common market' is potentially very broad indeed, and this interpretation is confirmed by numerous decisions on these provisions by the European Court of Justice. The only restrictive feature is the phrase 'which may affect trade between Member States', but it is clear from decisions of the European Court of Justice that the article is not limited to arrangements between persons in different member states. A domestic English transaction can therefore infringe it. Article 85 goes on to declare that any agreement which does infringe 85(1) is automatically void, a relatively insignificant sanction compared to the huge fines which can be (and increasingly are being) imposed on the parties to such an agreement.

It should also be noted that the European Commission has extensive powers to gather evidence of anti-competitive behaviour, including the power to seize documents. The Commission's inspectors usually arrive at a party's offices without notice in what has come to be known as a dawn raid.

A particular agreement which falls within Article 85(1) but is not considered anti-competitive can be exempted from the provisions of the Article altogether, either by means of a specific application by the parties to the European Commission or else under one of a continuing series of Commission Regulations which give block exemptions to certain classes of agreements or certain types of contractual provisions. Block exemptions have so far been granted in favour of:

- Bilateral exclusive distribution agreements.
- Bilateral exclusive purchase agreements.
- Patent licences.
- Motor vehicle distribution and servicing agreements.
- Know-how licences.
- Franchise agreements.
- Research and development agreements.
- Specialisation agreements.
- Insurance arrangements.
- Agreements regarding air transport.

The terms of these block exemptions are however very restrictive, often including numerous conditions which have to be met if a particular agreement is to be exempt, all of which contributes to the severe and increasing complexity of this area of European law.

Numerous other block exemptions are currently under consideration by the European Commission, but no final decision has yet been reached on them.

The standard English textbook on the subject of European competition law is Bellamy and Child's *Common Market Law of Competition*, 4th edition (1993) published by Sweet & Maxwell.

10.3.7 The new English Competition Act

The Competition Act 1998 will replace the English competition rules described above with effect from 1 March 2000. The new legislation is based closely on the European competition rules. The core of the new legislation is the prohibition of agreements between businesses or groups of businesses that have the objective of preventing, restricting or distorting competition in the United Kingdom and that may affect trade within the United Kingdom.

Businesses that break these rules will be liable to substantial fines and may also face claims by third parties that are affected by the anti-competitive agreement.

10.4 REPUGNANT CONTRACTS

10.4.1 Categories of repugnant contracts

Certain types of contract are void as a matter of public policy, and such contracts fall into nine well established categories. Six of these categories involve some kind of illegal, immoral or improper conduct, and it is no surprise that the courts will have nothing whatever to do with such contracts. They are generally referred to as 'illegal' contracts, a rather unhelpful description which it is nevertheless convenient for us to use. The illegal contracts are:

1. A contract to commit a crime, fraud or tort.*
2. A contract to defraud the Revenue.
3. A contract that is sexually immoral.
4. A contract prejudicial to public safety.
5. A contract prejudicial to the administration of justice.
6. A contract tending to corrupt public life.

The remaining three categories are void more as a matter of policy than principle. They are:

* A 'tort' is an actionable wrong other than a breach of contract, such as for example a nuisance.

7. A contract prejudicial to the institution of marriage.
8. A contract which ousts the jurisdiction of the courts.
9. A contract in restraint of trade.

The difference between the illegal contracts and the other three categories is reflected in their legal consequences, and for that reason we need to discuss them separately.

10.4.2 Illegal contracts and their consequences

The first three categories of illegal contract are too obvious to require illustration, but the others are less so. The classic example of a contract prejudicial to public safety is a trading contract made with a citizen of a country with which the United Kingdom is at war. Examples of contracts prejudicial to the administration of justice are (1) an agreement by which one person pays another not to give evidence against him and (2) an agreement by which one person finances a legal claim by another in return for a share of the proceeds. An example of a contract tending to corrupt public life would be if I agreed to pay a civil servant to propose me for a knighthood or a position on a quango.

An illegal contract is void, but the legal consequences can extend beyond this. Suppose for example that a landlord lets a flat to a tenant knowing that the tenant intends to use it for the purposes of prostitution. The lease is void since it is sexually immoral. It follows that any attempt by the landlord to sue for unpaid rent, and any attempt by the tenant to claim security of tenure under the landlord and tenant legislation, will fail. In addition however related transactions may also be tainted by the illegality of the lease. If the tenant borrows money to pay the rent from someone who is aware of the purpose of the lease, the loan agreement is also void. Similarly if the tenant pays the rent with a cheque which is dishonoured, and the landlord sues on the basis of the cheque (which he can do without making any reference to the lease), that action will also fail if the court becomes aware of the lease and its purpose. As we observed at the outset, the courts will have nothing whatever to do with an illegal contract.

10.4.3 One party unaware of illegality

It is of course possible for one party to be unaware of the illegal purpose of the other. A landlord may let a flat without realising that the tenant intends to use it for the purposes of prostitution, or alternatively the tenant may only form that intention at some point after the lease is entered into. In this situation the tenant's illegal purpose deprives him of all legal remedies under the lease, but the legal remedies of the innocent landlord are unaffected. The illegality will however deprive the landlord of his remedies if, having become aware of the illegality, he turns a blind eye to it.

There was considerable publicity in 1991 when it was reported in the press that a woman renting a flat from Mr Norman Lamont MP, then Chancellor of the Exchequer, was using it for immoral purposes. When Mr Lamont became aware of this he took the only legitimate course open to him, terminated the lease and took legal action to recover possession of the flat.

In between awareness and unawareness lies the grey middle ground of suspicion. You may suspect that a workman who insists on being paid in cash intends to defraud the Revenue, but this does not necessarily follow. If however the workman quotes a substantially lower price for payment in cash, then it is hard even to imagine an innocent explanation, so if you agree to pay cash your contract with him is in all probability void.

10.4.4 Contracts void but not illegal

We can now return to the remaining three categories of void contracts. Contracts and contractual provisions falling within these categories are not illegal in the sense we have been discussing: they do not have the effect of tainting related transactions, and an offending provision can be severed without making the rest of the contract invalid.

The first of these ill-assorted categories can be briefly disposed of. The courts will not enforce any contract which they see as prejudicial to the institution of marriage. Examples include:

1. A contract between two single people not to marry anyone else.
2. A contract where one person agrees to marry another in return for payment.
3. A contract to find someone a husband or wife.

The second category reflects the court's sensitivity to any attempt to undermine their jurisdiction. Accordingly any provision which prevents a party from going to court to enforce his contractual rights is void. What is perhaps surprising is that agreements which the parties do not intend to be legally binding, exclusion clauses and arbitration clauses, all of which have the effect of ousting the jurisdiction of the courts, do not fall foul of this principle.

For the purposes of business the third category, contracts in restraint of trade, is very much more important and requires a more detailed examination.

10.4.5   Restraint of trade

The principle underlying the doctrine of restraint of trade is this: it is in the public interest that every person should be free to carry on his trade, business or profession in whatever manner he sees fit. Any contractual restraint on that freedom is therefore void unless that restraint is reasonable in all the circumstances. Identifying such a restraint is generally very easy, but saying whether it is reasonable or not can be more difficult. Contractual restraints of this nature are commonly found in contracts of employment, contracts for the sale of a business, exclusive trading arrangements and the rules of trade associations, and we need to see how the doctrine of restraint of trade applies to each of them.

Contracts of employment
The terms of a contract of employment are generally imposed by the employer on the employee on a 'take it or leave it' basis. Sometimes those terms include provisions restricting the activities of the employee either during his employment or after his employment ends. A prohibition against competing activities during his employment will usually be reasonable and therefore valid. But restrictions on the employee's activities after his employment ends are likely to be unreasonable and therefore void unless they are necessary and proportionate to protect either the employer's trade secrets or else his business connections. Only in exceptional circumstances will any restriction other than a short term prohibition against poaching the employer's customers or clients be justifiable.

Contracts for the sale of a business
Whether he is buying assets or shares (a distinction discussed in section 2.1.9), the purchaser of a business has a legitimate interest in ensuring that the business is not undermined by the vendor continuing his trade with his old customers. It is therefore common in such contracts for the vendor to undertake not to run another business in competition with the one he is selling. Such restrictions are valid provided that they do not go further than is reasonably necessary to protect that business. A restriction which does go further, in terms of either its duration or geographical extent, or

which is designed to protect another business owned by the purchaser, is void and may also infringe the competition rules discussed in section 10.3.3.

Exclusive trading arrangements
Exclusive trading arrangements are very common. Familiar examples include:

1. Agreements between a garage owner and an oil company that the garage will sell only that company's products.
2. Agreements between a car dealer and a manufacturer that the dealer will sell only that make of car.
3. Agreements between the licensee of a pub and a brewery that the pub will sell only that brewer's products.

Typically the exclusivity undertaking is only half of the picture. The oil company and car manufacturer will in fact be financing the garage or dealership, the brewery will in fact own the pub which is leased to the licensee, and the goods will usually be supplied on advantageous terms. Generally such mutually beneficial arrangements are not considered to be contrary to the public interest and fall outside the doctrine of restraint of trade, but the doctrine can apply if the terms of the arrangement, considered altogether, are oppressive. Let us take two cases to illustrate this.

Esso Petroleum Co Ltd v *Harper's Garage (Stourport) Ltd* 1968 concerned a solus agreement. Esso financed the garage which was mortgaged to it for a period of 21 years. The mortgage could not be redeemed before then. The garage company undertook during that period to buy all its motor fuel from Esso, to keep the garage open at all reasonable hours and not to sell the garage without ensuring that the purchaser entered into a similar agreement with Esso. Esso allowed a rebate of ld a gallon on all fuels supplied. The terms of this arrangement went beyond a simple exclusive trading agreement because they restricted the way in which the garage conducted its business, and moreover did so for a fixed period which could not be terminated early. The House of Lords held that these features brought the agreement within the doctrine of restraint of trade and that it was unreasonable, especially as regards its duration, and therefore void.

In *A Schroeder Music Publishing Co Ltd* v *Macaulay* 1974, an unknown musician contracted with a publishing company on its standard terms. Under those terms he assigned to the company the world copyright in all music composed by him. The company did not undertake to publish any such composition, but agreed to pay him a royalty if it did. The agreement ran for five years but would be automatically extended if the total royalties paid under it reached £5,000. The company could terminate the agreement at any time on one month's notice, but the musician could not. The House of Lords held that the agreement was within the doctrine of restraint of trade and was unreasonably one-sided and therefore void.

An exclusive trading arrangement can therefore fall foul of the doctrine of restraint of trade as well as the competition rules, and legal advice on both issues should be obtained before entering into such an arrangement.

The rules of trade associations

The rules of trade associations operate as a contract between all the members of the association and also, if it is a distinct legal person, the association itself. Such rules commonly contain restrictions of some kind as to how members conduct their business, and such restrictions are subject to the doctrine of restraint of trade and are void unless they are reasonable.

CHAPTER 11

The involvement of third parties

The principle that a contract cannot confer rights or impose obligations on a third party should now be very familiar. There are however four quite different ways in which a third party may become involved in a contract or its performance, and they are as follows:

1. *Voluntary assignment:* A party voluntarily transfers some or all of his rights under the contract to a third party (section 11.1).
2. *Novation:* In effect a party transfers all his rights and obligations under the contract to a third party (section 11.2).
3. *Subcontract:* A party arranges for some or all of his obligations under the contract to be performed by a third party (section 11.3).
4. *Involuntary assignment:* In the event of the death or bankruptcy of a party, his rights and obligations under the contract automatically transfer to a third party (section 11.4).

A glance at any law textbook will show that voluntary assignment in particular is a hideously complex subject. In order to avoid an academic dissertation we will restrict our discussion to the commercial situations in which these subjects commonly arise, looking at the practical problems they can cause the other party and how he can avoid those problems.

11.1 VOLUNTARY ASSIGNMENT

11.1.1 The assignment of contractual rights

A contractual obligation cannot be assigned, but a contractual right can. The general rule is that a party is free to assign any or all of his rights under the contract to a third party, and he can do so without reference to the other party, provided that the terms of the contract do not prohibit him from doing so.* The other party is informed, after the assignment has taken place, that he now owes the obligations in question to someone else.

Usually of course a party enters into a contract because he himself wants the benefit of it, and there is only one commercial situation in which the voluntary assignment of a contractual right is at all common. This is where the party with the right to payment under the contract assigns that right to a third party, usually either one of his creditors or else a credit factor. Some businesses routinely assign their contractual rights to payment, at a slight discount, to a credit factor. This has the dual advantage of realising those debts early and leaving any problems in collecting them to the assignee.

11.1.2 The assignment of debts

The assignment of a right to payment is governed by Section 136 of the Law of Property Act 1925, which requires it to be in writing signed by the assignor, and requires the other party to be given written notice of the assignment. Suppose then that A, who has contracted to sell goods to B, assigns his right to the purchase price to C. The buyer B receives a letter from either A or C informing him of the assignment and instructing him to pay the purchase price to C rather than to A.

The legal analysis of the situation is very straightforward. It is now C rather than A who is entitled to the purchase price, and if B pays it to A he will have to pay it again to C. Any defence (including a counter claim or right of set-off) which B would have had to A's claim for the price will apply equally to C's claim for the price. In principle therefore B's position is not adversely affected in any way by the assignment. In practice however he needs to be careful. If having paid the purchase price to C it turns out that the

---

* *This general rule does not however apply to personal contracts – see section 11.5.*

assignment was invalid (because for instance it was not in the form required by Section 136), or else never took place at all, he will have to pay it again to A. So on receipt of written notice of the assignment, and particularly if that notice is from C, B needs to satisfy himself not only that the assignment really did take place but also that it was a valid one.

11.1.3   Practical conclusions on assignment

You will see why, having briefly opened this Pandora's box, we want to slam it shut again. The practical way to keep it shut is to include in your contracts a provision prohibiting any assignment by the other party, or at least prohibiting any assignment without your prior approval. The other party will want that prohibition to apply to you as well as to him, a point you can readily concede. Most substantial commercial contracts do in fact prohibit assignment and in this way prevent the difficulties to which an assignment can give rise. If in the absence of such a prohibition an assignment does take place, you should tread carefully, and will probably require legal advice.

11.1.4   The assignment of leases

Before leaving the subject of assignment, we need to note the special position as regards leases. A lease gives the tenant a proprietary interest in the land concerned. Unless the lease itself provides otherwise, the tenant can assign his interest in the land to someone else, who will assume all the rights and obligations of the tenant under the lease. But at common law the assignment does not release the original tenant from his contractual liabilities under the lease: since contractual liabilities cannot be assigned, he remains liable for the performance of all the continuing obligations under the lease. This is the position even if (as is usually the case) the lease requires the tenant to obtain the landlord's consent before he assigns the lease. So if the new tenant fails to pay the rent, the landlord can require the original tenant to do so.

This common law rule was abolished by the Landlord and Tenant (Covenants) Act 1995, but only as regards leases entered into after the Act came into force on 1 January 1996. With these new leases, as they are called, if the tenant assigns the lease he is released from all future liabilities under it. The old common law rule continues to apply to all leases entered into before 1 January 1996.

11.2 NOVATION

11.2.1 Meaning and purpose

Novation involves the replacement of an existing contract between A and B by a new contract on the same terms between A and C, and this requires the agreement of all three parties. Considering that the principles are so straightforward, it is surprising how much confusion the subject of novation causes.

The commercial situation in which a novation is necessary is where B sells the business to which the contract relates to C by way of an asset sale. (In the case of a share sale there is no need for any contracts to be novated, for the reasons discussed in section 2.1.9.) In the case of an asset sale B has no further need for the contract: he would like to assign all his rights and obligations under it to C so that he is no longer involved. But because contractual obligations cannot be assigned, he can only achieve this result if A and C agree to a novation. If they do, the effect is as if B has transferred his rights and obligations to C or, to put it another way, as if one party to the contract has been substituted for another, and it is common for the parties to express what has happened in this way. Legally however this is not the continuation of the old contract with a new party. The old contract between A and B has been extinguished and replaced by a new contract on the same terms between A and C. The fact that this is a new contract has significant practical implications.

11.2.2 The position of the other party

Suppose that you are party A in our example. B and C will have agreed, as part of the deal for the sale of the business, to try to novate all the existing contracts, including yours, which relate to that business.

If your contract with B is a substantial written agreement, such as for example a long term joint venture agreement, you will usually be asked formally for your consent to the novation. If you agree to this a novation agreement will usually be prepared for all the parties to sign, which will formally terminate your contract with B and substitute a new contract on the same terms with C. A formal novation agreement is a matter of good housekeeping and is not strictly necessary. Just as a written agreement can be terminated or varied informally it can also be novated informally. But if your agreement was important enough to be put in writing it will presumably be important enough to justify a written novation.

If however your contract with B is a more routine trading contract, B and C will usually take a different approach. C will write to you saying that, as the new owner of the business, he has taken over B's contract with you, and assuring you of his best attention at all times. Any act of acknowledgement on your part, including for example issuing your next invoice or some other document to C, will be taken as your agreement to the novation.

The important point, whether your consent to the novation is formally requested or not, is that you do not have to agree to it. You can tell C that you have no intention of contracting with him, and you can tell B that you are happy with your existing arrangement and have no intention of terminating it. Since B has sold the business, it is unlikely that he will want the contract to continue, and it may now be impossible for him to perform his obligations under it.

Businessmen are seldom in our experience awkward for the sake of it, but it may be to your commercial advantage to be awkward. If for example you are concerned about C's financial position, you are in a position to demand a third party guarantee as the price for agreeing to the novation. Alternatively you may want some improvement in the terms of the new contract or, if the existing contract is disadvantageous, you may decide to take this opportunity to try to escape from it altogether. Irrespective of which eventual outcome you desire, the correct first step tactically is to refuse to agree to the novation and to hold B to your existing contract. Unless B is willing and able to continue your existing arrangement, he will have to ascertain and ultimately meet your demands as the price for extricating himself from it.

11.2.3 A point to watch

There is a further practical point to watch out for if, in A's position, you decide that you will agree to the novation. In doing so you will have extinguished the old contract with B and released him from his obligations under it, and you must ensure that C undertakes to meet all those obligations.

Suppose for example that goods supplied to you by B under the existing contract are defective, but you only discover this after the novation has taken place. B may resist your claim on the grounds that you have released him from his obligations under that contract, while C may resist the claim on the grounds that it pre-dates the new contract and is nothing to do with him.

The way to avoid this situation is to require C to meet all B's outstanding obligations under the existing contract, either by insisting on the inclusion of that requirement in the novation agreement or, if none, by making it a condition of your agreement to the novation. C may be unwilling to assume those obligations because he is unaware of their extent, but you should stand your ground. Why should you be in a worse position as a result of the novation than you were before it?

11.3 SUBCONTRACTS

11.3.1 Meaning

While a party cannot assign his contractual obligations to a third party, he is generally free to arrange for a third party to perform them, provided that the terms of the contract do not prohibit him from doing so.* This involves a second entirely separate contract between that party and the third party, known for convenience as a subcontract. It is very common for a party to arrange for the performance of his obligations in this way, especially in the building and construction industry, so let us take an example from that industry to illustrate the principles involved.

11.3.2 The principles of subcontracts

Suppose that a builder B contracts to build a house for a client A. Unless the terms of that contract prohibit him from subcontracting, B can if he so wishes subcontract the whole job to another builder. In practice however it is much more likely that he will do the actual building work himself and subcontract only certain parts of the job such as the plumbing, heating and electrical work. For simplicity let us suppose that B subcontracts the electrical work to an electrician C but does all the rest of the work himself.

The essential point is that the main contract between A and B and the subcontract between B and C are entirely separate. C has no rights or obligations under the main contract because he is a stranger to it. A has no rights or obligations under the subcontract because he is a stranger to it. The fact that B has arranged for part of his obligations under the main contract to be performed by C does not relieve him of those obligations. So if the electrical work done by C does not meet the requirements of the main contract, B will be

* *This general rule does not however apply to personal contracts – see section 11.5.*

in breach of that contract and he cannot escape his liability to A for that breach on the ground that C failed to perform the subcontract. For his part C does not have to concern himself with the requirements of the main contract: he only has to ensure that he meets his obligations to B under the subcontract.

11.3.3 The reality of subcontracts

In theory then the existence of the subcontract does not affect A's contractual position in any way. In practice however he may be less than happy about it. He will no doubt have made enquiries into B's reputation before contracting with him, but he will not have had that opportunity with C. If C proves to be an incompetent electrician, A cannot terminate the subcontract or threaten to sue C under it because he is not a party to the subcontract. He is left complaining to B and threatening to sue him. On a practical level therefore B's use of a subcontractor has reduced A's control over the project.

It is for this reason that it is common for commercial contracts to prohibit subcontracting altogether or to restrict it in some other way.

11.3.4 Provisions which restrict subcontracting

The best course when negotiating a contract is to insist on a clause prohibiting the other party from subcontracting at all. If he resists this you will know that he is intending to subcontract and he will have to tell you what parts of the work he is intending to subcontract and to whom. If this is acceptable to you then write it into the contract as an exception to the prohibition: 'B shall not subcontract any part of his obligations except the electrical work which he will subcontract to C.' If B says he has not yet decided whether to subcontract or does not yet know who he will use, then prohibit him from subcontracting without your prior approval or, alternatively, without your prior approval of the identity of the subcontractor. If you have the bargaining power you may wish to go further, for instance by providing that if the work done by C does not meet the requirements of the main contract then B will on your request terminate the subcontract and engage a different subcontractor approved by you.

11.4 INVOLUNTARY ASSIGNMENT

11.4.1 Death

When an individual dies, his contractual rights and liabilities automatically transfer to his personal representatives (meaning his executors or administrators, as the case may be).* If therefore an individual who has contracted to sell goods dies before supplying them, his personal representatives acquire the obligation to supply those goods and the right to sue the other party for the price. However, the liability of the personal representatives under that contract extends only to the value of the assets of the deceased.

11.4.2 Bankruptcy

When an individual is declared bankrupt, the court appoints a trustee in bankruptcy whose main function is to realise that individual's assets and distribute the proceeds to his creditors. That individual's contractual rights and obligations automatically transfer to his trustee in bankruptcy.*

The position of the trustee in bankruptcy is therefore the same as that of a personal representative, subject to one important exception. Unlike a personal representative, a trustee in bankruptcy has the right to disclaim any existing contract which in his opinion is onerous or unprofitable, and if he does so no further rights or obligations arise under that contract. The existence of that right is of course highly disadvantageous to the other party, who will usually be released from the contract if it is profitable for him but held to it if it is not.

11.4.3 Receivership, administrative receivership and liquidation

When a company gets into financial difficulties it may be put into receivership, administrative receivership or liquidation. We need to consider in outline the differences among the three.

A receiver is usually appointed by a creditor under the powers conferred by a charge held by that creditor. A receiver deals only with the specific property of the company which is the subject of that charge. His function is to realise the value of that specific

---

* This automatic transfer of rights and liabilities does not take place where the contract in question is a personal one – see section 11.5.

property on behalf of that creditor, at which point the company will usually go into liquidation.

Like a receiver, an administrative receiver is appointed under a charge held by a particular creditor. An administrative receiver can only be appointed under a charge which covers all or substantially all of the property of the company. His purpose is to realise the assets of the company which are covered by that charge and distribute the proceeds to the creditor who appointed him.

By contrast the purpose of a liquidator is to realise all the company's assets and distribute the proceeds to the unsecured creditors generally.

Both an administrative receiver and a liquidator (but not an ordinary receiver) must distribute all proceeds of sale in the order specified by statute. Most significantly this means that the Inland Revenue and Customs and Excise take priority over all other creditors including, where there is an administrative receiver, the creditor who appointed him.

When an administrative receiver or a liquidator is appointed the company's contractual rights and obligations remain with the company and do not transfer to him. His position in this respect differs from that of a trustee in bankruptcy. Like a trustee in bankruptcy however, an administrative receiver or liquidator does have the right on the company's behalf to disclaim any existing contract which in his opinion is onerous or unprofitable.

11.5 PERSONAL CONTRACTS

We have seen that the law generally allows a party to assign his rights and subcontract his obligations, and that generally the rights and obligations of an individual automatically transfer to a third party in the event of his death or bankruptcy. The unspoken premise is that it does not matter who actually performs a party's obligations, or who he owes them to, so long as those obligations are in fact performed. Although with most contracts this premise is true, three short examples will show that it is not always true:

1. A young footballer signs a contract of apprenticeship with the current league champions, who subsequently assign their right to his services to a non-league club.
2. A couple agree to pay a famous artist £100,000 to paint a portrait of their daughter. He subcontracts the portrait to one of his students.

3. A highly paid nuclear physicist dies in a car accident. Her husband, a bricklayer by trade, tells her employer that as her executor he will be assuming all her rights and obligations under her contract of employment.

These examples show that some contracts are too personal to be performed by anyone other than the original parties. With personal contracts, as they are called, the normal rules on voluntary assignment, subcontracting and involuntary assignment do not apply: each party can insist on personal performance by the other, and if circumstances make this impossible the contract is frustrated. The classic examples of a personal contract are a contract of employment and a contract of apprenticeship.* Beyond this the distinguishing features of a personal contract are rather elusive. As a general proposition however it is very unlikely that a commercial contract of the kind we have been mainly concerned with will fall into this category.

* *Note however that an employee or apprentice can assign his right to his wages. The right to payment is the most impersonal of rights.*

CHAPTER 12

International transactions: the broader picture

So far this book has had a distinctly parochial flavour in that we have said virtually nothing about international transactions. We now need to look at the broader picture. Selling steel to a company in Pittsburgh or in Tokyo is a very different matter from selling steel to a mill in Sheffield: with international transactions you have to deal not only with different systems of law but also with different cultures and different ways of doing business. A global survey of business law and practice is of course out of the question. So far as law is concerned we can do no more than say a little about different systems of law and the jurisdictional issues which arise with transactions involving more than one such system.

12.1 SYSTEMS OF LAW

12.1.1 About systems of law

We have considered in outline the system of commercial law which applies within the jurisdiction of England and Wales. This is only one of the three jurisdictions which comprise the United Kingdom, the others being Scotland and Northern Ireland. Each of these three jurisdictions has its own separate and self-contained system of law, which deals not only with contracts and the other commercial matters we are concerned with but also with crime, families, trusts, land, wills, employment, tax, tort and a host of other topics.

Although the English, Scottish and Northern Irish systems of commercial law are (as you might expect) very similar, there are nevertheless significant differences between them. For example, under Scottish contract law there is no requirement of consideration for the formation of a valid contract, and a contract can confer rights on a third party. In other areas however these systems are very different. For example the English and Scottish criminal and land law systems have very little in common with each other.

As a general proposition, the legal system to which a person is subject at any time is dictated by his location and not his nationality. If an individual commits a crime in Glasgow, he is subject to and will be tried in accordance with the Scottish criminal law, irrespective of his nationality. If he starts a business in Glasgow, that business will be subject to the commercial law of Scotland.

12.1.2   Civil and common law systems

All the legal systems in the developed world owe their origin either to the law of ancient Rome or else to the law of England. Those that owe their origin to Roman law are known as civil law systems, while those that owe their origin to English law are known as common law systems. All the jurisdictions on the mainland of Europe are civil law systems, while the jurisdictions of the United Kingdom, Eire, Australia, New Zealand and (with one exception) all the United States of America are common law systems. The exception is Louisiana, which is a civil law system.

The essential difference between these two kinds of legal system lies in the source of the law. With civil law systems the entire law is set out in a series of codes – the criminal code, the commercial code, and so on. With a common law system the law developed originally as a result of court decisions in actual disputes, although legislation has largely overtaken judicial decisions as the main source of law in the common law systems.* So unless there is relevant legislation the law has to be discerned from an examination of the relevant cases, and as we have seen this means that it is not always possible to be sure what the law on a specific point actually is. But while the civil law systems enjoy the advantage of certainty,

---

* Within a common law system, the phrase 'common law' is used to mean that part of the law which is derived from cases rather than contained in legislation. Most of the English law of contract is, as we have seen, common law.

the common law systems have historically been better at adapting to changing social and commercial circumstances.

12.1.3 European law

At several points in our discussion of English law we have had to take account of the law of the European Union. We need to consider briefly European law and its relationship with English law.

The existence and powers of the European Union derive from a series of Treaties between the member states, of which the Treaty of Rome 1957 was the first and the Treaty of Maastricht 1991 is the latest. The law of the European Union is contained in these Treaties and in the legislation enacted by the various European institutions under the powers conferred by the Treaties. However, European law is not a separate and self-contained legal system in the sense in which English or French law is: there is for example no European system of commercial law or contract law.

In principle European law does not compete with the individual legal systems of the member states, but complements them, dealing only with those matters which affect the Union as a whole and cannot therefore be dealt with satisfactorily by the member states individually. However, it is for the European institutions and not the member states to interpret the Treaties and to decide when European legislation is appropriate and what form it should take. The harmonisation of the laws of the member states in the effort to create a single European market has been the pretext for a considerable volume of legislation on business matters. Much of this legislation is of an extremely detailed kind. There may be no European system of contract law, but there is for example a very long and complex directive on milk and milk products, and legislation on permissible noise levels for new cylinder mowers sold anywhere in the Union.

European law takes precedence over the laws of the individual member states. That is to say that the law of a member state is automatically invalid if it is inconsistent with European law, and the question whether there is any such inconsistency is decided by the European institutions and ultimately by the European Court of Justice in Luxembourg. In the United Kingdom the precedence of European law was effected by Section 2(1) of the European Communities Act 1972, but this is drafted in a very indirect way, presumably to disguise the momentous significance of the provision. From this perspective it appears that the recent debate about the sovereignty of Parliament is taking place 25 years too late.

12.1.4 Conclusions

Further generalisations about the characteristics of different legal systems cannot be justified in a book which is intended to be practical. On a practical level, if you are doing business in another jurisdiction it is not safe to assume that the commercial law of that jurisdiction is the same as the law of England and Wales. Usually you will require legal advice from a firm of lawyers within that jurisdiction as to what the law is and how it affects your business there.

In any jurisdiction the crucial issue is whether there is an effective mechanism for the enforcement of contractual obligations. Most jurisdictions, and certainly all the jurisdictions in the developed world, recognise the central principle that commercial agreements should be kept and provide legal redress through the courts against a party who fails to honour such an agreement. Usually, as with our own system, that legal redress involves the payment of compensation by the party in breach.

There are however some jurisdictions where there is no effective means of enforcing a contract. This is the situation in Russia and several of the other states which used to be part of the Soviet Union. As a result it is very difficult indeed to do business in these states. This is one of the main reasons why, despite the interest shown by Western businesses in these areas since the fall of communism, and despite their huge natural resources, very few significant investments have actually been made there.

A contract cannot exist in a legal vacuum. It can have no legal effect at all unless it is made by reference to some legal system which enables the parties, if it becomes necessary, to enforce their rights under it. The existence of effective legal remedies is an essential part of the fabric of any industrial free-market economy.

12.2 JURISDICTIONAL ISSUES

12.2.1 About jurisdictional issues

A purely domestic contract, that is a contract which is made in and is to be performed in England and Wales and whose parties are resident in England and Wales, raises no jurisdictional issues. The wronged party can commence legal action in the English (or Welsh) courts, the court will decide the dispute on the basis of English law, and if necessary the court can enforce its judgment against the party in breach in England and Wales by seizing his assets there.

A contract with one or more international elements can however raise two jurisdictional issues. The first is what law governs that contract, and the second is whether the English courts will have jurisdiction over a dispute under that contract. If the party in breach is not resident in England and Wales, there is the further issue of how a court judgment can be enforced against him.*

12.2.2 The governing law of a contract

We have seen that, as a general proposition, a business is subject to the law of the jurisdiction where it is located. A contract does not have a location in quite the same way, and we can demonstrate this by posing the sort of question which regularly appears in examination papers on the conflict of laws. Two businessmen, one Japanese and the other from Ohio, are in a Dutch registered airliner flying in Italian airspace when they enter into a contract for the sale and export of goods from Brazil to South Africa. The contract must be governed by a single system of law but, unless the parties have stipulated which law is to govern it, there are six possibilities which it will be very difficult to decide between.

In any contract the parties are free to stipulate which system of law is to govern it (e.g. 'this contract is governed by English law' or 'this contract shall be subject to English law'). The parties' choice of governing law is conclusive, even if the contract has no connection at all with that particular system of law.

If the parties do not stipulate which system of law governs their contract, then at common law the contract was governed by the system of law with which that contract had its closest and most real connection. The common law rule was however superseded, with effect from 1 April 1991, by the Contracts (Applicable Law) Act 1990, which gave effect to the Rome Convention on the Law Applicable to Contractual Obligations. That Act introduces a very much more complex system of rules for determining the governing law of a contract if the parties do not choose one. Since the main aim of this section is to stress the importance, in any contract involving one or more foreign elements, of stipulating a governing

---

* *These jurisdictional issues are not strictly part of English contract law, but part of another subject known as 'the conflict of laws'. The classic legal text is* Dicey and Morris on the Conflict of Laws *(4th edition 1993, published by* Sweet & Maxwell*), but for the uninitiated we would recommend its much shorter cousin,* Morris: The Conflict of Laws *(4th edition 1993, published by* Sweet & Maxwell*).*

law, we will not go any further into the rules which apply if no such stipulation is made.

The case of *James Miller & Partners Ltd* v *Whitworth Street Estates Ltd* 1970 (decided under the old common law rules) shows what can happen if the parties to an international transaction neglect to choose a governing law. Whitworth was an English company which owned premises in Scotland, and wanted to convert those premises into a bonded warehouse. It engaged James Miller, a Scottish company, to carry out the conversion. The contract was concluded in Scotland and was on the terms of a standard form published by the Royal Institute of British Architects, but did not stipulate which law would govern the contract. The finely balanced question whether the contract was governed by English or Scottish law went to the House of Lords, where three of the five judges thought that the transaction had its closest and most real connection with English law, while two judges thought that Scottish law governed the contract.

The sad thing about this case is that, had the parties considered the question of governing law at the time of contracting, it would probably not have been contentious. But because they failed to stipulate which law was to govern, they had to take that preliminary question to the highest court in the land.

Since you are reading a book about English law, you will presumably want English law to govern your contracts. If you have to agree to any other law, you will generally require legal advice in that jurisdiction before entering into the contract. It is however a serious mistake, in any contract with an international element, to leave the question of governing law either unasked or unanswered.

12.2.3 Jurisdiction over contractual disputes

You might expect the issue of jurisdiction automatically to follow that of governing law, so that the English courts would have jurisdiction if the contract is governed by English law, the New York courts if the contract is governed by New York law, and so on. This is not the case. The jurisdiction of the English courts over contractual disputes can be summarised in two propositions:

1. The English courts will hear any contract dispute, irrespective of which law governs the contract, where the parties submit to English jurisdiction.
2. Where the wronged party commences proceedings in the English courts but the party in breach has not submitted to

English jurisdiction, the English courts will still hear that dispute unless in all the circumstances it would be more appropriate for the dispute to be heard in another jurisdiction.

Submission to English jurisdiction can happen in either of two ways. First, the contract may stipulate that the English courts are to have jurisdiction ('the parties submit to the jurisdiction of the English courts in relation to any dispute under this contract'). Here neither party can subsequently object to the English courts hearing such a dispute. Second, where the wronged party commences proceedings in the English courts, the party in breach will be taken to have submitted to English jurisdiction if he takes any steps to defend those proceedings. Only if the party in breach takes no such steps but appears in the English court only to dispute its jurisdiction will the court consider whether it would be more appropriate for the case to be heard in another jurisdiction. If the court feels that would in all the circumstances be more appropriate (and the law governing the contract is one of the relevant factors) then it will stay those proceedings and the wronged party will have to pursue his claim in that other jurisdiction.

Obviously you do not want to become involved in jurisdictional disputes of this nature, and the solution is always to stipulate in any international contract which courts are to have jurisdiction. The sensible course is for the issue of jurisdiction simply to follow that of governing law.

Where the English courts do hear a dispute over a contract governed by a foreign law, the court will decide that dispute on the basis of expert evidence as to the relevant provisions of that foreign law.

12.2.4 Enforcement against a foreign defendant

Where the party in breach has no business or assets in England and Wales, it is not possible to enforce an English court judgment against him within the jurisdiction. This fact need not deter you, when contracting with a foreign business, from stipulating English law and jurisdiction: a system of treaties between most of the significant trading nations provides for court judgments in one country to be recognised and enforced by the courts in the others. With a liquidated claim however, the usual course is to sue the debtor directly in his local courts, since that will be more straightforward than trying to enforce an English court judgment. When you bring proceedings in a foreign court or seek to have an English court judgment enforced by a foreign court, you will of course need to instruct local lawyers. If our experience is typical, you may emerge with a new-found respect for the relative cheapness, speed and efficiency of the English legal system. When contracting with a foreign entity, it is all the more important whenever possible to protect yourself by requiring payment in advance, a letter of credit, a performance bond or one of the other devices discussed in Chapter 9.

12.2.5   Foreign parties choosing English law

It is quite common for a contract between two foreign parties with little or no connection with England nevertheless to stipulate that the contract is governed by English law. Usually these contracts also stipulate that disputes under them are to be submitted to the English courts or else to arbitration in London. As a result London is one of the world centres for the resolution of commercial disputes. This is a remarkable vote of confidence in English commercial law and court procedure, which are evidently regarded elsewhere as being efficient, cost-effective and impartial.

In this context we need to mention Section 27 of the Unfair Contract Terms Act 1977. This Section provides that where English law is the proper law (meaning governing law) of the contract only by choice of the parties, then Sections 2 to 7 of that Act do not apply to that contract. In other words the main operative provisions of the Act do not apply where the parties have stipulated that English is to be the governing law but, if no such stipulation had been made, the contract would have been governed by some other system of law.

12.3   UNDERSTANDING AND TRUST

An international transaction crosses cultural boundaries as well as legal ones. Business culture is an important subject, but it is an elusive one. The culture in which an individual operates is not generally something which he is even aware of, but rather which he knows intuitively and takes for granted. In a sense much of this book has been about culture, the culture of British business, although we have hardly mentioned the word. By exposing you to a different business culture, an international transaction can throw the more familiar domestic landscape into an entirely new light.

There are business cultures which are more legalistic than our own, North America being the obvious example, but many are less so. Japanese business relies very little on lawyers, and the Arabs tend to rely on personal understanding rather than signed agreements. But however great the legal and cultural differences between the parties, the human part of the equation is the same wherever you are.

Business is always personal, and in business the most important skills are the personal skills. The clue to this is that substantial deals are always done face-to-face. While there is of course no requirement that the parties or their agents actually meet, in practice no business would enter into a substantial contract to sell steel (whether the buyer is in Sheffield, Pittsburgh or Tokyo), without first meeting the individuals who represent the buyer. In legal terms this may be a transaction between two legal entities conducted by their respective agents, but in reality the critical factor is whether the individuals involved can establish personal understanding and trust between them. On this the success or failure of the negotiation, and of the transaction itself, will ultimately depend.

The key to successful business therefore is personal understanding and trust. This is true with domestic transactions as well as international ones, although with an international transaction cultural and linguistic differences can make understanding and trust more difficult to establish and maintain. You sometimes hear it said (though not by businessmen) that you should never do business with friends. This is untrue. The truth is that the best business is between old friends.

For a book about commercial contracts written by lawyers, this may seem a paradoxical conclusion on which to end. But every discipline must recognise its own limitations, and issues of understanding and trust are beyond reach of the law altogether. Neither promises nor words on a page can bind two people to trust each other.

Index

Lightning Source UK Ltd.
Milton Keynes UK
UKOW030208270613

212876UK00010B/1214/A